MONTGOMERY COUNTY LAND RECORD ABSTRACTS LIBERS H - I/J - K:

Covering the years 1797-1803

Abstracted by:
Patricia Abelard Andersen
Damascus, MD
2012

Colonial Roots
Millsboro, Delaware
2014

Land Records Read From: Microfilm WK 317-318 and WK 318-319, and the Maryland State Archives Land Records web site

The author may be contacted at:
GenLaw Resources
26810 Grace Court
Damascus, Maryland 20872

ISBN 978-1-68034-025-9

Published in the United States of America

CONTENTS

INTRODUCTION

This continues a series of Land Record Abstracts for Montgomery County, for Libers H, I/J and K. The deeds are indexed in the general indexes and are also available on line from the Maryland State Archives web site. Often times records, involving only chattel property were not contained in the current on-line indexes. Although some of the individual libers do possess indexes either at the beginning or end of the book, it can be time consuming to locate and use them, and do to aging and missing pages, some of these indexes are incomplete or missing. To find these original indexes, go to page 1 of each volume, and hit the previous page key. If there is an index at the front of the liber, this will find it. Not all of the books have these indexes unfortunately.

The slave records and other miscellaneous records of interest are included here to make easier the study of slavery in Montgomery County, and to assist family researchers in identifying origins of slave ancestors. An explanation of terms and the identification of some prominent players in these records follows. It should be noted that the index for slaves, servants, Negroes and Mulattos are by first name, in the first section of the index. Prior to 1800 surnames were rarely used. After that point in time, they begin to come into usage, but inconsistently so these individuals are indexed by their first names, and also in the surname index, if both were given. Even first names seem flexible and subject to change in their owners' recollections. When plantation owners of slave families are known, it is good to check their records for all of the slaves on that plantation.

Recording land records required that the witnesses be Justices of the Peace. This was not true for bills of sale, so often other family members, who may have had an interest in the slaves, will appear as witnesses. Also from this time, certain religious groups frowned upon holding slaves, notably the Quakers and the Methodists, and their ministers appeared as frequent witnesses to manumissions, so may yield clues to ancestry or location of the plantation and the slave family.

List of Some Terms and Abbreviations Used in the Abstracts

£	Pounds – still continued to be used as the common currency recorded in here as £10..10..10 read as 10 pounds, 10 shillings 10 pence. Dollars also became more common after 1803. Tobacco was also still being used as currency, especially in reference to old deeds, mortgages.
AAC	Anne Arundel County
ack	Acknowledgment of the deed by the grantor.
afd/afs'd	aforesaid
dower rights:	A wife or a widow's right to 1/3 of all her husband's real property. This right had to be released whenever he sold property. If not done at the time the deed was made, the widow could come back later and exercise a claim against the property, and sometimes later dower releases were recorded.
draught/draft:	One of the upper branches of a river or creek.
Indenture:	Any written contract. "Indentured servants" comes from this document.
lbs. tob.	Pounds of tobacco. (Legal money in Maryland)
M&B	Metes and bounds - description of real estate boundaries.
Manor of Monocacy	[or Calverton] - A unit of government similar to the Hundred, referred to in deeds.
PGC	Prince George's County
rsy/rsy'd	resurvey/resurveyed
SMC	St. Mary's County

Clerks of the Court and Justices of the Peace

ANDERSON, Richard. (1752-1835). Son of Richard and Priscilla Briscoe Anderson, he was born in St. Mary's County and died in Philadelphia, Pa. He served as a Justice of the Peace from 1795. His brother, James Anderson remained in Montgomery County.

BEALL, Brooke. (1742 -1795) First Clerk of the Court of Montgomery County, married to Margaret Johns, daughter of Thomas Johns, a Georgetown merchant. He resided at Brookmont, with a mill seat near the Potomac River, until at least 1783, when he purchased a lot and house in Georgetown from the confiscated British property of Dunlap & Sons for £1,910.. In partnership with Turner, he also had a mercantile business in Georgetown.

BEALL, Lloyd. (Ca. 1759-1817). Son of Benjamin Beall (d, 1765) and Mary Edmonston, who married second Robert Owen. He married Elizabeth Waugh Jones, daughter of Thomas Jones.

BEALL, Upton. (1770-1827). He was the eldest son of Brooke Beall, and generally called the second Clerk of the Court of Montgomery County, following the death of his father, Brooke Beall. He married Jane Neal Robb in 1810, daughter of Adam Robb, the local tavern keeper. He built the house at the corner of W. Montgomery Ave. and N. Adams, around 1815, now occupied by the Montgomery County Historical Society.

BELT, Joseph L. Qualified as Justice in 1796.

BURGESS, Edward Jr. (1733-1809). He was born in Anne Arundel County, and married Mary Davis, daughter of Thomas Davis and Elizabeth Gaither. Around 1773, he moved into the lower district of Frederick County and became involved in politics. He was an Anti-Federalist. He was a Justice of Frederick County, and held the same position in Montgomery County, at its formation. He was elected a representative to the Lower House of the Maryland Assembly ten times from 1777 to 1799. In 1776, he became a Captain in the Flying Camp of Revolutionary War soldiers. He settled near Logtown on the left side of the road from Georgetown to Frederick, somewhere near today's Gaithersburg High School. *Belt's Desire.* He also owned other real property, some with improvements. Between 1779 and 1790 he purchased about 1200 acres of land, much of this land was attached and sold by court order between 1792 and 1798 for debts. Therefore Edward Burgess was a prime example of the type of person who could take up the Anti-Federalist cause. He had debts which the issuance of paper money might help to alleviate.[1]

CAMPBELL, Aeneas. (Aens, other abbreviations) (1730-1812). He was born in St. Mary's County, moved to the Leesburg area in Loudoun County around 1757, and then into Frederick County in 1765. He served as a Justice of the Peace from at least 1771 in Frederick County. He lived on tracts in Sugarland Hundred, which became Montgomery County after 1776.

CORCORAN, Thomas (-1830). Qualified as Justice of the Peace in 1796. Active in Georgetown, Washington, D.C. Will presented there in 1830.

DAVIS, Thomas. Served as frequent witness with Richard Green.

FRENCH, George. Served as frequent witness to Georgetown deeds, from 1791.

GREEN, Richard. (1741-1818). Lived in Upper Newfoundland area of Montgomery County.

---

[1] *Montgomery County Story,* Vol. 30, no. 2, pg. 273.

HEUGH, Andrew. (1727-1789). Served as a Justice from around 1756 in Frederick County. He lived in Lower Potomac Hundred, which became part of Montgomery County after 1776. He was one of the twelve justices who repudiated the Stamp Act, November 23, 1765, and he served in the Lower House of the Legislature 1769-1770.

HOLLAND, Nathan, Jr., Qualified as Justice in 1797.

HOWARD, Greenbury. Served as frequent witness from 1796.

HUNGERFORD, Charles. Justice who represented Montgomery County in House of Delegates 1780-1781.

JONES, Charles. (1712-1798). Served as a Justice from 1754. He was one of the twelve justices who repudiated the Stamp Act, November 23, 1765. He lived on Clean Drinking Manor on the set side of Rock Creek, just north of the present line with the District of Columbia. In 1777, he became the first judge of the Orphans Court of Montgomery County.

MAGRUDER, Charles, served as justice from 1796.

McPHERSON, Josias Hanson (J.H.). Appointed a Justice of the Peace in 1798. Served until 1801, when he was listed as a commissioner to lay out town of Rockville. No later records found.

O'NEALE, Lawrence (1738-1815). Married to Henrietta (Neale) Brooke, widow of Clement Brooke. He served as Sheriff in Frederick County, 1773-1774, and held other local political offices as well as serving in the Lower House from Montgomery County from 1780-1796.

REINTZEL, Daniel, (1756-). Lived in Georgetown Hundred in 1776. Served as a Captain in the Revolutionary War.

SMITH, William. Served as Justice of the Peace from 1795.

SUMMERS, John L. Frequent witness to deeds from 1791.

SWEARINGEN, Elemelech . Frequent witness to deeds from 1797.

About the Author:

Patricia Abelard Andersen was born in 1948 in California, and graduated from San Diego State University, with a special major, combining Biology, Health Sciences Administration and Business Management. After graduation she worked as a claims representative with Social Security, and continued with graduate work, advancing to candidacy in an MBA program in Finance, before moving to Maryland in 1977, to take a job as a "medical logistician" at Fort Detrick in Frederick County. She is married to Robert Andersen, another SDSU alumni, who holds a masters degree in History.

In 1979, she went to work in Advertising Sales for the Washington Post. In 1994, she opted for an early retirement buyout, and obtained a paralegal certificate at Georgetown University, working in estates and trusts for one year, before taking on the job of librarian at the Montgomery County Historical Society, in 1996.

She has been working in genealogy research in Frederick County, since 1977, and was an editor and publisher of *Western Maryland Genealogy* for five years.

Pat's Maryland ancestors include William Offutt, through his son Samuel, and grandson, Hezekiah who married Sarah Odel, daughter of Keziah Offutt and Thomas Odel; William Burgess, through his granddaughter Elizabeth, daughter of Charles Burgess, who married Samuel Offutt; related lines of Prather, Brock; and James and Margaret (Wilson) Crawford, son of James Crawford of Baltimore. It was research on her husbands ancestors, Leonard Barnes who married Nancy Price in Frederick County in 1790, that started her abstracts of Frederick County land records. Their ancestry is still unsolved.

She began publishing land record abstracts in 1985. For a while, several volumes were out of print, but in 2010, an agreement with Colonial Roots in Lewes Delaware, to republish the out of print volumes in small quantities, along with the current Frederick County Abstracts was signed.

Now available from Colonial Roots, Millsboro, Delaware –

FREDERICK COUNTY ABSTRACTS:

Frederick County Land Records, Liber B, 1748-1752
Frederick County Land Records, Liber E:1752-1756 (reprint)
Frederick County Land Records, Liber F: 1756-1761 (reprint)
Frederick County Land Records, Liber G/H: 1761-1763 (reprint)
Frederick County Land Records, Liber J: 1763-1767 (reprint)
Frederick County Land Records, Liber K: 1765-1768
Frederick County Land Records, Liber L: 1767-1770
Frederick County Land Records, Liber M: 1768-1770
Frederick County Land Records, Liber N: 1770-1772
Frederick County Land Records, Liber O: 1771
Frederick County Land Records, Brief Abstracts, Libers P - S - T – U
Frederick County Land Records, Libers V, W, BD1, BD2, and RP1

MONTGOMERY COUNTY (MARYLAND) ABSTRACTS: LAND RECORD MISCELLANY,

Montgomery County Abstracts, 1777-1797, Libers A to G.
Montgomery County Abstracts, 1797-1803, Libers H, J & K

As many researchers are aware, deeds are presently available on-line. Unfortunately, there is no complete index to these records, so the abstracts still continue to provide value. The on-line site is through The Maryland State Archives, and at this time it is free. Anyone who has one of these abstract volumes and would like to obtain a complete copy of the record can print the record off from one's own computer, by applying for a password. For more information or questions, the author can be contacted via e-mail: patsdeeds@verizon.net or

Patricia Andersen
26810 Grace Ct.
Damascus, Md 20872

[this page intentionally blank]

Montgomery County Liber H, Land Record Abstracts

1-2. Frederick Duvall recorded 18 December 1797, deed made 26 September from Claudius Duvall for £40. Tract called *Hold Fast,* devised to him by his father Aquilla Duvall. Signed before Richard Green, Thomas Davis. Receipt.
2-3. James Hinton recorded 19 December 1797, from John D. Coffee, for £12, deed for part of *Moneysworth,* beginning at stone #1 to #2, with road. Containing 1 acre. Signed. Wit: Edward Burgess, Greenbury Howard. acknowledged. Dorcas Coffee relinquished dower rights.
3-4. Asher Leighton recorded 19 December 1797, from John D. Coffee, for £11, deed for part of *Moneysworth,* beginning at stone #6 with road. Containing 3/8 acre. Signed. Wit: Edward Burgess, Greenbury Howard. acknowledged. Dorcas Coffee relinquished dower rights.
4-5. Jonathan Browning Junr. recorded 19 December 1797, from John D. Coffee, for £15, deed for part of *Moneysworth,* beginning at stone #12, northeast side of road. Containing 1 acre. Signed. Wit: Edward Burgess, Greenbury Howard. Dorcas Coffee relinquished dower rights.
5-7. Jonathan Roads recorded 19 December 1797, from John D. Coffee, for £15, deed for part of *Moneysworth,* beginning at stone #11, with road. Containing 1-1/2 acre. Signed. Wit: Edward Burgess, Greenbury Howard. acknowledged. Dorcas Coffee relinquished dower rights.
7-8. William Duncan recorded 19 December 1797, from John D. Coffee, for £6..11, deed for part of *Moneysworth,* beginning at plat #7, containing 7/8 acre. Signed. Wit: Edward Burgess, Greenbury Howard. acknowledged. Dorcas Coffee relinquished dower rights.
8-9. William Duncan recorded 19 December 1797, from John D. Coffee, for £11..5, deed for part of *Moneysworth,* beginning at northeast side #7, containing 1/4 acres, on water courses.. Signed. Wit: Edward Burgess, Greenbury Howard. acknowledged. Dorcas Coffee relinquished dower rights.
9-10. Mathew Reed recorded 19 December 1797, from William Duncan for £4..13, deed beginning at stone on lot #7, on SE side of road, 1/4 acre. Signed, acknowledged, Martha Duncan released dower rights.
10-11. Samuel Craig of Alexandria, Virginia, recorded 20 December 1797, from Thomas J. Beatty of Georgetown, Washington, D.C. for £1450, sells parts of tract called, *Dann.* 1. Now in the possession of Baruch Prather, beginning at 1st line of James Moore's part of said land, E.100pc., N180pc., W50pc., ... 12 pc. W, 50 pc., containing 107 3/4 ac. 2. Part now in possession of Edward Harding, beginning at Edward Rigg's part: E, 125pc., N 71 pc., E 30 pc., then to beginning, 88 1/4 acres. 3. Part beginning at end of third line of land now occupied by James Moore: E 146 pc., N12 pc. E, 50 pc., N 8 pc., W 98 pc., then to beginning, 21 3/4 acres. 4. Part now occupied by Mr. Cawood, adjoining aforementioned land occupied by Edward Harding: S132 pc., E 10 pc., N 12 pc., E 102 ½ pc., N. 122 pc., 91 3/4 acres. 5. Part occupied by James Moore adjacent to land of Barruch Prather, E 100pc., N 120 pc., W 100 pc., then to beginning 105 acres. Signed Thomas J. Beatty before Charles A. Beatty, Daniel Reintzel.
11-12. Samuel Perry recorded 20 December 1797, bill of sale from Robert Perry for £40..2, and 4000 cut crop of tobacco, delivered to Georgetown Warehouse. If debt is paid, sale is void.
12-13. William Cecill recorded 22 December 1797, from Philip Hocker & Uriah Leaton, for £100, deed for *Pleasant Level,* 74 ½ acres.
13-14. Priscilla Brashear recorded 26 Dec. 1797, from Charles Brashear, for £61, bill of sale for personal property, Negro woman, Moll, a mare and small bay horse. Signed before Josiah Perry, Richard Wootton.
14-15. Edward Vellum recorded 26 December 1797, from Henry Vellum, bill of sale for £55, personal property, cattle.
15.William R. King recorded December 1797, from Richard King, for £400 bill of sale to deliver the following Negroes: Gerard, Patience, Peter, Priss, Joe and Silvy; 2 horses, 2 cows, 3 feather beds, tables, chairs, etc. Signed before Arnold Newton, Jesse Bailey. Acknowledged before Lloyd Beall.

15. Negro Sam recorded pass, 27 December 1797. "To Wit, Negro Sam has full liberty to transact for himself, and to buy and sell as a free man, and to do business on all occasions. Witness my hand, 9 August 1786, John H. Cromwell. [Marginal note: Examined & delivered. Recording paid.]
15-16. William A. Needham recorded 28 December 1797, from John Wynn Penn, deed for £40 sterling, 36 3/4 acres of *Addition to Rays Adventure.* Signed. Eleanor Penn released dower.
17-18. John Clark recorded 28 December 1797, from John D. Coffee, deed for £25..5, part of *Moneysworth,* starting at stone #8, NE side for 3/4 acres, and stone numbered #13 on plat, for one acre. Signed, acknowledged, Dorcas Coffee released dower.
18-19. John Clark recorded 28 Dec. 1797, from William Roby Owen, of Bullett Co., Kentucky. He sold tract, *Pleasure Plum,* on 16 Jan. 1779 to aforesaid John Clark, 211 acres. Made corrections to deed. Signed, also Frances his wife released dower in Kentucky.
19-21. Joshua Owen recorded 28 Dec. 1797, made 26 Oct., from John Clarke, for £450, deed for 97 acres of *Pleasure Plum.* Metes & bounds given. Signed before Henry Brookes, Greenbury Howard. Ann Clarke released dower.
21-22. Jonathan Rhodes recorded 28 Dec. 1797, made 26 Oct. from John D. Coffee, for £22..10, deed for part of *Moneysworth,* #5 on main road to #7. Dorcas Coffee released dower rights.
22-24. George King recorded 28 Dec. 1797, from Philip Hocker, for £1000, deed for *Buxton's Delight,* 50 acres and 2nd tract, *Addition to Trails Choice,* for 50 acres and 3d., *New Holland,* for 20+ acres. Signed Philip Hocker before Henry Brookes, Benj. Gaither. Dorcas Hocker his wife released dower.
24-25. Richard Waters recorded 28 Dec. 1797, from John D. Coffee, for £7..10, I beg. At 5thline of Wm. Shanks lot. Dorcas Coffee released dower.
25-26. John Clarke recorded 28 Dec. 1797, from John D. Coffee, for £212..5. deed for several lots and parcels, adj. To Frederick Sholl's lot on NW side of Great Road. Dorcas Coffee released dower. Also at same time, Ann Roberts, widow of Basil Roberts, and relict of James Coffee, came and released her dower rights in this tract.
26-27. John Orme recorded 1 Jan. 1798, made 14 Nov. 1797, from James Beall of James, for £217..19..4. Part of *Wet Beginning,* containing 193 3/4 acres. Elizabeth Beall released dower rights.
27-28. Joseph Gue recorded 3 Jan. 1798, from Basil Crow, for £75, deed for tract called *The Beginning,* originally patented by Lewis Duvall, Edward Crow and Samuel Farmer, 27 Nov. 1752.
28-30. George Gue recorded 3 Jan. 1798, from John W. Penn, made 23 Sept. 1797, for £100 sterling, deed for 100 acres. Signed. Eleanor wife of John Wynn Penn released dower rights.
30-32. Frederick Scholl recorded 3 Jan. 1798, from John D. Coffee, for £542.10, deed for part of *Moneysworth,* which was conveyed 2 April 1773, from John Belt to James Coffee, deceased, a part of *Hammer Hill,* on main road from Frederick Town to George Town, 97 3/4 acres. Dorcas Coffee released dower. Also at same time, Ann Roberts, widow of Basil Roberts, and relict of James Coffee, came and released her dower rights in this tract.
32. William Fitzgerald recorded 4 January 1798, from William Fitzgerald Junr., for £50, bill of sale for personal property.
33. Samuel & Rebecca Moxley recorded 7 Jan. 1798, from John Mullican, deed of gift granting personal property to his step children.
33. Samuel Robertson, certificate of Qualification as Deputy Sheriff recorded 8 January 1798.
33-35. John S. Crawford recorded 9 Jan. 1798, from James Marlow and his wife Febe, for £119, deed for part of *Snowden's Mill land,* conveyed by Samuel Baker to William Selby. Signed by mark before Aeneas Campbell, Thomas B. Beall.
35. Jesse Philips recorded 9 Jan. 1798, from Zadoc Pack, for £20, bill of sale for a white horse, other personal property.

35-36. Benjamin White recorded 13 January 1798, from Joseph Newton Chiswell, for £137..6..10 deed for part of *Second Resurvey on Wolf's Cow.* 36 5/8 acres. Signed before Lawrence O'Neal, Greenbury Howard. Eleanor Chiswell released dower.
36. George Ray & Amos Scott, qualification as deputy sheriff. Recorded 16 Jan. 1798
37-38. William Worthington recorded 17th January 1798, from Honore Martin, deed for lot #36 in town of Williamsburg, alias Montgomery Courthouse. Sarah Martin released dower.
38-41. Francis Lowndes and others recorded 17 January 1798, made 11 January 1798, between Richard Ober of Georgetown, and Francis Lowndes, Charles Lowndes, John Summers, merchants, trading under the name of John Suter & Co. [debt due £359..2..7]; Valentine Reintzel and George Reintzel, merchants [debt due £325..9..7]; and George King, merchant [note for $500 payable on Columbia Bank]; all of Georgetown. Whereas Richard Ober indebted unto above, makes over to secure debts, tracts *Drane's Final Conclusion,* adjacent to *Herbert's Chance,* about two miles above the Great Falls of the Potomac, and adjacent to *Offut's Pasture,* and *Outlet,* and *Resurvey on Thompson's Pasture,* 104 acres; also parcel called *Drane's Luck,* adjacent to tract *Smithfield.* Signed Richard Ober. Acknowledgment and Jane Ober relinquished dower rights.
41-42. Thomas Sprogell recorded agreement 18 January 1798, made 20 January, with Dolly Hardesty of Prince George's County, who binds her daughter Rachel Hardesty aged 7 years 9 mos. 10 days to learn mystery of housewifery, for term of 8 years, 2 months and 20 days; to feed, clothe and provide for her 6 months of schooling. Both sign by mark. Witness: Thomas Corcoran, Lloyd Beall.
42. Francis Boone recorded 19 Jan. 1798, made 1 Jan. from John Rabbit, bill of sale to cover debt of £120, mortgages three Negroes, Bob, a carpenter and woman Sarah and women Agnes. Signed before Thomas Corcoran.
43-44. Thomas Corcoran recorded 22 Jan. 1798, bill of sale from Richard Ober. Whereas he is indebted to Lloyd Buchanan & c. merchants of Baltimore, Richard Ober mortgages personal property and dwelling house in Georgetown to indemnify Thomas Corcoran.
44-45. John Hawley of Loudoun Co., Va., & Zachr Downs recorded agreement 25 January 1798, from Absalom Beddoe. Hawley and Downs made a deed 25 Oct 1783 to convey to Beddoe, tracts, *Resurvey on Deer Park and Bear Garden,* which lay foul of elder survey on *Snowden's Mill.* This is to correct errors, and modify deed.
45. Ruth Trundle recorded January 1798, Francis Deakins, made 16 November 1797 for £125..6, tract *Mount Carmel,* 2 ½ acres. Signed before Lloyd Beall, Thomas Corcoran. Eleanor Deakins released dower.
45-46. Edward Veirs recorded 6 January 1798, from John Hoggins, deed for £600, land tract *Resurvey on Hanover,* beginning at line between Levi Hayes plantation and field formerly owned by George Howard, except for use of well water to John Baptist Medley. Thamear Hoggins, wife of John released dower rights.
47. Bailey Erles Clark of Bladensburg, recorded 31 Jan. 1798, from Henry Culver Pierce, bill of sale for £65, sells one Negro boy, Abraham.
48. George H. Offutt recorded 31 January 1798. I Jeremiah Nicholson for £11..5, sell roan mare, 3 years old. Sale void if debt paid before 1 Feb. next. Signed by his mark, 27 January 1798. Ack.
48. John Bonifant recorded 3 February 1798, I Samuel Bonifant Senr. For natural love and affection to John Bonifant, give him one Negro girl, Catharine. Signed before James A. Beall, William Jones.
48-49. William Prather recorded bill of sale, 3 February 1798. I Thomas Prather for £200 deliver all my rights which are due from bill of sale to myself and William Prather, by Aaron Prather Senr. 7 November last. Signed before John L. Summers, Elemelech Swearingen.
49-50. Joseph Clagett recorded 3 February 1798, made 7 August 1797, between Samuel Clagett for £100, *Quince Orchard,* that part which was willed to Hezekiah and Josiah Clagett by their father Henry Clagett, for 218 acres. Signed Samuel Clagett, before same parties as above.

50. Order of Levy court 5 February 1798. We Henry Riggs, and Amon Riggs, are bound for £100 to perform as Levy Court Commissioners. Whereas Henry Riggs did contract with Benjamin Gaither and Edward Crow to build a new bridge over Seneca.
50-51. Elijah Williams recorded 8 Feb. 1798, from Lodowick Davis, deed made 2 September for £15, assigns part of real estate of Lodowick Davis, deceased. Signed before Thomas Davis, Elemelech Swearingen.
51. George Beall and Walter Clagett, appointment as inspectors of tobacco for the new Georgetown warehouse 9 February 1798. Signed by Ninian Pinkney Clerk of the Council.
51-53. James Hinton recorded 12 Feb. 1798, from John D. Coffee, deed for £15 sells lot on tract *Moneysworth,* on north side of road, from stone numbered 7, to fourth line of *Warfield's Vineyard.* Signed. Dorcas Coffee relinquished dower.
53. George & Patrick Magruder recorded 13 Feb. 1798, from Joseph Magruder, bill of sale for 5 shillings for two Negro slaves, William aged 8 years and Charles about 6 years, they being brothers. Signed before John T. Mason.
53-54. William Deakins Junior recorded 14 February 1798. Whereas Henry Chambers Junr., is indebted for 1800 lbs. Tobacco, he sells one sorrel horse, one black cow, one heifer. Bill of sale to be void if amount due paid.
54. Francis Toppass records agreement from Ninian Magruder of Samuel, to void Indenture effective 17 February 1798, of son John Toppas.
54-55. John Threlkeld, recorded 19 February 1798, in Georgetown, certificate of qualification as coroner, before Lloyd Beall.
55. Honore Martin recorded 20 February 1798, from Robert Davis, for $100, bill of sale for all my furniture, and crops of grain now growing and tobacco and corn. Signed before John L. Summers.
56. Philip Jenkins recorded 26 Feb. 1798, from Augustus Easton, bill of sale for £9, for one bay mare and other personal property. Signed by his mark before Elemelech Swearingen.
56-57. Philip Jenkins recorded 27 February 1798, from Thomas Appleby, bill of sale for £40, sells one small bay mare, 9 years old. Signed by mark before John L. Summers.
57-58. Thomas Cramphin recorded 1 March 1798, from Benjamin Rawlings, & Elizabeth Garrett Rawlings, his wife, deed for £600 for tract called *Garter Lost,* on Watry branch, formerly in possession of Edward Garrett and devised by his will to the said Elizabeth, as Elizabeth Garrett Gittings. Signed by mark by both parties before William Luckett. Dower release.
58. William Fitzgerald, recorded schedule 2 March 1798, including account due from John Holmes, Esq., to Sheriff Benjamin W. Jones. Signed by mark before John L. Summers.
59-60. [Marginal note: delivered to John Febrier, January 14, 1802.] Nicholas Febrier Junr and others recorded 3 March 1798, . from Nicholas Febrier, deed of gift for 5 shillings paid by Nicholas Febrier Jr., John James Febrier and Francis Febrier, sells Negro man slave Hyacinth, 50 years old; Negro Nicholas 25 years, boy Frederick about 14 years. Signed before David Peter, William H. Lyles.
60. [Marginal note: delivered to John Febrier, January 14, 1802.] Susannah Febrier recorded 3 March 1798. I Nicholas Febrier, for 5 shillings, release to her Negro man John Peter, 31 years; Negro man Zelim, 25 years and Lewis 15 years old together with all household furniture. Signed before William H. Lyles, David Peter.
60-61. Charles Gassaway recorded qualification 5 March 1798, as coroner.
61. Benjamin W. Jones recorded 5 March 1798, certificate of qualification as sheriff, sworn before Thomas Plater, Associate Justice.
61-62. George W. Moore recorded 6 March 1798, from William Bayley of Prince George's County, for £15 deed for *Fletchall's Quarter.* Signed before George French, Thomas Corcoran.
62-64. John Suter, Junr. Recorded 6 March, 1798, assignment from Richard Huff and Robert Stockton, administrators of Samuel Huff, deceased, made 28 February. Whereas John Suter Jr. and Samuel Huff were

partners and acquired jointly held property and debts, this sells all stock and trade of the Union Tavern to Suter, along with the debts.

64-65. William Hocker Senr. Recorded 6 March 1798, from Richard Bennett Hall of Prince George's County, deed for 3750 lbs. Tobacco, sells tract called *Killmain,* metes and bounds for 15 acres. Signed before Benjamin Gallaway, Francis Duckett.

65-67. Upton Beall recorded 7 March 1798, from Leonard Mackall, deed for 5 shillings, 200 acres, part of tract purchased of Ninian Beall Magruder by Brooke Beall, at lower end near Georgetown. Signed Leonard Mackall. (No dower release).

67-68. Catharine Mackall recorded 7 March 1798, from Upton Beall, deed made same date for 5 shillings. 200 acres. Same tract as above.

68-69. George & Patrick Magruder recorded 8 March 1798, from Joseph Magruder, bill of sale for 5 shillings, sells one Negro woman, aged about 34 years, Nanny. Also one bay mare and colt. Signed before John L. Summers.

69-71. Richard Andrews & c. recorded 8 March 1798, from William O. Magruder, for £107..7..6, part of tract, *Rich Land,* adjacent to part conveyed to Daniel Bennet containing 107 3/8 acres. Deed to Richard Andrews, Charles Andrews and Edward Andrews for 107 3/8 acre part. Signed before George H. Offutt, Greenberry Howard, acknowledgment.

71. Negro Thomas & others recorded 1 March 1798, from James Redman, manumission for Negro Thomas from and after 1 January 1806 and for Negro Darkey, from and after 1 January 1808. Signed before Stingfly Linthicum and William Smith.

71-73. Thomas Perry Willson recorded 9 March 1798, made 13 November from Edward Harding, for £225, deed for lot #35 in town of Williamsburgh. Signed by Edward Harding before Lloyd Beall, Thomas Corcoran. Receipt. Acknowledgment. Ann Harding released dower rights.

73. James Perry recorded 9 March 1798, Qualification as Coroner.

73-74. Henry Poole recorded 9 March 1798, for £6, deed from Jesse Hyatt, for lots #49 & #50 in Hyattstown, to pay yearly rents of 5 shillings.

74-76. Jesse Hyatt, recorded 9 March 1798, certificate and plan of Hyattstown. Plan copied from pages 75-76. [to right ▶].

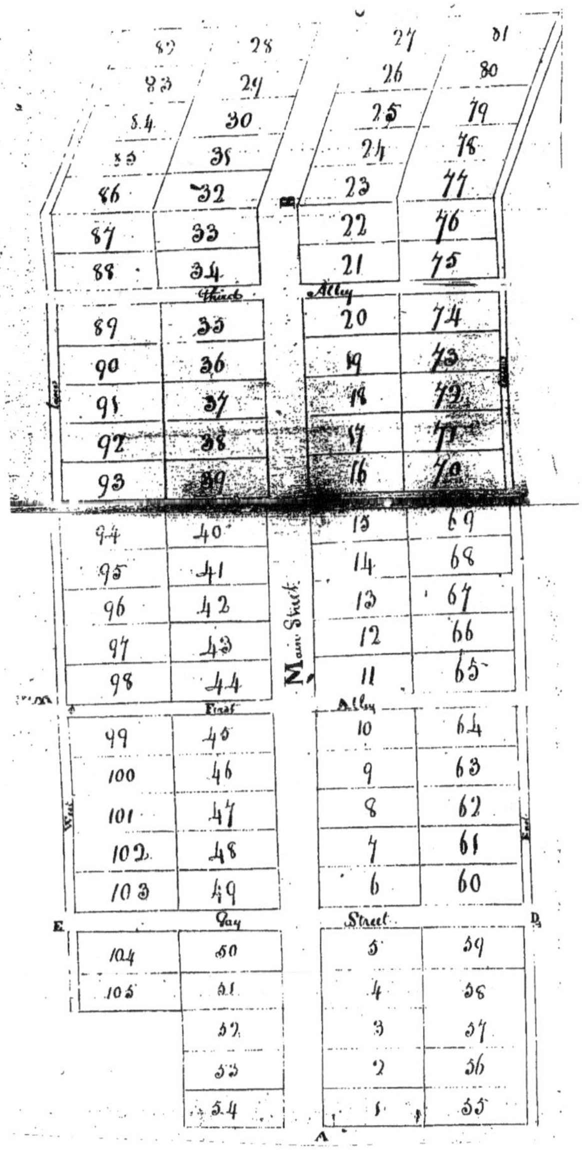

76-78. Henry Poole recorded 9 March 1798, made 10 Feb 1798, for 5 shillings from Jesse Hyatt, assigns all those streets, lanes and alleys called Main St., Gay St., First Alley, Second Alley, Third Alley, East Lane, West Lane, laid out by Jesse Hyatt in Montgomery County, called Hyattstown, on two tracts, called *Hard*

Struggle, and *Ivey Reach,* and also land to the Grist Mill lately belonging to William Richards. Signed by Jesse Hyatt. Nancy wife of Jesse Hyatt released dower rights.
78. Ann Sparrow, recorded 10 March 1798, list of Negroes imported from Virginia, and brought in 20 December 1797. A Negro girl called Beck, aged about 16 years old, left me by Thomas Sparrow, my husband, in his will.
78. John Baptist. Medley recorded 4 March 1798, from Solomon Simpson, receipt for payment of bond dated 1 January 1794, which was lost or mislaid, having received full satisfaction for it.
79. Thomas Orme recorded 4 March 1798, from Archibald Orme, bill of sale for 5 shillings, one Negro boy called James. Signed before Josias H. McPherson.
79. Richard Orme recorded 4 March 1798, from Archibald Orme, bill of sale for 5 shillings, sells one Negro boy called Sam, about 16 years old, the son of a Negro woman called Moll. Receipt and acknowledgment.
80-82. Andrew Scholfield & others, recorded commissions and depositions on 4 March 1798. To Messrs. Archibald Orme, Henry Brooke and Thomas Turner. Whereas Andrew Scholfield, Isachar Schoolfield and Mahlon Scholfield of Prince George's County, by their petition to resurvey, tract *Great Falls Branch,* commission appointed 6 March 1797. Depositions taken from Joseph Scholfield, age 37 years, and a Quaker, he solemnly affirmed the beginning of tract taken by his father and by his brother William Scholfield, now deceased. Affirmed before Samuel Turner, Richard Wootton.
82-84. Samuel Riggs recorded 4 March 1798, from Isaac Briggs and Hannah Briggs his wife, deed made 8th day, 12th month of 1797, for £1,001..5 sells Hannah Briggs part of *Fair Hill,* and *Surebind, Surefind.* Containing 222 ½ acres. Signed before Richard Green and Elemelech Swearingen.
84-.85. Richard Thomas Junr. Recorded 15 March 1798, From Caleb Bentley & Sarah Bentley his wife, deed made 22nd day 1st month, 1798. For 5 shillings, part of *Addition to Brooke Black Meadows.*
86-87. Thomas J. Beatty recorded mortgage 19 March 1798, from Middletown Belt for £67..14, one Negro woman, Peg, age 45 years and one Negro boy Harry, about 11 years old. If sums paid with interest by 20 September next, then the sale is void. Signed before John L. Summers.
87-89. John Edwards recorded 19 March 1798, from James Scott of Georgetown, bill of sale for £375, one Negro girl Nancy, one bay horse, one cow, billiards table, one desk, one bookcase, six feather beds, seven prints, 15 green windsor chairs, two cushion chairs, three walnut tables, and any other furniture in my shop in Georgetown. Signed 13 March 1798, James Scott before Lloyd Beall, Thomas Corcoran.
89. Henry W. C. Robertson recorded on 20 March 1798, certificate of qualification as deputy sheriff
89-91. Archibald Anderson Reed recorded 20 March 1798, from John Reed, deed made 17 Feb., for £117..5, part of *Johnson's Discovery.* Signed in the presence of Ans. Campbell, Greenberry Howard. Ann Reed released dower rights.
91-93. Richard Wootton recorded 29 March 1798, from Norman West, deed. Whereas Samuel West by his last will and testament, bequeath to his four sons land, and Norman West, one of the sons, sold his interest to Richard Wootton for £362..10, deed is for his undivided part of *Two Brothers,* 100 acres, and *Addition to Two Brothers,* 25 acres. Signed Norman West before John L. Summers, Elemelech Swearingen. Ann West, wife of Norman, released dower rights.
93. Schedule of Perry Beall, recorded 29 March 1798, property delivered to Benjamin W. Jones, sheriff, including one linen wheel, and accounts on Vachel Harding and Clement Green, and Michael Gladman, amount on judgment. Signed before John L. Summers, Elemelech Swearingen.
94-96. Samuel Wilson recorded 31 March 1798, from Honore Martin, deed for £132//7, part of lots #40 & 41 in Williamsburgh, alias Montgomery Courthouse. Signed before John L. Summers, Elemelech Swearingen. Sarah Martin released dower rights.
96-98. William Wilson recorded 31 March 1798, from Honore Martin, deed for £132..7, part of lots #40 & 41 in Williamsburgh, alias Montgomery Courthouse. His part is from stone at NW corner of lot bought of Honore Martin by James Day now in the possession of Hezekiah Viers, adjacent to Samuel Wilson's part. Signed before John L. Summers, Elemelech Swearingen. Sarah Martin released dower rights

98. George Killon, recorded schedule of property given to sheriff Benjamin W. Jones, on 2 March 1798. Notes on Dennis O'Bryan, Jeremiah Kale and a book containing accounts against sundry persons.
99-100. John. G. Jones, recorded 2 April 1798, bond under insolvent act, from James Heigh Blake, John Mountz Sr., Joseph Beck and James Simpson, for £50. John G. Jones now being in prison, his creditors claim that he concealed some of his property, and sold illegally some of it. Signed by creditors before Benj. Wilkinson, Paul Richards.
100-101. Moses Harvey, recorded schedule to sheriff on 5 April 1798, listed an account due from Dennis Magruder. Signed by his mark before John L. Summers, Josias H. McPherson.
101-102. Raphael Jarboe recorded 7 April 1798, from Hezekiah Veirs, mortgage for £150, for one lot in Williamsburgh, and contents, void if paid before 7 April 1799 with interest.
102-106. Samuel Davidson recorded 10 April 1798, from Robt Ferguson & Alexander Hamilton or Prince George's county. Whereas Walter Evans by deed, 31 August 1798 for part of *Dung Hill,* 143 acres. And whereas James Gordon, Henry Rudisel and others, obtained judgments against Walter Evans in the Western Court against Walter Evans. Sale of *The Dung Hill,* lately occupied by Joseph Evans deceased. Signed.
106-109. Thomas Cramphin recorded 10 April 1798, from Samuel Davidson, for $10,000. deed for part of *Dann* conveyed by John Heugh 26 March 1795, adjacent to *Leek Forest,* to beginning of part now in possession of Hugh Riley; to 3d line of tract now in possession of the heirs of the late Thomas Johns; to another part now leased by Edward Riggs, to the 5th line of a part in possession of Lewis Wilcoxon; to part conveyed by Lucy Brooke to Charles Clagett and Philip Berry, to tract purchased by Lewis Wilcoxon from Edward Tucker, to east side of the main branch of Rock Creek; along meanders of creek, also the boundary of *Joseph's Park,* containing 314 acres. Adjacent to part conveyed to him [Davidson] by Jesse Wilcoxon, 13 June 1795, it being the same tract formerly conveyed by Benjamin White Jones to John Heugh for 95 ½ acres. To Thomas Cramphin. Signed before George French, Daniel Reintzel. Acknowledgment.
109. Manumissions recorded 12 April 1798, from Samuel Nicholls, for Negro Rachel from present and for all future times, Jeremiah from and after 20 August 1819, Aran, from and after 3 May 1822, Amos, from and after 3 October 1827; Dinar, from and after 8 February 1807, and all issue born between now and then to be free at age 28; Charity, from and after 10 May 1811, and all issue at age 28; Anne from and after 15 August 1817. Signed 14 March 1798, in the presence of Thos Lucas, Wm Smith. Acknowledgment.
110-111. Richard Beall Junr. Recorded April 1798, From Capt. Richard Beall Senr. of Prince George's County, son of Ninian Beall Sr., deed of gift for natural love and affection, for large tract called *Largo,* now called *Beall's Good Will.* Signed before Ans. Campbell, Lawrence O'Neal.
111-112. Vachel Hall of Montgomery County, recorded 4 April 1798, from William Hayes of Baltimore County, & Notley Hayes of Washington Co., (Md.), for £270, part of tract called *Jeremiah's Park,* beginning at 12th line of land of Jeremiah Hayes, containing 120 acres. Signed before Alex. Clagett, Jacob Schnebley,. Sarah wife of Notley Hays released dower rights before same, Justices of the Peace of Washington County. Sarah Hays wife of William Hays relinquished dower rights before George Gould Presbury and Robert Gorsuch of Baltimore County. Elie Williams Clerk Washington County and Wm Gibson Clerk, Baltimore County attested to signatures of their justices of the peace.
113-114. James Cooke recorded schedule 17 April 1798, delivered to Benjamin White Jones, Sheriff, including amounts due on account from Richard Groomes, John Harper, William Groomes, Thomas Mockby, William Lowry Jr., Genl Jeremiah Crabb, Merchant Ricketts. Witnessed by John L. Summers, Elemelich Swearingen.
114. Thomas Owen recorded 14 April 1798, from John Hollings, of Virginia, bond of conveyance, to convey *Pigg Park,* his by right of inheritance. Signed before Richard Green (by mark) and John Dickinson (by mark.).
114-115. Richard Berry recorded 19 April 1798, assignment from Thomas O. Williams. Whereas Thomas Owen, sold *Pigg Park,* by bond of conveyance, and he afterwards passed bond to his nephew Thomas Owen, now of Virginia, Thomas Owen, long since dead, left an only daughter Barbara, who married William

Williams, both long since dead, for premises and 5 shillings to clear title, indenture made 10 March 1798, and signed by ? W. Williams, Elizabeth Berry, Zachariah Berry, Barbara Magruder, Francis Magruder, Walter Clagett, Martha Clagett, William P. Williams and Walter C. Williams. Witnesses: Edward Owen, Thomas Schley, John L. Magruder, Elijah Beall, Wingfield Tyrrol, Lloyd Beall, James Ward.

115. William A. Needham & John Wynn Penn, recorded agreement 19 April 1798. Whereas a deed dated in 1797 from John Wynn Penn to William Abbington Needham, put in the Clerks office for recording was not agreed to, we agree that said deed is void.

115. Leonard Gary of Anne Arundel County, for £50 sells to Andrew McDonald, one Negro woman named Mary, aged 33 years. Acknowledged before Lloyd Beall.

116. Caleb Bentley recorded 21 April 1798, deed from Richard Thomas Junr. And Deborah Thomas his wife, made 22nd day, 1st month, 1798, for 5 shillings, a part of *Addition to Brooke Grove* on the west side of Richard Thomas Junr.'s mill on the Reedy Branch, containing 4 acres. Signed before Richard Green and Elemelech Swearingen. Dower released.

117-119. Samuel Brooke recorded 21 April 1798, from Caleb Bentley & Sarah his wife, deed made 22nd day, 1st mo., 1798, for £750 assigns two tracts, part of *Addition to Brooke Black Meadows,* and part of *James Brookes Reserve,* beginning at a tract called *The Fork.* Lines given to Hawlings River, adjacent to a lot conveyed to Richard Thomas Junr. 71 acres of land. Signed before same witnesses as above.

119-121. Caleb Bentley recorded 21 April 1798, from Samuel Brooke for £937..10, parts of tracts *Addition to Brooke Grove, Resurvey on Brooke Park,* part of *Fair Hill,* and part of *Surebind, Surefind.* Metes & bounds given for 250 acres. Signed Samuel Brooke before witnesses above. Receipt. Acknowledgment. Sarah Brooke released dower rights.

121. Richard Stevens Junr., recorded 23 April 1798, from Richard Stevens Senr., deed of gift to his beloved son, of one gray horse, one feather bed, furniture, one brown heifer. Signed 23 April 1798, before John L. Summers.

121-122. Gerrard Brooke & John Stevens recorded 23 April 1798, from Richard Stevens, Senr. bill of sale for £100, sells one black horse, 6 yrs. Old, one bay mare 5 years, 2 black cows & calves; one red ditto, 16 old sheep, 5 lambs, 2 sows, 15 pigs, 13 shoats, 2 feather beds, 2 pewter dishes, 12 pewter plates, 2 iron pots. Signed before John L. Summers.

122. Charlotte Stevens recorded 23 April 1798, from Richard Stevens, Senr., deed of gift to my daughter for one feather bed, one red & white heifer. Signed before John L. Summers.

122-123. John Clark from Michael Tully for £700..15 and £12..1, paid to Tully by Jonathan Browning and 39 shillings paid by John Reed, have sold to the said Clark, Browning and Reed, 3 bay horses, one colt, feather beds and other housewares. Bill of sale to be void if debt redeemed by 1 December next. Signed before Mesheck Browning. Acknowledged before Henry Brooke.

123-124. John Forner of Baltimore recorded 24 April 1798, from Shadrach Penn, deed made 16 April, for part of *Prospect Hill,* on a line of *Friendship,* for 250 acres. Signed before John Clarke, Edward Burgess. Margaret Penn, wife of Shadrach, released dower rights.

125. James Scott recorded 24 April 1798, from Jesse Hyatt, for £14..10, deed made 7 February 1798, for lots #22, 23, 24 and 76, 77 & 78 in Hyattstown. Signed before Benjamin Gaither, Greenbury Howard.

126-127. Lewis Duvall recorded 24 April 1798, from James Scott for £100, deed made 21 April, for lots #23 and 77 in Hyattstown. Signed James Scott before Edward Burgess Junr., John Clarke. Acknowledgment.

127-128. Jonathan Browning Junr. recorded 24 April 1798, from James Hinton for £7..10, made 13 January for part of *Moneyworth,* conveyed from John D. Coffee. Signed before Greenbury Howard, Edward Burgess Junr. Catharine Hinton released dower rights.

128-129. Jacob Proctor recorded 24 April 1798, from William Duncan, for £20..8, deed made 13 Jan. 1798, for a lot, a part of *Moneysworth,* beginning at 3d line of lot of Asher Layton, lot #6. Signed before same witnesses as above. Martha Duncan released dower rights.

129-131. Godfree Waters recorded 26 April 1798, from John D. Coffee, for £20 deed made 10 April 1798, for lot #5, a part of *Moneyworth,* on east side of road. Signed before Edward Burgess Jr., and John Clarke. Dorcas Coffee released dower.

131. Edward Willett, Schedule recorded 28 April 1798, and delivered to Benjamin W. Jones, Sheriff. Accounts due of Rezin Fields, Robert Shaw, Joseph Joseph, Joseph Tippett, Daniel Dougherty, Joseph Wheat, William Fulks, Thomas McBee, John Harper, George Heathman, and William Groomes on a judgment. Signed before John L. Summers, Josias H. McPherson.

131-132. Basil Prather, schedule recorded 28 April 1798, and delivered to Benjamin W. Jones, Sheriff. Daniel Nicholls on account in hands of James W. Ward, constable. Signed before John L. Summers, Josias H. McPherson.

132-134. William A. Needham recorded 28 April 1798, from John Wynn Penn, for £72..5, deed made 7 April for part of *Addition to Rays Adventure,* beginning at *William and Mary,* containing 36 3/8 acres. Signed. Eleanor Penn released dower rights.

134-136. Archibald Campbell of the City of Baltimore, and Benj. Stoddert recorded 28 April 1798, from Joseph Forrest, deed of trust made 25 April. Whereas Joseph Forrest is indebted to sundry persons, he deeds his property to trustees, they to satisfy debts to Bank of Columbia, and others, and after sale return anything remaining to him. Signed before Thos Corcoran, James Beall.

136-137. Walter Roe of Baltimore Co., recorded 30 April 1798, from Francis Deakins, devisee of Wm Deakins, deed of bargain for 236 acres part of *Conclusion.* [See deed for more details – question whether this is a fictitious sale to clear title. ?]

137-139. Walter Magruder recorded 3 May 1798, from Nathaniel Magruder of Alexander, deed for 5 shillings, made 30 April for part of tract *Grubby Thicket,* 136 acres and part formerly conveyed by Andrew Heugh to Nathaniel Magruder for 52 acres. Signed before Joseph S. Belt, George H. Offutt. Receipt, acknowledgment.

139-140. Walter Magruder recorded 5 May 1798, from Nathaniel Magruder of Alexander, for 5 shillings, a bill of sale to my son, he delivers a Negro man Pad, and woman, Fan, and boys Ned and Sam, and Negro girl Massey the children of Fan. Signed before witnesses as above.

140. John Hawkins recorded 5 May 1798, from Nathaniel Magruder of Alexander, for 5 shillings, bill of sale for my title to a Negro woman called Grace and her child Ned, and a Negro girl Flora, and a Negro boy Parker, now in Hawkins possession. Signed before witnesses above.

140-141. Francis Deakins recorded 5 May 1798, from Richard M. Taylor, for £264, deed for tracts called *Rays Venture,* and tract called *Mount Carmel,* containing together 38 ½ acres, as in deed from Thomas Reed to Richard Taylor, made 4 December 1794. Signed before Aeneas Campbell and Lawrence O'Neale. Receipt & acknowledgment.

142-143. John Kelly recorded 6 May 1798, from Jacob Howard of Prince George's County, and James Riley, for £352..10, deed made 22 March for part of *Riley's Chance* ____ *Hills,* and a part of *Harrison's Delight,* 141 acres. Signed before Richard Cramphin, Gass. P. Van Horne. Receipt and acknowledgment. Lucy Howard released dower rights. Justices of the Peace were certified by John Read Magruder, Clerk of Prince George's County.

144. Patrick Durham recorded 6 May 1798, from Samuel Hepburn of Prince George's County, for £112..10, bill of sale for one Negro woman Nancy and her two children Daniel and Henry. Signed before Thomas Contee, Rd Marshall.

145. Jesse Phillips recorded 7 May 1798, from Samuel Asbring, for £10, bill of sale for one feather bed and furnishings. Signed by mark before Thos B. Beall, Thos. W. Riggs.

145-147. William Kelly recorded 7 May 1798, from Samuel Hepburn of Prince George's County, mortgage made 12 April. Whereas 28 January 1798, conveyed by bond to William Kelley and Samuel Hamilton, 200 acres of *Hanover,* (the whole tract is 2200 acres), adjacent to lots now rented and occupied by John Wayman, and to a lot now occupied by Edward Wathen, said bonds amounting to £527..8..6, principal with interest. Signed Samuel Hepburn before John Smith Brookes, Robt Bowie. Acknowledgment.

147-149. Richard Ridgely of the City of Annapolis, Attorney at law, recorded 7 May 1798, made 12 February, Between Sarah Griffith, relict and widow of Col. Charles Greenbury Griffith deceased, and Jeremiah Crabb & Elizabeth his wife. Whereas the said Charles Greenbury Griffith in his life time was seized in sundry tracts of land in Montgomery County, to wit, two tracts, one called *Resurvey on Benjamin's Square,* and the other, *Lodowick's Range,* containing the quantity of 382 ½ acres of land, in virtue of sundry conveyances from a certain Lodowick Davis deceased, to the said Charles Greenbury Griffith, and also in virtue of a decree of the Hon. Chancery Court, 22 December 1791, wherein the said Griffith, was complainant and the devisees of the said Lodowick Davis defendants, also the said Griffith was seized of part of a tract of land called *The Cow Pasture,* by virtue of a deed of conveyance from a certain Caleb Griffith, 10 March 1787, containing 82 1/4 acres of land, on the 9th day of February 1787, returned a survey by the name of *Brandenburgh,* containing 478 ½ acres, and whereas the said Charles Greenbury Griffith, departed this life intestate leaving the said Sarah Griffith his widow, and Elizabeth Crabb his only child, with whom the said Jeremiah Crabb had intermarried; they have agreed to convey the said tracts to Richard Ridgely, in consideration of £2000. Signed Sarah Griffith, Jeremiah Crabb, Elizabeth Crabb before John L. Summers, Henry Brookes. Acknowledgment, and dower release.

149-150. Richard Ridgely recorded 7th May 1798, from Eleanor Palmore, assignment of dower as widow to Lodowick Davis deceased for £25, to which she may be entitled to on one hundred acres of land, it being a part of the *Resurvey on Benjamin's Square,* which the said Lodowick Davis sold to Charles Greenbury Griffith in his lifetime, which the said Griffith obtained by decree against the heirs of Lodowick Davis in the Court of Chancery for 100 acres. Signed Eleanor Palmore, Benj. Gaither, Henry Brookes.

150-152. Harry Woodward Dorsey of Anne Arundel Co. recorded 7 May 1798, from Richard Ridgely, attorney of the City of Annapolis. He conveys the same properties that were conveyed to him in the deed recorded above. Receipt for £2000. Elizabeth Ridgely released dower.

152-153. Nathan Musgrove recorded 7 May 1798, from Tush Clark & his wife, Arra Clark, of Huntington County, Pennsylvania for £50 ..5 sells tract called *Gaither's Purchase,* 100 acres; *What's Left,* 54 acres, conveyed by Benjamin Gaither to John Musgrove, 4 October 1779, and *Hannah's Purchase,* 55 acres, *Treed Land,* 40 acres, *Addition to Plummer's Content,* 25 acres, and a second part, 66 acres, conveyed by John Prather to John Musgrove, 1 December 1784, and also *Resurvey on John and Sarah,* 10 1/4 acres, land from John and Betty Welsh to John Musgrove, 15 December 1785, in the fork of Hawlings River; also *Bear Garden Forest Enlarged,* part in Montgomery County and part in Anne Arundel County. Signed by mark before Richard Green and Thomas Davis. Receipt, Acknowledgment and dower release recorded.

153-155. Nathan Musgrove recorded 7 May 1748, made 16 February 1798, from Joshua Plummer & wife, for £37, deed for tracts listed as above. Signed by marks before Thomas Davis, Benj. Gaither.

155. William Darne, Junr., recorded 8 May 1798, list of Negroes before James M. Lingan of Georgetown. On 15th March from the state of Virginia, brought Negro boy Nat aged 10 years, which did before belong to his father for the past three years.

156-158. William O. Neal Sr., recorded 10 May 1798, from William Pritchett, deed made 1 March for £700 sells parcel called *Cuckold's Delight,* for 140 acres. Signed before John L. Summers, Josias H. McPherson. Acknowledgment. Eleanor wife of William Pritchett released dower.

158. Rebeckah Casey & Elizabeth recorded 10 May 1798, from George Riley, bill of sale for £100, for Negro girl called Vilet, 12 years old and one Negro boy called Charles, about 8 years. Signed before Thos Corcoran, Lloyd Beall.

158. Richard Orme recorded 1 May 1798, from Aquilla Beall, for £60, bill of sale for a mulatto slave named Bob. Signed before J. H. McPherson.

159-160. John Suter & c. recorded 15 May 1798, from Zachariah Maccubbin, mortgage for Negro man Jack, 50; Will, 42; Frank, 32; Sam, 35; Dick, 13. Signed Zachariah Maccubin before Thos Corcoran, Lloyd Beall.

160-161. Rezin Beck recorded 15 May 1798, from Joseph Beck, for $200, bill of sale for personal property: one desk, 4 beds & furniture, 3 walnut tables, one dozen chairs. Signed 28 April 1798 before John Long, Lloyd Beall.

161-162. James Dunlap of Georgetown recorded 15 May 1798, from Benjamin Ray, Junr., late sheriff. A writ of vendition issued 24 January, James Gordon, Henry Riddell, John Campbell, John Campbell Junr., Alexander Lowe, and William Ingram plaintiffs against John Saffell ,son and heir of James Saffle dec'd and Charles Saffle, son and devisee of Mary Saffle deceased, widow & devisee of Samuel Saffle deceased, defendants. Sells land *Fellowship,* on a draught of Seneca Creek, conveyed by Benjamin Kelley in 1756 to Samuel Saffle. Signed by Sheriff before John L. Summers, Josias H. McPherson.

162-163. Ninian Willett recorded 13 May 1798, from Edward Willett, of Fairfax County, Virginia, for £25, deed for part of an island in the Potomac, known as *Trammells Island,* Signed before John L. Summers. Josias H. McPherson.

163-165. Ann Roberts recorded 15 May 1798, from William Robertson, Sheriff, deed made 6 April. Whereas William Deakins Jr., deceased and Bernard O'Neal obtained a judgment against Basil Roberts, now deceased, and by writ of fieri facias, took two tracts, and William Deakins Jr. was highest bidder at sale. Afterwards he sold his right to Ann Roberts, but never made deed. In consideration of the above premises, deed signed by William Robertson before Dan'l Reintzel, Thos Corcoran.

165-166. Jacob Shuh recorded 17 May 1798, schedule of debts goods, etc. to Benjamin W. Jones, sheriff. Amounts owing from Josiah Shoals, Mathias Tesiter, Thomas Halfpenny and Salome Miller, signed before George H. Offutt, Elemelech Swearingen.

166. Robert S. Smithy, recorded schedule 17 May 1798. Those itemized as owing him money were W. H. Dorsey, Thomas S. Lee Jr., Alex'r Peter, Thos Worthington, Thos Turner, Dr. W. Murphy, David Crawford, Henry Trail, Robert Peter Sr., Joseph Boone, Clement Hill, Wm Robertson, James Harris, John Miller, Alex'r McIntire, Doctor Gantt, Wm Thompson, John Pringle, Robert Peter Junr., V. Bogengrieff, N. Traverse, Richard Ober, Capt. John Thompson, George King, Wm Whann, Jesse Melin, D.S. McDugall, John Pringle, Matthew Bowne - several large notes, and suits against Js Young, and Capt. Hand of Philadelphia. Signed before Elemelech Swearingen, George H. Offutt.

167-168. Negro Harry recorded 18 May 1798, from John Suter, Junr., for valuable consideration, manumission, Harry being healthy and sound and able to get his living.

168-169. Thomas Beall of George, Wm Smith and Samuel Williams, recorded 27 June 1796, from Francis Deakins, deed. Whereas Bernard O'Neale and William Deakins did convey certain parcels at the mouth of Seneca, 19 July 1793, recorded in Liber E:498-502.

169-171. Frederick Duvall recorded 26 May 1798, from Aquilla Duvall for £320, Sells all his rights to *Hold Fast To What You Have Got.* Signed before Francis B. Sappington, William Beatty.

171. Henry Forrest, recorded 29 May 1798, certificate as deputy sheriff, sworn before Thomas Corcoran.

171-172. Joseph Nevit recorded 30 May 1798, from Norman Goodear, bill of sale, as a mortgage of personal property for £10, owed to Andrew Schofield. Signed before Lloyd Beall.

172-173. Zachariah Maccubbin, Thomas Nicholls and John Kelly, recorded 31 May 1798, from Thomas Nicholls of John bill of sale for £225, one bay horse, two milch cows, 21 head of hogs, 25 barrels Indian corn, three feather beds, other items of personal property listed. Signed before J. H. McPherson.

173. James L. Anthony, recorded 1 June 1798, qualification as deputy sheriff, before Benjamin W. Jones.

173-174. Lewis Duvall recorded 1 June 1798, from James Scott, deed made same date for £50, sells all his estate both real and personal lying in Montgomery County, including 4 lots in Hyattstown #23, 76, 75 & 78, three feather beds, 4 head of cattle, etc. Signed James Scott before Elemelech Swearingen, Josias H. McPherson.

174-175. Archibald Dunn, Hugh S. Dunn and Jesse Phillips recorded recognizance 18 March 1798 before Greenbury Howard. Whereas a certain Massa Dowden made oath that Archibald Dunn was the father of her illegitimate child, he is now bound to maintain same from becoming a ward of the county.

175. Isaac Owens recorded 6 June 1798, from Thomas Nevitt, bill of sale for $100, for one half of a scow now in my possession the other half in the possession of John Templeton. Signed Thomas Nevitt and acknowledged before Charles Beatty.
175. Robert Wallace recorded 7 June 1798, from William Prather Williams, deed made 6 June for £18..15, for lot #77 in town of Williamsburgh, part of a tract called *Exchange and New Exchange Enlarged,* signed before John L. Summers, Josias H. McPherson.
177. Thomas B. Offutt recorded 7 May 1798, from Richard Ober, bill of sale for Negro woman Rachel and her child Harriet. Signed before George H. Offutt.
177-178. Joseph Brooke recorded June 1798, from Samuel Turner, bill of sale for Negro girl Hannah 17 years old. Taken before Ignatius Newport, Anthony Rothwartz.
178-179. John Belt recorded 9 June 1798, from Rezin Johnson, deed made 19 May for £450 for part of *Resurvey on Friends Advice,* conveyed by Abigen Johnson to Rezin Johnson. Signed before Greenbury Howard and John Clark, and Henry Davidge and Anthony Ricketts on the premises. Acknowledged by Rezin Johnson and Lydia Johnson wife of Rezin released dower rights.
179-180. Richard Beall, Margaret Beall, Charlotte Myers and Lucretia Gartrell, recorded 12 June 1798, From Peter Kemp, for £5, deed for a parcel called *James and Mary.* Signed before J.T. Beall, Allan Bowie.
180-181. Richard Beall recorded 12 June 1798, from Charles Miles, Elizabeth Miles his wife and Amelia Beall, for £33. Deed for part of a tract called *Snowden's Mill,* lying near Paint Branch. All three signed by marks before James A. Beall and Horatio Beall. Acknowledgment and dower release before Allan Bowie.
181-182. John Thompson & James Thompson recorded 12 June 1798, from James Fling, bill of sale for £300, a 2/3 share in the following Negroes: Negro man Jacob, Negro woman Nan (or Ann) and Negro girl named Suk. Signed by mark of James Fling.
182-183. James Hunt, Ruth Hunt, Thomas P. Hunt and William Hunt, children and co-heirs of William Pitt Hunt, late of same county deceased, from Samuel Brewer Magruder, for £279..2, deed for tract called *The Mills,* 25 acres granted to Samuel Magruder on 2nd or 3d December 1738; also part of *Maguder and Bealls Honesty;* a part formerly conveyed by Ninian Magruder, to part conveyed to Robert Peter. Signed before Daniel Reintzel and George H. Offutt. Rebecca Magruder wife of Samuel B. Magruder released dower rights.
183-185. Lewis Bealmear & Saml Bealmear, recorded deed 14 June 1798, from Elizabeth Bealmear of Ann Arundel County. Whereas Francis Bealmear by his will did devise to them part of *Valentines Garden Enlarged*, reserving rights to his widow Elizabeth; she for £400 devises all her rights to them. Signed before John Swearingen and Josiah H. McPherson.
185-187. Lewis Bealmear and Samuel Bealmear, partition deed made 14 June 1798, tract containing 146 1/4 acres. Signed by both parties before same witnesses as above.
188-191. William Cranch, recorded 14 June 1798, power of attorney. I William Hollingsworth of Nine Elms, Battersea in the County of Surrey appoint John Warder, of Philadelphia, merchant my true attorney to recover of Mr. Walter Hellen of Georgetown, such sums due him. Signed before Samuel Crosley and William Ouchenberry, Notary Publick of London. Joshua Johnson, Consul of the Port of London attested. I James Scott of Durham Place, Lambeth in the County of Surry appoint John Warder of Philadelphia, merchant attorney to obtain payments due from Mr. Walter Heller. Signed before same witnesses as above. I John Warder of Philadelphia appoint George Gilpin of Alexandria, attorney to the annexed letters. Signed before Clement Biddle, Notary Public.
191-193. Absalom Beddo recorded deed 16 June, 1798, made 15 March, from Richard Beall, Amelia Beall, Solomon & Charlotte Myers, Charles & Elizabeth Miles, Margaret Beall, John & Lucresia Gartrell, all of Montgomery County, for £74..12, parcel, *Addition ???,* on east side of Paint Branch, 30 1/4 acres. Signed and acknowledged before James A. Beall, Horatio Beall. Charlotte Myers, Elizabeth Miles, Lucretia Gartrell and Elizabeth Beall wife of Richard Beall, all released dower rights.

193-194. Jacob Snider Junr. recorded 16 June 1798, made 2 January, from William Ballinger, deed for £157..10, tract called *Henry and Elizabeth,* containing 5 acres. Signed before Val. Brother, Belt Brashear. Lydia Ballinger released dower rights.
195-196. John Baer recorded 16 June 1798, made 2 January, from William Ballinger, deed for part of *Henry and Elizabeth*, adjacent to *None Such,* containing 106 acres. Signed and witnessed as above.
196. Philemon Plummer Junr. recorded 15 June 1798, from John Nicholson, bill of sale for personal property. Signed before Thomas Davis.
197-198. William Kelly recorded 19 June 1798, from Richard Mockbee, deed for £150, for part of tract called *Clean Shaving.* Signed Richard Mockbee before Henry Brookes, Benj. Gaither. Acknowledgment.
198-199. Honore Martin recorded 20 June 1798, made 18 June, from Nicholas Umstatd & Mary his wife, deed for £50, sells all title to the real estate of John Allison, late of Montgomery County by virtue of his will. Signed Nicholas Umstattd, Mary Umstattd, before John L. Summers, Josias H. McPherson.
199-201. Patrick Durham recorded 22 June 1798, deed made 5 May for £800 from John Kelly. Part of *Riley's Chance,* and part *Harrison's Delight,* and *Addition to Higgs,* and *Let me no more Deceive You,* 194 ½ acres all together. Signed John Kelly before Greenbury Howard, Benjamin Gaither. Catherine Kelly his wife released dower rights.
201. William Glaze recorded, from Ruth Glaze, for love and affection and 5 shillings from son William, sells all my estate both real and personal. Signed by mark, Ruth Glaze before William Awbrey, Baruch Prather, John Clagett of Thomas. Acknowledged before Josias H. McPherson.
201-202. Ruth Glaze recorded bond 23 June 1798, from William Glaze, for £200. The obligation is that the above bound William Glaze and John Clagett of Thomas shall well and truly, board, lodge and provide for the aforesaid Ruth Glaze, she continuing to live in the house of the aforesaid William Glaze during her natural life. Signed by William Glaze and John Clagett of Thos. Before Baruch Prather, William Awbrey.
202. Thomas Plater of Maryland record bond from Henry O'Neale & Anthony Tracy to State of Maryland, for £30, date 1 November 1797. The obligation of the bond is that Anthony Tracy will indemnify Montgomery County for all charges by reason of a female base born child called Maria Murphy, begotten on the body of Priscilla Murphy by the said Anthony, until she come of age. Signed by Anthony Tracy by mark, before William Smith.
202. Samuel Busey of Anne Arundel County, recorded 26 June 1798, from John Busey, bill of sale for one horse, 5 years old, 2 feather beds, etc. Signed before Joseph Belt.
202-204. Peter Arnold and David Arnold, brothers, recorded 26 June 1798, made 28 February, from Philip Hammond Hopkins, of Anne Arundel County, for £518, deed for part of parcel, *Labyrinth,* from the 42nd line, adjacent to *Plummer's Hunting Lot,* and the land of Joseph Jones, containing 60 acres. Signed before Edward Hall, Leonard Sellman. Acknowledgment.
204. Josias F. Beall from William Perry, bill of sale for a horse, etc. Signed before James F. Beall.
205-206. Nathan Cooke recorded 26 June 1798, made 24 February, from Thomas Selby, deed for £300, for part of *Resurvey on Charles and John's Choice,* lately resurveyed as *Fair Rosamond's Bower,* for 110 acres willed to him by Thomas Selby Senr., deceased. Signed before John S. Summers, Benjamin Gaither. Sarah Selby released dower rights.
206-207. Thomas Dunn recorded 27 June 1798, made same date, from John George Snider, weaver, for £7 with interest from 19 January last, mortgage note as security on note due to Philemon Plummer. Signed in German Script, Johan Georg Schneider, before Richard Green.
207-208. Thomas Contee of Prince George's County, recorded 29 June 1798, from Benjamin Ray Junr., late sheriff of Montgomery County, by virtue of writ, issued by the General Court of the Western Shore, 1 August 1797, Thomas Contee plaintiff against Edward Burgess, Ephraim Burgess, and Edward Burgess Junior, defendants, sells property at public sale, a part of *Addition to Snowden's Manor,* containing 91 acres for £180.

208. Thomas Contee from Benjamin Ray Junr., late sheriff. Same parties as above involved. Tract called *Second Addition to Snowden's Manor,* 237 acres. Sold to highest bidder.
209-214. George Chandler and Bernard Gilpin, partition deed
214. Philip Jenkins recorded 2 July 1798, from Job Medley, for £15, bill of sale for bay mare colt, 2 years old, 13.5 hands, etc. Signed by mark.
214. Thomas Clagett Wilcoxon recorded, from Jesse Wilcoxon, deed of gift for 5 shillings and natural love and affection "for my son," tract called *Drane's Purchase,* containing 100 acres. Signed before Aneas Campbell, Greenberry Howard. Acknowledgment.
215-216. William Worthington, from Judith Chaney, assignment of dower for $20. to all her rights in land that did belong to her late husband, John Chaney, situated in Anne Arundel County and elsewhere. Signed before Josias H. McPherson, Elemelech Swearingen.
216-217. Horatio Tuel, schedule to sheriff Benjamin W. Jones, recorded 5 July 1798. Accounts due from Nathan Neighbors, Peter McBride, Zachariah Tucker, William Collyer, George Wilson, Bernard Greenwell, Henry Stallings, Thomas C. Wills, William Sharp, John Jenkins, Robert Webber, Hutcherson, and William Redman on judgment. Horatio Tuel swears to statement before John L. Summers, J. H. McPherson.
217-220. Thomas Cramphin of Montgomery County recorded 7 July 1798, made 10 May, 1798 from Rev. Doctor John Carroll of Baltimore; Notley Young and Robert Brent of Prince George's County, trustees, devisees and executors of Daniel Carroll, late of Montgomery County for £2170..10 sells part of tract *Joseph's Park,* beginning at stone on east side of Rock Creek, it being the beginning of the whole tract, to west side of a small branch running through the tenement of Timothy Lyddane, to a road leading by tenement, to corner of parcel formerly possessed by Dr. Andrew Beall and a corner of Benjamin Becraft's land, following to the beginning of Benjamin and Peter Becraft's lands, and the end of the second line of Conn's land ... to the road leading from Newport Mills to Georgetown, then with meanders of Rock Creek to a small parcel sold by Daniel Carroll deceased to Thomas Johns deceased, then to beginning, containing 403 3/4 acres. Signed J. Carroll, witnessed by A. Boyle; Notley Young, Robert Brent and Thomas Cramphin, witnessed by Daniel Reintzel, George French.
220-221. Greenberry Griffith Jr., recorded 13 July 1798, made 21st March 1798, from Philemon Griffith of Frederick County, & Joshua Griffith, of Montgomery County, executors of the Will of Henry Griffith of Montgomery County, deceased. Deed for £133..2..1, for tract.
221-223. Basil Beckwith recorded 14 July 1798, from Rezin Spates, deed made 21 April for £81..10, part of *Resurvey on Brandy,* to part conveyed to Martin Fisher for 120 acres, to part conveyed to Charles Decandry and Peter Bowie for 120 acres. To end containing 11 3/8 acres. Signed before Aeneas Campbell, Thomas B. Beall. Acknowledgment. Henny, wife of Rezin Spates released dower rights.
223-224. Thomas Beall of George recorded 17 July 1798, from Levin Magruder for 5 shillings. Whereas Samuel W. Magruder, late of Montgomery County held tract *Piney Level,* 130 acres devised to his two sons Levin and Charles, and Charles sold his undivided share to Thomas Beall, this is a deed of division for 50 acres. Signed before Benjamin Griffith, Josias H. McPherson. Elizabeth, wife of Levin Magruder released dower rights.
224-225. George H. Offutt, recorded 17 July 1798, indenture made 20 January 1798 between Thomas Drane, executor of Thomas Sparrow, for £126, sells tract, *Hold Fast,* adjacent to *Williamsborough,* 48 acres. Signed by Thomas Drane Jr., before Lawrence O'Neale, Greenbury Howard. Ack. Receipt.
225-227. Edward Crow recorded 11 July 1798, made 18 January 1798 between William Gaither, whereas William Gaither, entered into a contract with William Ridgely to convey to him, part of *Samuel's Chance,* for consideration agreed upon, 14,000 lbs. tobacco, and Ridgely further contracted with Edward Crow to convey tract. Deed made to him. Signed William Gaither before Francis B. Sappington, Dan'l Dorsey.
227-230. Leonard Holliday Johns recorded 8 July 1798, made 2 February 1798, between John Wilcoxon for £354..10, sells parcel called *Dann,* formerly conveyed by William Ridgely to William Wilcoxon 6 September 1768, and afterwards conveyed by William Wilcoxon to Jesse Wilcoxon 15 September 1777, at beginning

of William Ridgely's part of *Dan,* running the meanders of Rock Creek, N 41 deg W, 10, N3.5E, 6; N28W,1; N10 to Rock Creek, N21W,12, N34W,12; N7W8; N19W9; N37.5E,12 to third line of whole tract to the beginning of *Joseph's Park;* N29W36; N44W38; S44W,124; ??; S74.5W,68; S16W,11 and line to beginning containing 70.5 acres; beginning at second part of *Dan* conveyed by Rebecka Brooke to William Wilcoxon, 1 June 1772, and conveyed to Jesse Wilcoxon 15 September 1777; beginning at 7th line formerly conveyed by William Dent, for 25 acres. Also one other part conveyed by Lucy Brooke to Charles Clagett and Philip Berry for 200 acres, then conveyed to Thomas Wilcoxon and by Thomas Wilcoxon conveyed to Jesse Wilcoxon and Levin Wilcoxon. Signed Jesse Wilcoxon before Wm Smith, Laurence O'Neale, 22 Feb 1798. Elizabeth wife of Jesse released dower rights.

230-231. Stephen B. Balch & George Thompson recorded 21 July 1798, made 19 July, from Thomas Offutt of Wm, for £48, grants parcel called *Goose Island,* confined all around by Potomac River, about 1/4 mile below Mr. Cloud's or Edward's Ferry, 9 ½ acres. Signed Thomas Offutt Jr., before Dan'l Reintzel, Lloyd Beall. Marcia wife to Thomas Offutt released dower.

231-232. Negro Rachel records enfranchise, 25 July 1798. I Solomon Holland for good causes, manumit Rachel aged about 22 years, now in possession of Benjamin Ricketts, after the decease of the said Benjamin Ricketts, after term of service above. Signed 23 July 1798. Solomon Holland before John L. Summers.

232. Philip Selby recorded 24 July 1798, from John Mitchell and Francis Deakins, administrator of Wm. Deakins Junr., both of Georgetown. Release of prior sale of £174 on writ of fi fa, signed by John Mitchell and Wm Deakins on 25 August 1795.

232-234. Richard Bennett Hall of Prince George's County recorded 1 August 1798, from David Luckett, deed for £376..12..6, two tracts. Part of *Resurvey on Allison's Adventure,* adjacent to *Killmain,* and Sugarland Road, containing 22 ½ acres and also *Pleasant Plains,* a contiguous tract containing 52 ½ acres. Signed D. Luckett before Aeneas Campbell, Greenbury Howard. Susannah Luckett released dower rights.

234-235. Patrick Durham recorded 2 August 1798, from John Kelly, for £150, bill of sale for live stock and furniture. Signed before Edward Burgess, Jr.

235-236. Patrick Durham recorded 2 August 1798, from John Dubois, of Frederick County, Md., for £70 bill of sale for one Negro woman Bridgett, 32 years old and child Tom, aged 3 months. Signed before Jacob Young.

236-237. Stephen Lewis recorded 6 August 1798, from Mathew Reed, for £40 bill of sale for lot and tenement and contents in town of Clarksburg, 1/4 acres. Signed before Edward Dunnigall, Levy Tucker. Schedule of goods attached: one black walnut table, 4 chairs, one chest, one washing tub, one wooden bucket, one tin bucket, one stone pitcher, one griddle, one iron tea kettle, one iron pot, one copper pot, one fish barrel, two flour barrels, one 10 gallon keg, one pewter dish, half dozen knives and forks, one Dutch oven, one frying pan, one spinning wheel.

237. John Jeans recorded 6 August 1798, from William Carline, for $20, bill of sale for two beds, bedsteads, furniture, woolen wheel, linen wheel, taylors goose, chest and bright bay mare 10 years old. Signed by mark before Aeneas Campbell.

237-238. Joseph Catro, recorded 10 August 1798, schedule delivered to Benjamin W. Jones Sheriff, before John L. Summers, Benjamin Gaither.

238. Solomon Holland, Edward Owen and Caleb Sommers, recorded bond for £8037..14..10, to State of Maryland, to be collector of tax for the levy court. Signed before Benjamin Jones and Thomas Gatton of Richard.

238-239. Adam Ramsower recorded 14 August 1798, from Jesse Hyatt, deed made 7 April for £25, for lots #51, 52, 53, 105, 106 & 177 in Hyattstown; to pay annual rent of 5 shillings. Signed before Edward Burgess Junr., John Clark. Ack. Receipt.

239-240. Levin Magruder recorded August 1798, from Thomas Beall of George, deed. Whereas Samuel W. Magruder, late of Montgomery County held tract *Piney Level,* 130 acres devised to his two sons Levin

and Charles, and Charles sold his undivided share to Thomas Beall, this is a deed of division for 80 acres. Nancy Beall wife of Thomas Beall of George released dower rights.
240-241. Francis Paster recorded 14 August 1798, from Jesse Hyatt, deed made 7 April, for £18, for lots #5 & 59 in Hyattstown; to pay annual. Signed before Edward Burgess Junr., John Clark.
242. A summary list of real and personal property in Montgomery County, recorded in chart form on one page, listed the number of acres in each hundred, the number of slaves in each of the following categories: Ages 8-14; females 14 to 36; males 14 to 45; under the age of 8 years; Above the ages of 36 and 45; ounces of silver plate, other property and the values of each category. The districts recorded included the 1st District: Georgetown, Lower Potomac and Middle Potomac Hundreds; 2nd District: Upper Potomac and Sugarland Hundreds; 3d district: Sugar Loaf and Linganore Hundreds; 4th District: Upper Newfoundland and Seneca Hundreds; 5th District: Lower Newfoundland, Rock Creek and Northwest Hundreds. Report signed by Thomas Davis, Richard Wootton, Allen Bowie and J. B. Beall. The summary census numbers of slaves were as follows:

Place	Age 8-14	F 14-36	M 14-45	Under 8	Over 36, 45.
District 1	302	337	349	334	190
District 2	260	274	354	445	183
District 3	178	229	223	329	74
District 4	199	203	227	274	154
District 5	192	249	272	365	200
TOTALS	1131	1292	1425	1947	801

243. Robert Peter recorded 24 August 1798, from William Smallwood, for balance of rent due for 1797, the sum of 7688 lbs. crop tobacco, a bill of sale for annexed schedule of goods which included a sorrel horse, a bay horse, other livestock, furniture and dishes.
243-245. Richard Gott recorded 24 August 1798, from Robert Peter of Georgetown, deed for 5 shillings, parcel, *The Fertile Plains,* 396 ½ acres. Signed before Daniel Reintzel, Lloyd Beall. Receipt. Elizabeth, wife of Robert Peter released dower rights.
245-246. Charles Perry recorded 24 August 1798, with William Worthington and Upton Beall, to State of Maryland, Supervisors Bond for £725. Signed before Brice Selby, Levi Connor.
245-246. Caleb Peddicoat, Greenberry Peddicoat and Carlton Peddicoat recorded 25 August 1798, from Jasper Peddicoat, bill of sale for £150, for a Negro girl Charity 12 years old, Rachel 10 years old and Maria 3 years old, and furniture. Signed before J. H. McPherson.
246-248. Ann Clagett recorded 25 August 1798, from Robert Peter trustee of Thos Wilson, deed made per order of the Chancellor of Maryland, 23 August for £245..6 with interest; land on south east side of *Archibald's Lot,* to 39th line of *Resurvey on Exchange and New Exchange Enlarged,* and adjacent to *Black Oak Thicket,* containing 104 acres. Signed Robert Peter as trustee before George French, Daniel Reintzel.
248-249. Philip Jenkins recorded 25 August 1798, from Jasper Pedicoat, for £25 bill of sale for 4 feather beds, bedsteads and furniture. Signed before J. H. McPherson.
249-250. Thomas Cramphin recorded 28 August 1798, from Nathaniel Beall, for £75..17..2, deed of trust for Negro slaves: Ben 25 years, Will 30 years, boy Tom 12 years and Negro Rachel 45 years old. Sale void if sum paid by 1 June next. Signed before Benj. Perry and J. T. Beall.
250-252. Robert Peter recorded 30 August 1798, from Hezekiah Thomas, deed made 16 August for £210, tract called *Conclusion,* originally granted to Daniel Dulaney, for 1930 acres. M&B given from 17th line of

Resurvey on Drought, and *Resurvey on Partnership.* For 93 ½ acres. Signed before Wm Smith, George H. Offutt. Jane Thomas released dower rights.

252-254. William Fulks recorded 2 September 1798, from John Beckwith, deed made 22 June for £191..6..10, for tract (*Hobson's Choice,)* which William Williams Sr. on 9 Nov. 1775 conveyed to John Beckwith, [FCLR BD1:333] beginning on 4th line of *Conclusion,* to tract laid off for Charles Williams, containing 117 3/4 acres. Signed before Henry Brookes, Josias H. McPherson. Receipt. Martha Beckwith wife of John, released dower rights.

254. Robert Smith recorded 8 September 1798, one Negro woman named Linn, devised to me from my father John Smith, formerly of Prince George's County, now deceased by deed of gift made in Prince George's County, which said Negro was brought from Virginia to Maryland about 1 July last, aged about 18 or 20 years. Signed R. Smith.

254-255. Abraham Snyder recorded 13 September 1798, from John D. Coffee, for £15 deed made 7 April for one lot, part of a tract called *Moneysworth,* lot beginning at stone #10. Signed before Henry Brookes, and John Clarke. Dorcas Coffee released dower rights.

255-258. Talbott Alnutt recorded 14 September 1798, from Basil Darby, deed. We Richard Pack and Mary Pack his wife of Rowan Co., North Carolina, appoint Basil Darby our lawful attorney to sell tract of land on Seneca called *Thomas's Discovery,* which was by the will of James Allnutt, devised to his five daughters, except for 1/3 of same which was given to his wife Jane Allnutt during her life. This deed, made by Basil Darby, sells their undivided 1/5 part of her third part, by Mary Pack, one of the daughters of James Allnutt and Richard Pack her husband, for £30 by their lawful attorney, Basil Darby.

259. Gustavus Scott, recorded 17 September 1798, a list of Negroes brought from Virginia into this State: Sal from Virginia, a slave before 1783, devised to me by the will of Wm Scott Esq., late of Fairfax County, Va. Signed before Upton Beall.

259-260. Samuel Knox recorded 17 September 1798, from Stephen B. Balch, for £112..10, bill of sale for Negroes, boy George 9 yrs and Harry 4 years old, and Negro woman Charity 24 years old, to hold them until they arrive at age 30 and no longer. Signed 14 September 1798, Stephen B. Balch before John Hewett and George French Jr.

260-261. Richard Anderson recorded 17 September 1798, from George Riley, for £100, deed for tract where Basil Thompson lived last year called *Discontent,* on the second line of *Two Brothers,* signed by George Riley before John L. Summers, Josias H. McPherson.

261-263. Ninian Magruder & Nathan Cooke recorded 25 September 1798, from William Leach, for £343..13..9, deed for two tracts of land, *Owens Resurvey,* and part of *Resurvey on Abel's Levels.* Metes and bounds given for 136 1/4 acres and 16 ½ acres. Signed by mark before John L. Summers and Elemelech Swearingen. Receipt. Acknowledgment. Althea Leatch, wife of William released dower rights.

263-264. Stephen Lewis recorded 1 October 1798, from Mathew Reed, for £40, bill of sale for a lot and tenement in town of Clarksbugh, 1/4 acre with all household stuff and furniture contained in annexed schedule. Signed Matthew Reed before Edward Hannegan and Lucy Tucker by mark. Items: feather bed, bedstead, bed cloaths, black walnut table, four chairs, chest, washing tub, wooden bucket, tin bucket, stone pitcher, iron griddle, iron tea kettle, iron pot, coffee pot, fish barrel, two flour barrels, 10 gallon keg, pewter dish, half dozen knives and forks, Dutch oven, frying pan and spinning wheel.

264-266. Gerard Gaither, devisee under the will of Henry Gaither, deceased, from Lewis Duvall, executor of the will of Aquilla Duvall deceased. Whereas Aquilla Duvall on 21 December 1772 for sum of £5..10 sterling, paid by Henry Gaither, now deceased, made a bond obligatory to sell 110 acres, but died before deed was executed. Now a good deed is being made, metes and bounds recorded. Signed by Lewis Duvall before Benjamin Gaither, Edward Burgess Junr.

266-267. Negro Bob & others recorded 2 October 1798, from Benjamin Waters, manumissions. Bob aged 29 to be free at age 39; Lulu 27 to be free at 39. All their offspring to be free at 25 years. Jack now age 8 to be free at age 31 years; Janny aged 3 years and Maria just born, and Frederick age 4 years to be free at 31 years old.

267-268. Ninian Magruder recorded 3 October 1798, from William Offutt Magruder, deed of gift made same date in consideration of the natural love and affection and for his better maintenance and support assigns tract deeded to our father, Ninian Magruder by William Pritchett, part of *Pritchett's Purchase,* at end of second line of *Huntington,* for 50 acres, and also part of *Addition to Magruder's Purchase,* for 18 acres. Signed Wm O. Magruder before Henry Brookes, Benjamin Gaither.

268-270. Richard Jones recorded 4 October 1798, from Evan Thomas, deed made 1st day 8th month called August, for £93, for tract called *New Purchase,* a part of *Two Farms,* beginning at 1st line of *Beall Christie.* Metes & bounds, adjacent to *Easy Purchase,* laid out for 17 ½ acres. Signed Evan Thomas before Dan'l Reintzel, Thos Corcoran. Receipt. Acknowledgment.

270-271. Hezekiah Thomas recorded 4 October 1798, from Nancy Crow wife of Basil Crow, of Bullett County, State of Kentucky, deed made 10 August for 5 shillings, sells all her interest in tracts on the Hawlings River, given by Basil Crow and Priscilla Caldwell, Wm Singleton.

271-272. Patrick Lyddane, Michael Lyddane and Thomas Lyddane recorded 4 October 1798, from Evan Thomas, for £22..15, tract of land called *Joint Purchase,* a part of *Two Farms,* beginning at tract, *Bealls Manor,* adjacent to *Radnor,* containing 6 3/4 acres. Signed before Dan'l Reintzel and Thos Corcoran. Receipt, Acknowledgment.

273-274. William Candler recorded 4 October 1798 from William Hammond Dorsey and Ann Dorsey his wife, deed made 16 August 1798 for £60, sells part of *Pleasant Plains of Damascus,* containing 100 acres, being the same tract conveyed by Mathew Pigman to Richard Brooke, deceased. Signed before Thos Corcoran, Lloyd Beall. Dower release recorded.

274-275. Charles Bucy Junr, son of Charles recorded 4 October 1798, from Jesse Hyatt, deed made 25 August for £13..10 for lots #3, 21, 57 & 75 in Hyattstown. Signed before John Clarke, Greenbury Howard. Acknowledgment.

275-278. Charles Lowndes recorded 4 Oct. 1798, from Isaac Polock of the City of Washington, Territory of Columbia, mortgage made 28 April 1798, for $2,340 parcel in Montgomery County consisting of parts of two tracts, one *Magruder's Purchase,* the other, *Addition to the Resurvey on Magruder's Purchase,* on the 31 Jan. 1797 conveyed by Thomas Johnson of Frederick Town to the said Isaac Polock containing 295 ½ acres, recorded among the land records for that part of the territory of Columbia which lies in Maryland. If Isaac Polock pays the sum with 6% per annum interest from the 1st November last past, until sum is paid, then sale is void. Mortgage for two year term. Signed Isaac Polock, Charles Lowndes, before Thos Corcoran, George French.

278-279. Lawrence O'Neale recorded 5 Oct. 1798, from Edward Veirs, bill of sale in consideration of a debt owed, assigns one Negro man called Noble, four horses, six head of cattle, four feather beds and furniture, all my crop of corn, wheat, rye and tobacco. Signed same date before John L. Summers.

279. John Riddle recorded 9 October 1798, from William Ray son of John, bill of sale in consideration of the natural love and affection I bear to John Riddle, assigns and confirms one Negro girl, Elizabeth, about six years of age. Signed before John L. Summers.

280. James Norwood Junr., recorded 9 October 1798, from James Norwood, Senr., deed of gift in consideration of the natural love and affection I bear to my son, assigns all right, title & claim to the property of my late son Stephen Norwood. Signed by mark before Edward Burgess, Jr.

280-282. Basil Magruder Perry recorded 9 October 1798, made 8 October from Andrew Jackson Hoskinson, deed made 8 Oct. for £190..10, tract called *Hoskinson's Delight,* deeded from Allen Beall to John Hoskinson, deceased, a part of *John and Mary, Bear Garden Enlarged, Trundles Folly, Greenland, Jane and Mary,* and resurvey thereon; containing 97 1/4 acres devised to the said Andrew Hoskinson by his father John Hoskinson. Signed Andrew Jackson Hoskinson before Lloyd Beall, Thos Corcoran. Receipt. Acknowledgment. Elizabeth Hoskinson, wife of Andrew J. Hoskinson, released dower rights.

282-284. George Ray & John Ray Junr., recorded 9 October 1798 from John Ray Senr., deed for natural love and affection I bear toward my sons, and for five shillings, assigns tract called *General Montgomery,* a resurvey made 18 March 1783 on *Rays Town,* beginning at a tract called *Joseph,* to a tract called *Tree Bottom,* to a tract called *Good as one Can Get,* to third line of a tract *Hunting Hills,* containing 226 ½ acres. Signed before John L. Summers, Josias H. McPherson.

284-285. William O. Neale recorded 9 October 1798, from John Young & Precious Young his wife of Berkeley County, Virginia, deed. Whereas John Allison, late of Montgomery County, did by his will devise his real and personal estate to be sold at the death or remarriage of his wife Elizabeth Allison, and the money to be divided among his children, of whom Precious Young is one, for £22..10, sells their share. Signed John Young and Precious Young by mark before Lawrence O'Neale, Josias H. McPherson.

285-286. Rachel Ray & Dorcas Ray recorded 9 October 1798, from John Ray Senr., deed of gift for natural love and affection for his daughters, gives them Negroes Minty, age 25 years; Nan, 7 years, Thomas, 5 years, Ben 4 years, Bill 2 yrs and Daniel 3 months old, plus all my furniture and plantation utensils and stock. Signed John Ray Senr. before Josias H. McPherson.

286-288. Gerard Brooks recorded 9 October 1798, from Ezekiel Jackson, bill of sale for £40 sells one bay mare, saddle and bridle, tobacco and flax. Signed by mark before John L. Summers.

288-289. Josias Ray of Prince George's Co., recorded 9 October 1798, from William Ray, son of John, deed in consideration of the natural love and affection for my brother, and for his better maintenance and support gives him tract in Montgomery County, called *Conjunction,* adjacent to *Hunting Hills,* and on the whole of *Day Ending*. Signed before John L. Summers, Josias H. McPherson. Acknowledgment.

289-291. Sarah Robertson, Samuel Robertson, Elizabeth Robertson, Anna Robertson, and William Robertson, children of the late George Robertson, recorded 9 October 1798, deed from David Lynn, for part of tract called *Bradford's Rest,* containing 40 acres. Signed David Lynn before George Murdock. Mary Lynn released dower.

291-293. Margaret Davis of Frederick Co., wife of Ignatius Davis, recorded 9 October 1798, from Richard Wootton, deed made 4 September, in consideration of his natural love and affection, and for £10 makes over part of second resurvey on *William and James,* which he purchased of William Littlefield; and also part of *Friend in Need,* purchased of Jacob Waters, on the North side of Seneca Creek. Signed before Allen Bowie, Josias H. McPherson. Martha, wife of Richard Wootton, released dower rights.

293-294. Josias Ray of Prince George's County, recorded deed of gift, from William Ray son of John Ray, 10 October 1798. For the natural love I have for my brother, grants one Negro man, Hannibal aged 40 years, John age 18; Joe 13 years; Dinah 33 years, Sophia 16 years, Jane 12 years and Suck 6 years of age. Also all my household kitchen furniture and plantation utensils and 25 head of sheep, 12 head of horned cattle and crop of corn and tobacco. Signed before John L. Summers, acknowledgment.

294-295. John Howse recorded 13 October 1798, from John Bales, for £100, bill of sale for one dark bay gelding, cattle and other property. Signed by mark before John L. Summers.

295. Robert Peter from William Smallwood, transfer of schedule, recorded 13 August 1798, including amount for rent due in1797, delivers one gray mare, cow and calf, furniture, barshare plow. Signed by mark before Thomas Fletchall, J. Thompson.

296. Alexander Whittaker recorded assignment 18 October 1798, from Joseph S. Belt for £45..15, a Negro girl Nanny. Signed before Robert A. Whitaker.

296-297. Negro Charles recorded 18 October 1798, from William Craik, manumission for good causes, released from slavery. Signed before Dan'l Reintzel, Samuel Davidson.

297. William Collings recorded 18 October 1798, from John Scrivener, for £50, bill of sale for all my crop of tobacco now in the houses, stripped; and all my crop of Indian Corn now in the field, one gelding, 9 head of hogs, 4 horned cattle. Signed by mark before Gass. W. Harwood.

297-299. Isaac Webster Senior recorded 19 October 1798, from Solomon Holland, late sheriff of Montgomery County, deed made 16 June. Whereas a judgment was obtained by Richard Morgan and his wife

against Lewis Duvall, on 23 March 1792 a writ was issued for tracts *Richards Range* 140 acres; *Bristol,* 50 acres, and *Rogues Harbour,* 206 acres, the property of Lewis Duvall was taken and exposed to public sale. Nathan Musgrove was the highest bidder, and he assigned his right to Isaac Webster Sr. Signed Solomon Holland, and acknowledged before John L. Summers, Josias H. McPherson.
299-300. Robert McClan, Schedule recorded 25 October 1798, property turned over to Benjamin W. Jones, sheriff. Credits due from Jonathan Newhouse on note £50..10..10 and others in small amounts on account: Anthony Gogler, John House, Walter Mitchell, Thomas White, Hazel Butt, John Traverse, Daniel Maginnis, Jacob Powell, Doct. Charles Worthington, Stewart Williams, A. B. Edmonstone, Benjamin Haines, George Craigg, Thomas Sandard, Abraham Wingard, Aaron Dyer, James Simpson, John L. Lovejoy, John King, Thomas Hill, James Read, Nathaniel Magruder, James Doyle, Jacob Wilson, Barton Harris, Benjamin Swann, ___ Brown, John Deakins, Nathan Collins, Edward House. Signed Robert McClan, before John L. Summers, Josias H. McPherson.
300-301. Edward Magruder recorded 25 October 1798, from Benjamin W. Jones, sheriff, deed. Whereas by writ of fieri facias issued by the Montgomery County Court, 8 December 1797, Edward Magruder plaintiff against Leonard Cooke, defendant. Sold lot #24 in Beatty & Hawkins Addition to Georgetown at auction to the highest bidder, Edward Magruder for £55. Signed before John L. Summers, Josias H. McPherson.
301-303. Elemelech Swearingen recorded 26 October 1798, from Charles Burress, bill of sale for £100 specie, sells Negro woman, Easter 12 years old and Negro Mary 45 years, one mare, and one bay horse, cows, hogs, feather bed and furniture. Signed by mark before Josias H. McPherson.
303-304. Elemelech Swearingen recorded 29 October 1798, from Walter O. Daniel, bill of sale for £90..7..2. Sells one bay mare 6 years old, one black mare one bay horse and colt, crop of corn and tobacco. Signed before Josias H. McPherson.
304-305. Elemelech Swearingen recorded 1 November 1798, from Charles Burress & Ruth, his wife, for £50, deed for part of *Bradford's Rest*, adjacent to William P. Williams, formerly owned by Anthony Wilcoxon, deceased, which is the dower right of aforesaid Ruth Burress. Both signed by mark before Benjamin Gaither, Josias H. McPherson. Deed acknowledged and dower released.
305-308. Joseph Aud recorded 1 November 1798, from Francis Deakins, devisee of William Deakins, made 13 October 1798, for £200, parts of *Conclusion*, adjacent to *Troublesome*, and *Grandmother's Good Will.* 218 acres. Signed, and wife of Francis Deakins (not named) released dower rights.
308-310. Solomon Simpson recorded 3 November 1798, from Michael Ashford. Dowden, deed made 1 September for tract called *Apple Orchard,* at tract called *St. Thomas,* containing 3/4 acre. Signed before Laurence O'Neale, Greenbury Howard. Mary Dowden released dower rights.
310-312. Solomon Simpson recorded 3 November 1798, made 13 June from Richard Bennett Hall, of Prince George's County, deed for £942..10, sells two tracts, *Saint Thomas,* adjacent to tract *Saturday Night,* and *Succession,* containing 139 ½ acres; and the second tract a part of *Friendship,* conveyed by John Baptist Pierce, to Richard Bennet Hall for 57 acres, now laid out for 49 acres. Signed Richd B. Hall before Thos Duckett, Wm. M. Hall. Receipt, acknowledgment. Margaret wife of Richard B. Hall released dower rights. Attested to by John Neal Magruder, clerk of Prince George's County.
312. Thomas Gatton, recorded 3 November 1798, Qualification as Deputy Sheriff, at the request of Benjamin Jones, taken before J. H. McPherson.
313-315. Daniel Luckett recorded November 1798, from Richard Bennett Hall of Prince Georges County, deed made 13 June, for £269..5 part of two parcels, *Good Will,* adjacent to *Saint Thomas,* containing by patent 40 acres, and *Saturday Night,* containing 5 acres, and a third tract, part of *Friendship,* adjacent to *Saint Thomas*, for 8 1/4 acres, in all 53 1/4 acres. Signed before Thos Duckett, Wm. M. Beall. Margaret Hall released dower.
315-318. Daniel Luckett recorded 5 November 1798, made 21 July from Solomon Stimpson, for £402..10, part of two tracts, one *Simpson's Dwelling place,* and part of *Friendship,* for 80 ½ acres. Signed before Aeneas Campbell, Greenbury Howard. Dorcas Stimpson released dower.

318-319. Benjamin Berry Junr. and Isaac Lancaster Lansdale recorded 5 November 1798, from Andrew Hoskinson of Prince William County, Va., for £17..10, deed made 8 October 1798, he assigns all his claim to their mill dam, on Paint Branch, and from damages arising from its overflow. Signed before Ans Campbell, Greenbury Howard.
319-321 Michael A. Dowden recorded 5 November 1798, made 13 June, from Richard Bennett Hall of Prince George's County, for £52..10, part of a parcel called *Saint Thomas,* adjacent to a tract *Saturday Night,* containing 10 ½ acres. Signed before Thos Duckett, Wm M. Hall. Receipt. Acknowledgment. Margaret Hall released dower.
321-323. Caleb Summers recorded 7 November 1798, deed made 24 October, from Solomon Holland. Whereas Caleb and John L. Summers, did on 6 February 1787 purchase from William P. Williams, a lot #39, in Williamsburgh, alias Montgomery Courthouse, divided between them, on which now stands a house, now occupied as a tavern by John Wayman, beginning at the northwest corner of the courthouse lot. Signed Solomon Holland, before Josias H. McPherson, Elemelech Swearingen.
323-325. Thomas B. Beall recorded deed 7 November 1798, from Azariah Weaver Sanders of Nelson County, Kentucky, and his power of attorney to his friend Henry R. Whitacre to execute the deed, which he had obligated himself to convey tract called *Widow's Lot,* which was devised to him by Azariah Davis. Signed before Benjamin Grayson, Clerk of Nelson County.
325-326. Tyson Beall recorded 7 November 1798, from Nathan Hoskinson, for £33, deed for *Trundle's Folly,* for 22 1/4 acres from the dividing line between Nathan Hoskinson and Andrew Hoskinson. Signed by Nathan Hoskinson and acknowledged.
326-328. John L. Summers recorded 7 November 1798, from Caleb Summers, deed for part of lot #39 and lot #38, in Williamsburgh, beginning at the NW corner of the courthouse lot, on the south side of West land, near the NW corner of Caleb Summers brick house, to lot #37, then to First Street, to a stake at the NW corner of Honore Martin's stable on lot #37, to that part conveyed by Solomon Holland. Signed Caleb Summers. Rachel Summers wife of Caleb released dower rights.
329. Negro James & others recorded 7 November 1798, from Benjamin Stoddert, manumissions for the following Negroes. James, a.k.a. James Brown, aged 30 years; Grace Thomas age 18 years, and Fanny Ridgely 15 years old. Signed by Benjamin Stoddert before Uriah Forrest, Charles Wayman.
329-331. Shadrach Turner of Prince Georges County, recorded 7 November 1798, from Henry Baggerly, deed made same date, for £30, a part of *Beall's and Edmonston's Discovery,* adjacent to 100 acre part formerly belonging to Samuel Blackamore, now Turner's, to a part conveyed to Henry Baggerly and Charles Phillips. Signed before Allan Bowie, Thomas Davis. Receipt. Mary Baggerly released dower rights.
331. Leonard MacDaniel, a "mulatto Negro man" recorded 8 November 1798, from Richard Parrott, enfranchisement from and after date hereof. Signed 20 October 1798 before Elijah Beall, Lloyd Beall.
332-335. William Fulk recorded 8 Nov. 1798, land commission granted to perpetuate bounds of *Hobson's Choice,* and *Conclusion,* granted 25 August 1798, to Richard Wootton, Richard Anderson, James Anderson, and John L. Summers. They met at a tree to take depositions from Charles Williams, age 54 years, who deposed 23 or 24 years ago, he was present as a chain carrier when his father, William Williams Senr., caused to be surveyed and laid out to John Beckwith a part originally called *Conclusion,* to a line of division, nearly in a line between William Fulk's dwelling where John Beckwith formerly lived and house where Mrs. Verlinda Williams now lives. Mary West, aged 40 years deposed that in 1775, before tract was deeded to John Beckwith by her father, William Williams Sr., he marked an oak which was the boundary between Amos Williams and John Beckwith.
335-337. Robert Dorsey merchant of Baltimore County, recorded deed 8 November 1798, from Joseph Barnes, for $3590., part of *Addition to Brook Grove,* and part of *Fairhill,* contiguous to each other, and adjacent to trees in certificate for Anne Dorsey's allotment of her part of her deceased grandfather's lands, the lands of James Brooke deceased, as filed in Chancery to a part conveyed to John Howard for 391 ½ acres,

as *Addition to Spring Garden,* to new road leading from the mouth of the Monocacy to Ellicott's Lower Mills. Signed Joseph Barnes before Thomas Davis, John Clark. Mary Barnes released dower rights.
338-341. Thomas Beall of George recorded 8 November 1798, from Wm Smith & Samuel Williams, deed made 27 June 1798. Whereas Thomas Beall has borrowed $3,420 from the bank of Columbia for the use of Wm Smith and Samuel Williams, this deed is to indemnify him from harm if sum not repaid. Deed is for land called *Seneca Ford,* a part of *Middle Plantation,* sums are to be paid by 18 June 1800. Acknowledgment.
341-342. Charles Green & D. English recorded 9 Nov. 1798, from James Blake, bill of sale for Negro man slave, "Saul" for $235.
342. Easter Want recorded recognizance 10 November 1798, from William Thomas a black man, Thomas Moore, Samuel Brooke and Roger Brooke. Acknowledgment of sum of £7..1. Whereas a certain Easter Want did on 25 January 1798, discover under oath before Thomas Davis that she had an illegitimate male child born September last, and William Thomas, a black man was the father, he agrees to support and maintain said child until it shall arrive to seven years of age. Signed before Richard Green.
342-343. Solomon Holland recorded 10 November 1798, from Zachariah Maccubin, bill of sale for £211..6..6, sells Negroes, Paul 32 years, Luce 12 years, Jane 5 years, Harry 5 years; Jill 3 years. Signed 22 October 1798 before Josias H. McPherson.
343-346. Joseph Hodgson of the City of Washington, State of Maryland, recorded indenture 12 November 1798, from Joseph Green, master and half owner of the Schooner Columbia, the other half owned by Robert Dashiel and Peter Dashiel of Somerset County, state of Maryland, which now lies in Georgetown, and is licensed there to be employed in coasting trade and fisheries. The vessel has one deck and two masts, 62 ft by 18 ft. 6 inches wide. For $435, he assigns his undivided moiety in the schooner, signed by mark before Thos Corcoran, James Beall.
346-347. William Holmes recorded 12 November 1798, from Richard Waters, son of Richard, bill of sale for 900 lbs. crop tobacco and £9..4..5, one bay mare 17 years old and one sorrell mare. Signed by mark before Ann Leatch, Eleanor Estep. Acknowledged before J. F. Beall.
347-348. Thomas Pack Senr. recorded 15 November 1798, from Thomas Pack Junr. for £30..5, bill of sale for two feather beds, bedstead, table, cubbard and crockery and other household items. Signed 11 Nov. 1798, before Laurence O'Neale, and Barbara Neale.
348-349. Benjamin White Jones, recorded bond as Sheriff to State of Maryland, for £10,000 with sureties: Henry Jones, John Belt, Nacy Waters and Solomon Holland.
349-351. Basil M. Perry recorded 15 November 1798, from James Beall of James for £66..10, sells 33 1/4 acres of *Greenland,* beginning at the dividing line between Nathan Hoskinson and Andrew Hoskinson, land given them by their father, John Hoskinson, deceased. Signed before Benjamin Gaither, Josias H. McPherson. Elizabeth Beall released dower.
351-353. Tyson Beall recorded 15 Nov. 1798, from James Beall of James, for £114, deed for 71 acre part of *Greenland,* and also part of *Bear Garden Enlarged,* adjacent to *James and Mary.* Signed as deed above.
353-355. Honore Martin recorded 16 November 1798, from Edward Veirs, deed made 25 September 1798 for £600 sells part of *Resurvey on Hanover,* beginning at a stone fixed in a lane between Levi Hays plantation and the field formerly occupied by George Howard for one acre of land, except for the free use and privilege of well and water hereafter unto John Baptist Medley. Signed before Henry Brookes, Josias H. McPherson. Receipt. Acknowledgment. Mary Viers, wife of Edward released dower rights.
355-357. Hezekiah Wilson recorded 29 November 1798, made 17 November, from William Sears Senr., deed for £63..10, part of tract called *Narrow Lane,* a part of *Rich Bottom,* part *Progress,* part *The Slipe,* containing a 10 3/4 acres, and part of 4 1/4 acres + ½ acre together 15 7/8 acres. Signed William Sear before Ans Campbell, Laurence O'Neale. Elizabeth Sears released dower rights.
357-362. John Veatch & Solomon Veatch, deed of partition recorded 29 November 1798, made 17 November 1798, both sons of Ninian Veatch deceased. Division of land called *Progress,* a part of *Narrow*

Lane, and part of the *Resurvey on Cool Spring,* and called *Three Tracts Resurveyed.* Signed by both parties before Ans Campbell, Lawrence O'Neale. Nancy Veatch, wife of John Veatch and Mary Veatch, wife of Solomon Veatch released dower rights on the other's respective parts.

362-363. John Baker recorded 29 November 1798, from Thomas Williams, of Bladensburg, Prince George's County, for £75 in property, bill of sale for a Negro woman slave named Matilda, aged about 18 years. Signed before J. F. Beall, James A. Beall. Receipt, acknowledgment.

363. Negro Jack recorded manumission 2 December 1798, from James Orme in consideration of the faithful services of Negro Jack and 5 shillings, he is to be set free and discharged a free man 14 November 1798. Signed James Orme.

363-365. Edward Talbott of Loudoun County, Virginia, recorded 12 December 1798, from Ninian Magruder deed made 10 Dec. for part of *Magruder and Bealls Honesty,* on road leading from Georgetown to the Mouth of Watts Creek. Signed before Thos Corcoran and Joseph S. Belt. Receipt for £5. Eleanor Magruder released dower.

365-366. James Hurdle & others recorded 13 December 1798, from Robert Hurdle, deed of gift for the love and affection which I have for my son James Hurdle and his heirs, one bay horse, and also my crop in the ground. James is to pay the rents that are due. To my daughter Eleanor Hurdle, one bay horse and weaving loom; to my daughter Ann Hurdle, one feather bed, three cows and 15 hogs. Signed by mark by Robert Hurdle before Benjamin Gaither.

366-367. Joshua Perry recorded 13 December 1798, made 11 December, from Francis Deakins, exec. Of Wm Deakins, deed for part of a tract called *Nameless,* a part of *Fruitful Plains Resurveyed,* beginning at a tree of *Happy Choice,* to a tract called *Hobson's Choice,* containing 44 acres. Signed Joshua Pearre before Lloyd Beall, Thomas Corcoran.

367-368. William Belt, recorded 14 December 1798, qualification as deputy sheriff, at the request of Benjamin W. Jones, sheriff. Sworn before Daniel Reintzel.

368-369. John S. Browning recorded 18 December 1798, from Jonathan Browning, deed of gift for the natural love and affection, I bear unto my son, I grant all and singular my goods and chattels, and also lot in Clarksburg. Signed Jonathan Browning before Mescheck Browning, Stephen Lewis and Greenbury Howard. Margaret Browning his wife, examined separately acknowledged deed.

369-370. Carlton Belt recorded 19 December 1798, from Solomon Veatch, deed made 17 November 1798, for $150. sells tract formerly called *Progress,* and *Narrow Lane,* which were resurveyed and called *Three Tracts Resurveyed,* containing in whole 7 ½ acres. Signed before Aneas Campbell, Laurence O'Neale. Mary Veatch released dower rights.

370-372. Carlton Belt recorded 19 December 1798, from Thomas Veatch, deed for £41..5, part of a tract called *Poplar Spring,* to a tract called *Whole Included,* to be conveyed to Thomas Veatch for 7 3/4 acres, now laid out for 16 ½ acres. Signed Thomas Veatch Senior, before Ans. Campbell, Laurence O'Neale. At same time Lurania Veatch, wife of Thomas released dower rights.

372-373. Carlton Belt recorded 19 December 1798, from William Sears, deed made 17 November 1798, for £30, part of *Poplar Spring,* 14 ½ acres, and a second part containing 1 ½ acres, a third part beginning at end of 16 perches on 2nd line of *Resurvey on Cool Spring,* containing ½ acre and 32 perches. Signed before Aneas Campbell, Laurence O'Neale. Elizabeth Sears released dower.

373-375. John Freeman recorded 20 December 1798, from Edward Crow, deed made 30 June for $337, assigns two tracts of land, *That's All,* containing 22 acres, and *Silver Brook,* beginning at end of second line of *Inman's Plains,* to *Resurvey on Griffith's Chance,* to tract called *Silence.* Signed Edward Crow before Greenbury Howard, John Clark. Receipt. Acknowledgment.

375-376. Brice Lowery, recorded 28 December 1798, schedule of all property deeded to Benjamin Jones, Sheriff, including debts on accounts due from Thomas Comes, Robert Thomsburgh, George Wolfe and James Scott. Signed by mark before Benj. Gaither, Greenberry Howard.

376. Commission for Justices of the Peace for 1796 recorded by Montgomery County 19 January 1796, Justices of the Peace: Aneas Campbell, John Holmes, William Smith, Lawrence O'Neale, George French, Charles Magruder, Richard Green (H's Run), David Reintzel, Henry Brookes, Thomas Davis, Allen Bowie, George Ham. Offutt, Thomas Corcoran, Lloyd Beall, Solomon Holland, John L. Summers, Greenberry Howard, Edward Burgess Jr., and Joseph S. Belt.
376-377. Commission for Justices of the Peace for 1797, recorded 12 January 1797. To Aneas Campbell, John Holmes, William Smith, Lawrence O'Neale, George French, Charles Magruder, Richard Green (H's Run), David Reintzel, Henry Brookes, Thomas Davis, Allen Bowie, George Ham. Offutt, Thomas Corcoran, Lloyd Beall, Solomon Holland, John L. Summers, Greenberry Howard, Edward Burgess Jr., Joseph S. Belt, Thomas Brooke and Josias Fendall Beall, Elemelech Swearingen and Benjamin Gaither. Be it known that reposing great trust and confidence in your knowledge, equity and love of justice, you and each of you are jointly, severally appointed and assigned Justices of the Peace of Montgomery County, 5 December 1797. Alexander Contee Hanson, Esq. Chancellor.
377. Commission for Justices of the Peace for 1798, recorded 25 February 1798. Aeneas Campbell, John Holmes, William Smith, Lawrence O'Neale, George French, Richard Green, (H's Run), David Reintzel, Henry Brookes, Thomas Davis, Allen Bowie, George Ham. Offutt, Thomas Corcoran, Lloyd Beall, Solomon Holland, John L. Summers, Greenberry Howard, Edward Burgess Jr., Joseph S. Belt, Thomas Brooke and Josias Fendall Beall, Elemelech Swearingen and Benjamin Gaither, Joseph Forrest, John Clarke, Josias Hanson McPherson, John Beall Magruder. Appointed Justices of the Peace.
377-380. Isaac Webster Senr., of Harford County, [son-in-law of Joseph Richardson,] recorded deed from Isaac Webster Junr. Isabel Webster, Isaac Massey and his wife Margaret; William Webster, Thomas Webster and Samuel Webster, all of Harford Co., Md., his children, the grandchildren and heirs of Joseph Richardson. Deed made 30 August. Whereas Joseph Richardson Sr. delivered to him around 1762 part of *Charles and Benjamin,* and *James Brookes Reserve,* and several other tracts including 50 acres of *Rogues Harbour,* and *Bristol,* 50 acres; and part of *Richardson's Range,* all lying at the head of Seneca Creek in 1765. The said Richardson by his will entailed all his lands to his grandchildren, the children of his daughter Sarah who was married to Isaac Webster. These lands were sold to William Waters and Lewis Duvall, the latter not having paid for them, for want of a regular title from the heirs of Richardson. This deed to Isaac Webster Senr. is to clear the title of the sales. Signed by all the parties before Jacob Forward and Wm Smith, Justices of Harford County.
380-382. Thomas Davis recorded 24 December 1798, from Mary Davis, admin. Of Amos Davis of Frederick County for £162..7, and for carrying into effect the disposition made by Betsy Welsh in an instrument of writing, to deliver the Negroes and goods conveyed by John Welsh to Amos Davis. Deed to which this was annexed was not recorded here.
382. Negro Tom recorded 27 December 1798, from Samuel Douglass manumission to be from and after 15 November 1820. Signed before Wm Smith, Lenox Martin.
382-383. Director Smallwood recorded 29 December 1798, from Edward Talbott, of Loudoun County, Virginia, for £37..10, deed for part of *Magruder and Bealls Honesty,* signed before Thomas Corcoran, Joseph Belt. Acknowledgment.
383-385. Director Smallwood recorded 29 December 1798, from Edward Talbott, for £27 deed made 10 December 1798, for part of land resurveyed 25 July 1787 by William Bates Wilson, by the name of *Ravenspring,* beginning at 22nd line of *Honesty,* to the termination of a line of part of *Friendship,* granted to Zachariah Magruder 25 March 1765. Containing 6 acres. Signed before Thomas Corcoran, Joseph S. Belt.
385-386. Samuel Offutt recorded 31 December 1798, made 15 October 1798, from John Rawlins, tract *Final Conclusion.* Signed before Edward Burgess Junr., John Blake.
386-387. Richard Gatton recorded 31 December 1798, from Thomas Shadrach, of Saint Mary's County, for £105, bill of sale for one Negro man, Moses. Signed before H. H. Young, Marsham Waring.

387-389. Samuel Riggs recorded 2 January 1799, from George Plummer, of Kentucky, deed made 10 November 1798. Whereas Thomas Riggs, late of Montgomery County, deceased, did on 22 July 1797, give his bond to Samuel Riggs for £1000 to convey 100 acres of tract *Bordley's Choice,* deed made from George Plummer for £120 part to dividing line of Thomas Riggs and John Riggs and the late James Riggs part of said *Bordleys Choice*. Metes and bounds given for 100 acres. Signed George Plummer before Greenbury Howard and Benjamin Gaither.

389-390. Charles Beckwith recorded bond 4 January 1799 to State of Maryland made by Charles Beckwith, Jeremiah Crabb, Thomas West and Richard Wootton. The condition, being that an Act of Assembly of the November Session 1797 appointed Allen Bowie, Samuel Turner Sr., Charles Perry and Benjamin Ray Senr. to contract for the building of a gaol in Montgomery County. The above Charles Beckwith for £874 agreed with the commissioners to erect, finish, and complete said building, and posts bond for performance.

390. John Traverse, certificate as deputy sheriff, recorded 7 January 1799 before Thos Corcoran.

390-391. Thomas Burrows, recorded schedule 8 January 1799, of goods delivered to Benjamin W. Jones, Sheriff: one bed and furniture, one iron pot, one table and chest, one narrow axe, one weeding hoe, one barshear plow, and swingle trees; a parcel of pewter, 12 knives and forks, one saw, one chair, two stools. Signed before Josias H. McPherson, Dan'l Reintzel.

391. Charles Burrows, recorded schedule 8 January 1799, of goods delivered to Benjamin W. Jones sheriff. six head of sheep, one barshear plow, one shovel, two chairs. Signed by mark before same witnesses.

391-393. John Busey recorded lease 11 January 1799, from Francis Valdener, made 289 December 1798, for tract called *Friendship,* containing 230 acres, from 1 January next (1799) for five years. John Busey to sustain and repair said property, and pay annual rents. Signed Frances Valdener, John Busey before Hezekiah Ford.

393-394. Griffith Davis recorded 12 January 1799, list of Negroes, imported man Ben aged 17 years, left to me by the will of my deceased father Charles Davis, by will dated 16 May 1796, recorded in the Clerks Office of Fauquier County, Virginia, and owned by Charles Davis in Virginia at least three years, and before a resident of Maryland before 21 April 1783. Signed Griffith Davis.

394. David Crawford, recorded 17 January 1799, bill of sale from Richard Forrest of Prince Georges County, for £131..5, Negro woman Sal 20 and her child Bet; also Negro Sarah the wife of my Negro man named Sampson. Signed before John Smith Brooke.

395. Ruth Suter, Nathan Suter and Alexander Suter recorded list of Negroes 18 January 1799, brought from Virginia to this state on 24 November 1798: Negro man Sampson 64 years, Negro man Alexander 20 years; Negro woman, Sall about 25; Negro girl Rachel 6 years old. Said Negroes were residents of Virginia for at least three years before importation into state. Signed by Nathan Cook, agent for Ruth Suter, Nathan Suter and Alexander Suter.

395-396. John Belt recorded 25 January 1799, from Evan Belt, deed for £184, sells *Resurvey on Benjamin's Square,* 4 1/4 acre, as deeded by Jeremiah Davis to Ignatius Pigman, except for 5/8 acres. Signed before Daniel Reintzel, Josias H. McPherson, Receipt, Ack.

396-399. Beal Gaither recorded 29 January 1799, from Samuel Thomas, of Anne Arundel County, miller, deed made 24 September 1799 for £258 sells two tracts, *Gaither's Forest,* and *Hard to Get and Dear Paid for,* beginning at *Barron Ridge,* bounding on the River. The second part, *Gaither's Forest,* begins at 7th line of Linthicum's part, containing 86 acres, and also adjacent to *Mount Calvary.* Signed before Alexander Warfield, Thomas Hobbs. Anna Thomas released dower.

399. Thomas L. Washington recorded 1 February 1799, certificate of Negro, Lewis Clark a slave, brought from Virginia into the state with intention to settle.

400-401. Elizabeth Skerrett and others recorded 4 February 1799,from William Skerett, bill of sale, first to Elizabeth Skerrett a Negro boy, Beal for £3; to Teresa Skerrett, a Negro girl, Charlotte for £3; to Harriett Skerrett a Negro child, Ned for £3 and to Maria Skerrett a Negro boy, Archy for £3; and to all four, a Negro woman slave Jenny, for £9. Signed before Adam Robb and Daniel Reintzel.

401. Samuel Thomas of Samuel 3d recorded 4 February 1799, from Richard Thomas Senr., deed made 2nd Feb. 1799, for love and affection I have for Samuel Thomas Jr. and for one dollar, grant him part of the *Fourth Addition to Snowden's Manor and Snowden's Manor Enlarged,* beginning at the 20th line of *Addition to Charley's Forest,* to part formerly conveyed by Richard Snowden to William Richardson for 200 acres, containing 120 acres. Signed before Richard Green, Thomas Davis.

402-403. Samuel Thomas recorded 7 February 1799 from Richard Thomas, bond for £1302 promising to make a good and lawful deed for part of *Snowden's Manor Enlarged,* which Richard Snowden conveyed to Richard Thomas for 650 acres. Signed before Richard Thomas Jr., Bernard Gilpin, John Thomas 3d.

404. Thomas Hall recorded 7 February 1799, from John Chambers, manumission from this date, 7 February 1799, signed before John L. Summers.

404. James Clagett of Georgetown, ship carpenter, recorded 9 February 1799, bond from Elias Wheatley, of St. Mary's County for £2000. Whereas James Clagett conveyed property in trust for the sole and separate use of Elizabeth, wife of the said James, which she has agreed to receive in full satisfaction of any claim she may have hereafter, should she survive the said James Clagett to dower in lands or real estate, and also to a distributive share, but she being by law, incapable of entering into a contract binding upon her, the said Elias Wheatley has agreed to be bound, that she the said Elizabeth Clagett will keep the aforesaid agreement. Signed before Thomas Reader, and Thomas Corcoran.

405-406. Elias Wheatley of St. Mary's County, recorded 9 February 1799, deed made 23 January 1799, from James Clagett, ship carpenter of Georgetown, for consideration of trust herein and five shillings, grants the following slaves: Charity, Sarah, Jane, Anna, Notley, James, George, Nace, and James, and their future increase, for the use and benefit of Elizabeth, wife of the said James Clagett. Signed James Clagett, Elias Wheatley, before Thos Corcoran, Charles A. Beatty.

406-408. Thomas Owen Williams of Prince George's County, recorded 11 February 1799, from Thomas Sim Lee & Mary Lee, his wife, deed made 31 January 1799 for £87..10, an undivided moiety in *Wickham's Range,* on Horse Pen Branch, containing 50 acres. Signed before Lloyd Beall, Thos Corcoran. Receipt, acknowledgment, dower release.

408. George Beall and Walter Clagett, recorded 11 February 1799. Appointment of the inspectors to the Center Warehouse, and for the new warehouse at Georgetown. Oaths made before Ninian Pinkney, Clerk of the Council.

408-409. William Fisher recorded 12 February 1799, from Martin Fisher, deed of gift for 7 shillings and natural love and affection, gives to him a Negro woman Sal, 25 years old and her daughter Fan, 5 years old. Signed 8 February 1799, before John L. Summers.

409-410. John Clarke recorded 12 February 1799, from William Shank, deed for $350 for lot #4 in Clarksburgh, conveyed to him by John D. Coffee. Signed before Greenbury Howard, Edward Burgess Jr. Elizabeth wife of William Shank released dower rights.

410-412. James Hawkins recorded 12 February 1799, from James Hinton, deed made 9 February for £55 a lot, part of *Moneysworth,* containing ½ acre. Signed before John Clark, Greenbury Howard. Catherine Hinton released dower right.

412. Hezekiah Wilson recorded 12 February 1799, from John Veatch, deed made 17 Nov. 1798 for £34..10..6, part of *Resurvey on Cool Spring,* for 13 acres. Signed by John Veatch before Aeneas Campbell, Laurence O'Neale. Nancy Veatch, released dower rights.

413-415. William Norris of George recorded 12 Feb. 1799, from William Jarrell Senr. of Monongahela Co., Virginia, for £446..16..3, deed for part of *Hopewell,* 65 1/4 acres. Signed by William Jarrell before John Clarke, Edward Burgess, Jr.

415-416. Leonard Hays recorded 12 Feb. 1799, from William Jarrell, Senr. of Monongahela Co., Virginia, for £270..18..9, part of *Hopewell,* for 96 1/4 acres. Signed as above.

417-418. Matthew Reed recorded 12 Feb. 1799, from William Hoggins, executor of Peter Hoggins, late of Montgomery County, deceased. For £79..1, deed for part of *Resurvey on Friends Advise,* 13 1/4 acres, adjacent to 7th line of a tract called *Dry Spring.*
418-420. Hugh Coupland recorded 12 February 1799, from James Hinton, for £60, deed for lot in Clarksburg, on east side of Great Road. Signed before Greenbury Howard, John Clarke. Acknowledgment. Catherine Hinton released dower rights.
420. Commission for Justices of the Peace for 1799 recorded 15 February 1799, to: Aeneas Campbell, William Smith, Laurence O'Neale, Richard Green, H. Keen, Daniel Reintzel, Henry Brookes, Thomas Davis, Allen Bowie, George Ham. Offutt, Thos Corcoran, Lloyd Beall, Solomon Holland, John S. Summers, Greenbury Howard, Edward Burgess Junr., Joseph Belt, Thomas Brooke Beall, Josias Fendall Beall, Elemelech Swearingen, Benjamin Gaither, Joseph Forrest, John Clarke, Doctr. Josias Hanson, Patrick Magruder and James Lackland of Montgomery County. Signed by Alexander C. Hanson, Esq., Chancellor.
420-421. Commission for the Levy Court for 1799, recorded 15 February 1799, to Thomas Davis, Allen Bowie, John S. Summers, John Clarke, John B. Magruder, Charles Wayman and James Lackland. Signed as above.
421-422. William O. Wyvill recorded 18 Feb. 1799, from Edward H. Wyvell, bill of sale for £90, one old black horse, wagon and gears, cow and all title to parcel where I now dwell in a lease I obtained from William Deakins. Signed before Edward Burgess Sr., Edward Burgess Jr.
422-424. Zachariah Linthicum recorded 18 February 1799, from Hardage Lane, deed made 1 February for £378, for part of tract *Partnership,* adjacent to *Wolf Pitt,* and *Good Luck,* and *Second Resurvey on William and John,* and the *Second Survey on Friend in Need* which was conveyed by Ninian Beall to Thomas Birdwhistle, for 116 acres. Signed before Wm Smith, John S. Summers, acknowledgment.
424-426. Ozias Offutt recorded 24 Feb. 1799, made 20 October 1798, between Elizabeth Offutt, James D. Offutt and Baruch Offutt all of Montgomery County, for $1300 sells part of *Clewerwell* and *Clewerewell Enlarged,* from the 4th line, containing 145 acres. Signed Elizabeth Offutt by mark, James D. Offutt, Baruch Offutt. Wit: George H. Offutt, Josias H. McPherson. Acknowledgment. Mary Offutt wife of James D. Offutt relinquished dower rights.
426-427. James Offutt recorded 21 Feb. 1799, made 20 October 1798 between David Lowe, Margaret Lowe, wife of David, and Catherine Magruder for £400, part of tract *Hemsley*, and *Hemsley's Addition.* Signed before George H. Offutt, Josias H. McPherson. Acknowledgment. Dower release of Margaret Lowe.
427. Nathan Jones recorded 1 March 1799, from Ninian Willett, deed made 15 Oct. 1798, for £260, part of a tract called *Boons' Good Luck,* 52 acres. Signed before John S. Summers, Josias McPherson. Ann wife of Ninian Willett released dower rights.
429. John Lee recorded 1 March 1799, from Thomas S. Lee, deed of gift for the natural love and affection I bear to my son, and also to place him in the same situation as his brother and sisters who had four Negroes given to them by their late grandfather, Ignatius Digges Esq., I give him one Negro
430-431. Samuel Hanson Wheeler recorded bond 5 March 1799, from Walter B. Beall, of Allegany County, Maryland, made 19 December 1798, for £700, sells lot #1, in writ of partition between Clement Wheeler of Prince George's Co., and the heirs of Richard Beall of Samuel, deceased, for 66 ½ acres, it being Walter B. Beall's proportion. Signed by Walter B. Beall before Aeneas Campbell, Thomas B. Beall. Jane Beall his wife released dower rights.
431-432. Ann Doyle, daughter of Alexander Doyle, deceased, recorded 6 March 1799, from George King, bill of sale for 5 shillings, one Negro woman named Sarah and her two youngest children, Mary and Henny. Signed George King before Isaac Tenney, Frances Dodge. Acknowledged before Lloyd Beall.
432-434. Thomas Beall of George, William Smith and Samuel Williams recorded 6 March 1799, from Richard Thomas, deed made 6 February. Richard Thomas on 22 November 1765 conveyed to William Deakins 20 acres, part of the *Resurvey on Thomas Discovery,* and where he resurveyed it in 1788, and the resurvey ran considerably into elder surveys as *Thomas Discovery Fortified,* he is making this deed to make

good on the 20 acres. Wm Deakins Jr. having sold his interest in the 20 acres along with other tracts to Richard Parrott, the above named William Smith and Samuel Williams, and the said Richard Parrott afterwards sold his interest to Thomas J. Beatty, who sold the interest to the aforesaid Thomas Beall of George. Richard Thomas in consideration of the premises and for 5 shillings, deeds to them a part of *Resurvey on Part of Thomas Discovery, and part of Thomas Discovery Fortified,* laid out for 20 acres. Signed before Richard Green, Thomas Davis. Receipt. Acknowledgment.

434-435. Thomas Simpson recorded 6 March 1799, from Joseph Gittings, bill of sale for $450 sells several horses, mares, colt, 16 barrels corn, 2 barshear ploughs, one wagon, one feather bed and all household goods. Sale to be void if sum redeemed. Signed 2 March 1799 by mark before Richard James, Joel Simpson.

435. Negro Cate recorded 6 March 1799, from Jesse Harris, manumission signed before Elizabeth Martin, William Smith.

435-437. Zachariah Linthicum recorded 6 March 1799, from John Worthington Warfield, for £42, deed for *Mount Airy,* adjacent to *Buck Bottom,* and Seneca Creek, to the dividing line of tract of Charles Gassaway. 23 ½ acres. Signed before John L. Summers, Josiah H. McPherson. Mary wife of John W. Warfield released dower rights.

437-438. Patrick Orme recorded 7 March 1799, from Evan Thomas, deed made 12th day, 2nd month, 1799, for £148, tract called *Orme's Lot,* a part of *Two Farms,* at end of part conveyed by Evan Thomas to Richard Jones, containing 28 1/4 acres. Signed before Allen Bowie, J. F. Beall. Rachel Thomas released dower rights.

438-439. Caleb Darby recorded 8 March 1799, from William Hoggins, executor of Peter Hoggins late of Montgomery County, deceased, deed made 7th February for £233..5, part of *Resurvey on Friends Advise,* adjacent to tract called *Dry Spring,* containing 38 acres. Signed before John L. Summers, Benjamin Gaither.

440-441. Solomon Simpson recorded 8 March 1799, made 7 March, from Abiel Jannero & Deborah Jannero his wife, of Prince George's County. The said Deborah, one of the children of William Young, deceased, for 10 shillings, sells her undivided sixth share in tract called *Wilson's Delay,* signed before Thos Plater. Receipt, Acknowledgment and dower release.

441. William Magrath recorded 9 March 1799, from Joseph Smith & David Smith, deed for their undivided claim to the property devised from James Smith, and also any claim they may have to the share of Alice Smith, our deceased sister. Signed before John L. Summers, Josias H. McPherson.

441-443. Phillip Barton Key of City of Annapolis, recorded 13 March 1799, made 15 October 1798, from William Bayley & Susanna Frazier Bayley his wife, both of Prince George's County. Whereas they are indebted to Key in the sum of £3957, they are conveying parcels: *Contention,* 236 acres and part of *Hughes Disappointment,* on the west side of the Main Road from Georgetown to Frederick Town, if sum is paid by 1 Jan. 1804, sale is void.

443-444. Hezekiah Viers recorded 15 March 1799, from Jeremiah Nicholson, for $100. bill of sale for one bay horse, 6 years old, one roan mare, 2 feather beds, iron traces, barshear plow, other items. Signed by mark before Josias H. McPherson.

444. Clement McDermott & William Ray Junior recorded Certificate as Deputy Sheriff 18 March 1799, before John L. Summers.

445. James Crafford, recorded 18 March 1799, schedule of debts due, given to sheriff. Accounts due from Wentsworth Watson, William Barnes, James Hinton, Henry Wathan, Samuel Sprigg, and John Nicholas Jun. On judgment.

445-446. Thomas Howard recorded 18 March 1799, from Nathan Harris, for £40, bill of sale for Negro man, Cato. Signed before Greenberry Howard, Leonard Watkins.

446. James Gannon, barber, of Georgetown, recorded 18 March 1799, from Dr. John Weems of Georgetown, bill of sale for $200, for possession of Negro woman Nelly, and her daughter, a mulatto girl named Leithy. Signed before Thomas Corcoran.

446-448. Mary Morton recorded 19 March 1799, from Thomas Morton, for £300 deed made 28 February for part of *Beall's Good,* whereon he now dwells, also his half of the grist and saw mill now held and occupied jointly with Ignatius Davis; and also the times of the following Negroes: James for 3 years; Ned Brown for 8 years; and Booth for 3 years; Susanna for 6 years and Jane for 6 years; 10 head of hogs, 16 head of cattle, 8 head of horses and wagons; 4 beds and furniture and all household and kitchen furniture. Signed Thomas Morton, before Lloyd Beall, Thomas Corcoran.

448-449. Samuel Beall recorded 21 March 1799, from James Gannon of Georgetown, for £68, Bill of sale for a Mulatto woman Nelly and her child, Leithy. Signed before James S. Morsell.

449-450. John Connelly recorded 22 March 1799, from Allen Bowie, tract called *Good Luck,* for establishing the lines of *Beall's and Edmonston's Discovery,* beginning at *Good Luck,* conveyed by Allen Bowie to Evan Thomas, from the given line of *St. Winnexburg,* to a north line of the *Hermitage.*

450-451. General Henry Lee of Virginia, recorded 22 March 1796, from Francis Deakins, deed for tract *Slago,* on waters of a branch called *Slago,* about 311 acres, five or six miles from Washington. Signed before Charles A. Beatty.

451-452. Marsham Waring recorded 29 March 1796, from Bernard O. Neill for 10,000 lbs. tobacco, a mulatto boy Bill and a mulatto boy Alfred, and mulatto girl Liddia, and all my horses, colts, etc. Whereas Marshall Waring has this day become security for me in a bond given to a certain James Fee against me in general court, if condition of bond met, this sale is void.

452-453. James Offutt recorded 30 March 1796, from Ninian Willett & Ann Willett his wife, deed made 22 March for $110. all their interest in tract *Hensley.* Signed by Ninian Willett and Ann Willett by mark, before Dan'l Reintzell, John L. Summers

453-454. Elizabeth Richardson recorded 2 April 1799, from Robert E. Yates, for £108, bill of sale for 3 feather beds and furniture, four chairs, table, trunk, cart, all my plantation utensils and kitchen furniture, one pair stilyards, one gun, one bay horse, three cows. Signed Robert E. Yates, before Thos. B. Beall, Henry Horrell.

454-455. Robert Peter recorded 2 April 1799, from Evan Thomas, for £292..18..9, deed assigns part of tract, *Two Farms,* west 9 perches from tract called *Easy Purchase,* and from *Beall's Industry.* Signed. Rachel wife of Evan Thomas released dower rights.

456. John Clarke recorded 3 April 1799, from John Breise, for £10..10..10, bill of sale for one dark bay horse and one bay mare. Signed by mark. Witness: Greenbury Howard.

457. Samuel Turner's schedule recorded by Benjamin W. Jones, sheriff, on 5 April 1799. Amount due from Thomas Sylvestor, of £12..13..6.

457-459. Charles Porter recorded 5 April 1799, from David Stewart of Baltimore Town, deed made 1 April. Tract called *Brandy Hall,* to last line of *Wickham's Good Will,* and *The Pines,* and tract *Addition to Rays Town,* conveyed by David Crawford and Wm Deakins Jr. To David Stewart. Signed. Elizabeth Stewart released dower rights.

459-460. Elijah Beall recorded 6 April 1799, from Elias & Elizabeth Harding, his wife, deed conf. For tract called *Labyrinth,* signed before Lawrence O'Neale and Thos B. Beall.

461-462. William Sears Senr., recorded 9 April 1799, from Hezekiah Wilson, deed made 17 November 1798, for part of tract called *London,* containing 2 1/4 acres. Signed. Bersheba Wilson released dower rights.

462-463. John Laird of Georgetown recorded bond 9 April 1799, from Sarah Heugh & daughters: Elizabeth, Mary, Harriett, Nancy, Jane and Sarah Heugh, all of Montgomery County, for £400 bill of sale for the following Negro slaves: Ben 23 years, Jerre 20 years, Hannah 18 years, Jane 18 years, Jarrett 6 years son of Negro woman Ally; Harry 3 years old son of Nell; and Poll about 9 years old daughter of Rachel; bond provided that if they shall pay sum with interest to John Laird by 14 May next this is void. Signed by all seven ladies before William Needham, Dan'l Reintzel. Acknowledged by Mrs. Sarah Heugh, Miss Elizabeth Heugh, Miss Mary Heugh, Miss Harriett Heugh, Miss Ann Heugh, Miss Jane Heugh and Miss Sarah Heugh.

463-466. Thomas Fletchall recorded 9 April 1799, from Elizabeth Pierce, relict of John Baptist Pierce. Whereas William Cummings and James Edmonston did some time in 1736 lease to Thomas Gatton 200 acres of *Preston's March* for 99 years from 10 March 1736 and Thomas Gatton on 25 June 1759 conveyed to James Gatton his right to 100 acres part (see Frederick County Land Records F:795) and James Gatton by his will devised residue to Azariah Gatton and on 9 April 1789 he made over his right in John Baptist Pierce (Montgomery County Land Records D:195-196). At his decease Elizabeth Pierce became entitled to a half part of her deceased husband's estate, and was appointed administrator, had said tract surveyed and found it to contain 102 3/4 acres, and sold her right to Thomas Fletchall for 15 shillings per acre. Signed before Ans Campbell, Dan'l Reintzel.

466-467. Negro Abraham recorded 9 April 1799, from Thomas Green, for diverse good causes sets free his Negro boy, now about 16 years, to be free at the expiration of 12 years from this date. Signed before Greenberry Howard.

467-469. William Sears Sr. recorded 9 April 1799, from Carlton Belt, for £30 deed for parcel called *Slipe,* also part of *Resurvey on Gore's Adventure,* together with parts of tract called *Whole Included,* 1st adjacent to *Progress,* containing 2 acres; 2nd part 3 1/4 acres; and 3d containing 2 acres and 15 sq. perches. The whole of 4 parts contains 15 1/4 acres. Signed before Aeneas Campbell, Laurence O'Neale. Anne wife of Carlton Belt released dower rights.

469-470. Thomas & Samuel Turner recorded 9 April 1799, from William Robertson, bill of sale in consideration of my being indebted in two suits recovered, sell the following slaves, Nace, 35 years; his wife Minna, about 25 years and Janis about 20 and her child Tibb about 8 months; Dinah 18 years and her child Dinah 10 months; Florah about 25 and her two children, Henry 2 years and an infant; Jack about 50 years and his wife Abigail, 45 years, and Orange about 53 years. Signed 3 April 1797 before Samuel Harwood, Wm Holmes.

470. Dr. Jeffrey Magruder recorded 11 April 1799, from Robert Fish Junr., bill of sale for one Negro woman, Hannah and Sam, her son. Signed before John L. Summers.

470-471. Ninian Willett recorded 12 April 1799, from Nathan Jones for £8..15, deed made 15 October, for part of tract called *Jones Inheritance,* for 1 3/4 acres. Signed by mark before John L. Summers, Josias H. McPherson. Ack. Ann, wife of Nathan Jones released dower.

471-473. Basil Darby recorded 12 April 1799, from Edward Veirs, for £39, deed made 13 March for part of *Resurvey on Non Eaten;* beginning near line formerly conveyed by Daniel Veirs to George Dyson for 150 acres, to the last line of Basil Darby's tract *Mary,* heretofore conveyed to George Darby by the name of *Resurvey on Non Eaten,* containing 7 ½ acres. Signed Edward Veirs before Lawrence O'Neale, Greenbury Howard. The wife of Edward Veirs (name not given), examined apart and relinquished dower rights.

473-474. John Reid recorded 16 April 1799, from John Richards for £26..10, deed made 25 October 1798, for tracts *Slipe,* beginning at first line of *Resurvey on William's Tryal,* to 31st line of *Johnson's Discovery.* Containing 4 1/4 acres. Signed before Greenbury Howard, John Clarke. Ann Richards wife of John released dower.

474. Edward H. Wyville, recorded 16 April 1799, delivery of schedule to Benjamin W. Jones, sheriff of Montgomery Co. Includes one punch bowl, two iron pots, 5 pewter plates, one jack plane, one smoothing plane, 2 schissels, one hand saw, one adze, 2 moulding planes, 2 augers, one old chest, one old cupboard. Signed before John L. Summers, Josias H. McPherson.

475. Robert Beall, recorded certificate 16 April 1799. "I have no just cause to say anything disrespectful of Zadock Willson and that all the wood he had he bought and honestly paid for. January 23rd, 1799. Robt Beall.

475. Elias Perry recorded, from Erasmus Perry, deed of gift in consideration of the love I have for my son, one Negro man, named Mark. March 28, 1799.

475-476. Charles Carroll from Joseph Compton Senr. & Joseph Compton Junr., bill of sale recorded 23 April 1799 for £184..16..4, sell Negro Rachael and her son John, her daughter, Ann, her daughter Jane, and her son

Robert, three mares and one horse, wagon and gears, 14 head black cattle, 4 feather beds. Sale void if sum with interest paid by 19 April 1801. Signed 16 April 1799 before Laurence O'Neale, Elizabeth O'Neale.
476-477. Walter Clagett recorded 29 April 1799, from Charles C. Jones, deed made 19 April 1791 for $740, sells part of tract called *Labyrinth,* containing 13 ½ acres. Signed before Thos Corcoran, Charles Beatty. Receipt. Acknowledgment.
477-479. Edward Magruder recorded 29 April 1799, from William H. Dorsey, deed made 13 April for £912, part of *Addition to Brooke Grove,* 729 acres. Signed before Thos Plater, Wm Magruder. Acknowledged, and Ann, wife of Wm Dorsey, released dower rights.
479-480. Thomas Higdon recorded 2 May 1799, from Elisabeth Pearce, widow of John Baptist Pearce, deed for $70, tract called *Future,* which Pearce purchased from Basil Jewell. She sells her right of dower. Signed by mark before Ans Campbell, Thomas B. Beall. Acknowledgment.
480. Levi O. Conner & others, recorded 8 May 1799, Qualification as Deputy clerks, by Levi Orme Connor, John Peter and Lloyd Magruder.
480-481. Marsham and Henry Waring, recorded 9 May 1799, from Richard Turner, for $300, bill of sale for one Negro man, Lin. Signed before John L. Summers.
481. Negro Peter recorded manumission, 9 May 1799, from Benjamin Waters. He is to be free after 25 December 1809. Signed before Samuel Williams, William Smith.
481-483. Francis Lowndes recorded May 1799, from Benjamin Lowndes, deed for 5 shillings, 3 tracts: *Edmons Good Will,* 162 acres conveyed by Zachariah White to Christopher Lowndes, deceased in 1767, in Frederick County Records, and parcel called *Beall's Manor,* 29 acres, and *Charles and Jane,* 100 acres, deeded by right of inheritance to Benjamin Lowndes as eldest son and heir at law. Dorothea Lowndes, his wife, released dower, before R'd Cramphin, Richard Lowndes.
483-484. Charles A. Beatty recorded 10 May 1799, from Thomas J. Beatty, power of attorney. In order to meet the several claims which may come due against me in my absence, he may sell personal property and collect all debts due to me. Signed before Thomas Corcoran, Joseph Forrest.
484-485. Carlton Belt Senior recorded 12 May 1799, from John Young, for £35, he assignes tract *Williams Delay,* containing 14 1/4 acres. Signed before Aeneas Campbell, Laurence O'Neale. Keziah, wife of John Young released dower rights.
485-486. Hezekiah Willson recorded 12 May 1799, from Carlton Belt for £7..10, sells part of *Whole Included,* containing 1 1/4 acres. Signed with witnesses. Ann Belt released dower.
487. Joseph West recorded 15 May 1799, from Margaret Hayman, power of attorney to manage the estate of my two children George Haymand and Elizabeth Haymand. Signed before Daniel Reintzel, 1 April 1799.
487-488. William Norris Silver recorded 19 May 1799, from James S. Steel, for £500, bill of sale for Negro Charles 50 years old, Negro Cloe about 38 and Solomon age 15 months; two bay mares, one gelding, 2 black colts, 6 head cattle. Signed by mark before John L. Summers, Edward Been.
488. Harriet Beall recorded 8 May 1799. "I, Samuel Beall, of James City County, Virginia, for love and affection to my daughter, give one Negro girl, Little Judy about 14 years old. Signed 10th day -------, 1788, before B. Holmes, J. Smith.
488-489. James Brown recorded 20 May 1799, from Beall Gaither for £70, made 25 Feb. 1799, tract *Resurvey on Leeks Lott,* 44 acres. Signed before Thomas Davis, Benjamin Gaither.
489. Aquila Magruder recorded 22 May 1799, Certificate of a Negro woman named Amy, 18 years old, which fell to Aquilla Magruder by intermarriage with Mary Ann Magruder of the Commonwealth of Virginia. Removed to his plantation with intention to use here, 22 May 1799.
490. Robert P. Magruder recorded 24 May 1799, from Zadock Magruder, for the natural love and affection, for him conveys tract called *Joseph and James,* part of *Conclusion;* resurveyed into *Betsy's Fancy* on 7th May 1799. Signed before John L. Summers, Benjamin Gaither.
491. Richard Wootten recorded 25 May 1799, from Alexander C. Hanson, deed. Whereas William Willson purchased 203 ½ acres, formerly the property of Dunlap & son, for £203..10 by his assignment of the tract,

Younger Brother, to John Peter 13 May 1799 transferred his right to Richard Wootton. Now Alexander C. Hanson, Chancellor of Maryland, in consideration of the premises in pursuance of an Act of Assembly in that case, provided, confirms sale.
491-492. Charles Saffle recorded 28 May 1799, from Nathan Oden for £25, bill of sale for furniture and livestock. Signed before John L. Summers.
492-493. Robert Peter recorded 29 May 1799, from James Beeding, for 2158 lbs. crop tobacco, and full sum of £79..9..6, bill of sale for all household goods in schedule hereunto annexed, including one Negro woman named Rose. Signed before Thomas Corcoran, Alexander S. Peter.
493. Patrick Magruder Esq. qualified as Justice of the Peace 30 May 1799.
493-494. Thomas Sim Lee recorded 31 May 1799, from Thomas Beall of George & John Peter as trustees of the will of John Murdoch deceased, and Thomas Beall as guardian of the Addison, Eliza and Catharine Murdoch, infants and heirs of John Murdoch; confirms sale contracted by John Murdoch for part of tract called *Friendship.* Signed in the presence of Thomas Plater.
495. Elizabeth Fenwick & others from Richard Fenwick, for five shillings, and the natural love and affection for my children, Elizabeth Fenwick, Mary Fenwick and Susanna Fenwick, Margareta Fenwick and Richard D. Fenwick, deed for Negro Jacob, one sorrel horse, one black horse, one black mare, one colt, 2 cows, 8 head of hogs, 2 beds and furniture, one walnut desk, 6 chairs, all my cooking ware and kitchen furniture. Signed before Daniel Reintzel.
495–496. Solomon Simpson recorded deed 5 June 1799, from Alexander Young of Prince George's County, one of the children and co-heir of William Young, for 10 shillings, grants his undivided sixth share of the tracts called *Williams Delay,* and the resurvey called *Willson's Delay,* signed before Abiel Jenners, acknowledged before Thos Plater.
496-497. David Luckett recorded 7 June 1799, from John Yates, for £56..4, bill of sale for all household goods and a ferry boat which was particularly mentioned, as well as 3 beds, 2 bedsteads, 4 sheets, 2 quilts, 2 pillows, one walnut chest, one pewter dish, 8 plates, sundry crockery ware, one sow and 10 shoats, one black horse, all situated in a certain tenement, north of the Monocacy in Montgomery County, now the property of Larise (?) Luckett and in occupation of John Yates. Signed 24 May 1799 before Thos B. Beall.
497. James Summerville recorded 8 June 1799, from William Dent Beall, for £275, bill of sale for Negro men, Prince and Nace; wagon and gears, 2 horses and 3 mares. Signed before Charles A. Beatty, Benjamin Lacey.
497-498. Thomas Contee recorded 8 June 1799, from William Dent Beall, for£186..6, bill of sale for Negro woman Nan and Negro man David. Signed before witnesses as above.
498-500. Thomas Veatch recorded 9 June 1799, from Carlton Belt, for £189..7..6 deed made 11 May, for part of the *Whole Included,* beginning at the 18th line of *Poplar Spring,* to the end of the 4th line of a tract formerly conveyed by Elizabeth Goslier to Thomas Veatch. 68 acres, and the 3d part at *Allison's Adventure,* contains 7 3/4 acres. Signed by Carlton Belt before Ans Campbell, Laurence O'Neale. Ann Belt released dower rights.
500. Aquila Vinson recorded 11 June 1799, from Isaac Lansdale, for £93..15 deed for part of *Resurvey on the Farm,* containing 50 acres. Signed before Lloyd Beall, Thos Corcoran. Cassandra, wife of Isaac Lansdale released dower.
501-502. Robert Peter recorded 11 June 1799, from John Scrivener & Elizabeth, his wife, for £150, deed of bargain & sale made 18 April 1799, on *Resurvey on Brandy,* on the 12th line of *Barsheba,* containing 50 acres. John Scrivener signed by mark, Elizabeth Scrivener signed deed before Aeneas Campbell, Thos B. Beall. Acknowledgment and dower release.
502-503. Aquila Johns recorded 11 June 1799 from William Bayley of Prince Georges Co., for £350, lot in Georgetown, part of #17, to line of Elizabeth Duncastle Senr., Sarah Duncastle and Elizabeth Duncastle, Junr's part of said lot, to falls street. Signed William Bayley before Robert Brent, John Addison. Susanna Bayley released dower.

503-504. Honore Martin recorded 17 June 1799, from John Day, for £37..10, bill of sale for 2 feather beds, one walnut chest, one trunk, bureau, half dozen windsor chairs, one sow and seven shoats, signed John Day before John L. Summers.

504-505. John Clarke & John Howes recorded 17 June 1799, from Clement Harding for £52..1, sells one dark bay horse 14 years, one roan mare 10 years, one bay year old colt, several head of cattle, 4 feather beds, bedsteads, 6 chairs, sale void if sums paid by 25 December next.

505. Thomas Kirk Junr. recorded 17 June 1799, from Abram Snider, for £20 deed made 9 March for one lot on a part of *Moneysworth,* on the NW side of road, #10. Signed by mark before Greenbury Howard, John Clarke. Receipt. Ack. Susannah Snider released dower.

506. Negro Samuel recorded 18 June 1799, from Vachel Hall, manumission from and after 1 January 1807. Signed before Thomas Morton, John Clark.

506-511. Certificate and survey of plat of road leading from Georgetown by Montgomery County Courthouse to the Mouth of Monocacy in Frederick County, recorded 19 June 1799. Metes and bounds given, agreeable to an Act of Assembly, surveyed by Thos Howard, Benj. Ray. Plat appears between pages 510-511, but not legible on microfilm.

512-513. Deed recorded by Nathan Cash 21 June 1799. Deed for Jonathan Cash from John Cash for £40 his undivided fifth share of 153 3/4 acres of land which he holds with William Cash, Jonathan Cash, Reason Cash and Isaiah Cash, in *Resurvey on Pascalham.* Signed John Cash before Greenbury Howard, John Clarke. Margery, wife of John Cash released dower.

513-514. John Poole Junr., recorded 21 June 1799, from John Poole Senior, for £30, deed made 11 May, for 15 acres of *Pooles' Right.* Signed before Lawrence O'Neale, Greenbury Howard.

514. Uriah Forrest recorded certificate of qualification as Justice of the Peace, 24 June 1799, signed before Joseph Forrest.

514-515. Edward Burns recorded 26 June 1799, from Philip O. Connell, for $105, four good feather beds and furniture, provided that if I pay by 1 March sum due with interest, bill of sale is void. Signed before J. H. McPherson.

515-516. Zadock Magruder recorded 26 June 1799, from Zadock Magruder Junr., deed in consideration of the duty and affection he hath for his father grants during his natural life, tracts *Turkey Thicket,* 350 acres; and *Robert and Sarah,* part of *Dickenson's Lott,* other tracts named. Signed before John L. Summers, J. H. McPherson.

516-517. Zadock Magruder Junior recorded 26 June 1799, from Zadock Magruder Senr., deed made 14 June 1799, for the natural love and affection, all of the tracts which were named in deed above, were granted from Senr. to Junior. Signed before same witnesses.

517-519. Martin Fisher recorded 27 June 1799, from Richard J. Orme, for £116 deed for tract *Troy,* beginning at *Piney Thickett,* adjacent to *Wickham and Pottinger's Discovery,* signed before Dan'l Reintzel, John L. Summers. Acknowledgment.

519-520. James Waters recorded 28 June 1799, from Deletha Taylor for £220, part of *Forest* to a dividing line between Deletha Taylor and Isaac Hite, by estimation 55 acres. Signed by mark before Ens Campbell, Thos B. Beall.

520-521. Henry Knowles recorded 1 July 1799, from Thomas Fearro, for £76..12, bill of sale for one pair andirons, one fire shovel and tongs, one dozen windsor chairs, one walnut table, one mahogany stand, 2 feather beds, 3 sheets, 6 blankets, one rug, 2 looking glasses, 3 pine tables, 3 bed quilts, 3 window curtains, other items listed. Signed before Thos Corcoran.

521. Henry Sparrow recorded 1 July 1799, from Thomas Davis, for £60, mortgage on Negro man, Nat, about 45 years old, provided that if sum is paid by 12 December next, sale is void. Signed before Charles A. Beatty.

522-523. John Pleasants &c recorded 2 July 1799, from Patrick Durham, mortgage. Whereas John Kelley is bound for £380..14..9, and Patrick Durham is willing to be security to John P. Pleasants, Israel Pleasant

and Samuel Pleasants trading under the name of John Pleasants and Co., they agree to deliver tracts, *Riley's Chance, Appenine Hills, Harrison's Delight, Addition to Higgs,* and *Let no Man Deceive You,* totalling 195 ½ acres together. Signed Patrick Durham, before Dan'l Reintzel, John L. Summers.
523-524. [Marginal note: Delivered John Orme, 21 October 1803.] Richard J. Orme recorded 3 July 1799, from Archibald Orme, for £7..10, deed for *Resurvey on Rich Meadows,* lying on west side of Muddy Branch, the following tracts, *Hamilton's Lot,* late the property of Richard Ricketts, *Lucas Adventures, Hartley Hall, Maiden's Bower, Cornelius Chance and Deakins Range,* containing 155 acres.
525. Charles Davis, schedule recorded listed no assets, 17 July 1799. Wit. Daniel Reintzel, J. H. McPherson.
525. Harry W. C. Robertson recorded 17 July 1799, from William Robertson, bill of sale for $320. Sells one Negro man Nace, 35 years old; Negro woman Minney, 30 years old and her four children: Pegg, Sally, Phebe and Basil; one Negro woman Susie 18 and her child, Desire; Negro man Jack 50 years old and his wife Abigail. about 40 years old; Negro woman Venus and her child Abe and Negro man George, 50 years old.
526-527. John Fletchal recorded 15 July 1799, from Basil Beckwith, deed for £18..10 for part of *Resurvey on Brandy,* for 10 acres
527-528. Green and English recorded 17 July 1799, from James H. Blake of Georgetown, bill of sale for two Negroes, one Gail, and one called Chaney.
528-529. George Riley recorded 20 July 1799 from George Beckwith, for £100 bill of sale for all household stuff in attached schedule. [Not recorded.] Signed before Elemelech Swearingen, William O. Lodge.
529-530. Elizabeth Ellicott of Baltimore County, recorded 22 July 1799, from Richard Thomas, Sr., deed for 5 shillings, for part of tract called *Charley Forrest,* laid out for 9 acres and 2 perches. Signed before Richard Green, Thomas Davis. Acknowledged.
530-532. Richard Thomas Senr. recorded 22 July 1799, from George & Elizabeth Ellicott, deed for 5 shillings for part of tract called *Brother's Content,* beginning at 4th line of a tract called *Addition to Charley Forrest,* containing 9 acres and 8 sq. perches. Signed before Wm Owings, Elias Ellicott.
532-533. Ann Sanders recorded 22 July 1799, From Henry Tayman of Ann Arundel County, bill of sale for any right to property which Elizabeth Sanders had at my marriage with her, entitled by the decease of her father, James Sanders, uncle Robert Sanders or any other person. Signed before John L. Summers.
533. Henry Tayman of Ann Arundel Co. recorded 22 July 1799, from Ann Sanders, bill of sale for £50 one Negro boy called Ben, 9 years old, now in his possession.
533. James H. Blake recorded 25 July 1799, from Charles Green & David English, of Georgetown, bill of sale for right to Negro man, Saul, previously mortgaged by James H. Blake.
534. Charles Perry recorded 27 July 1799, bond as supervisor, made by Charles Perry, William Worthington, Thomas P. Wilson.
534-535. Felix D. St. Hillaire, recorded 27 July 1799, delivered schedule of real and personal property to Benjamin W. Jones sheriff, including accounts due from Lawrence O'Neall, Aneas Noland, William Jones, Patrick McDermitt, Carlton Belt, Henry Garrett, Edward Thomas. Signed before John L. Summers, with attestation: "I have not directly or indirectly at any time since my imprisonment or before, sold leased or otherwise conveyed any of my property.
535-536. Nathan Musgrove recorded 29 July 1799, from Zachariah Musgrove, deed for £30..10 *Resurvey on John and Sarah,* 10 1/4 acres; part of *Resurvey on Gaither Purchase,* 38 acres; on the waters of Hawling and Snowden Rivers, as devised by the late John Musgrove, father of Zachariah to be divided among his children. Signed before Richard Green, Francis Davis.
536-537. Ephraim Gaither recorded 29 July 1799, deed made same date from Margaret Brooke, for $2000. Parts of *Addition to Brooke Grove, Sure Bound Sure Found, and Fair Hill,* beginning at a tract called *Ridgeley's Ridge,* 245 acres. Signed Margaret Brooke before Richard Green, Thomas Davis.
537-538. Ephraim Gaither recorded 29 July 1799, from Thomas Davis, trustee for the sale of the real estate of John Prather, deceased. For £`164..16, the remaining 2/3 parts of purchase price, grants tract, *Resurvey on John and Sarah,* 103 acres. Signed Thomas Davis, trustee, before Allen Bowie, John Clarke.

539. James Perry recorded 1 August 1799, from Samuel Williams, bill of sale for £160, Negroes Jacob age 22 years, slave for life, and boy Magee, 15 years old, a servant to age 25 years; and two horses. Signed by Samuel Williams, before John L. Summers, Bruce Selby. Samuel Williams recorded agreement to secure payment of debt to William Taylor of Baltimore, 1 August 1799. Signed James Perry.

539-541. Benjamin Reeder, recorded 6 August 1799, made 5 August, from Francis Hammerly, of Fairfax County, Virginia, deed for 5 shillings. All his right and title to tract called *Conclusion,* adjacent to *Pork and Potatoes,* and Richard Hoggins's part of *Conclusion.* Elizabeth Hammerly, wife of Francis released dower rights.

541-542. Benjamin Reeder, recorded 6 August 1799, made 21 June, 1799 from Henry Hammerley and Ann Digges, deed for 5 shillings, for all their title to tract called *Conclusion,* adjacent to *Pork and Potatoes,* and Richard Hoggins's part of *Conclusion.* containing 258 acres. Signed before Henry Gardner and James Egerton of St. Mary's County.

542-543. Benjamin Reeder recorded 6 August 1799, from Edmond Plowden, Jane Plowden his wife; Henry Neale and Eleanor Neale his wife; and Betsy Lewellen, all of St. Mary's County, for 5 shillings, deed for all their title to tract, *Conclusion,* surveyed for William Hammersley, adjacent to *Pork and Potatoes,* and Francis Thomas's part and Richard Hoggins's part, containing 248 acres. Signed before Henry Gardner, James Egerton of St. Mary's County. Acknowledgments and dower releases recorded.

543-545. Benjamin Reider recorded 6 August 1799, made 13 June, from Baker Brooke & Mary Brooke, for 5 shillings, all their title to tract *Conclusion,* containing 248 acres, adj. To Francis Thomas's part and Richard Hoggins's part. Signed Baker Brooke, Mary Brooke, and Dan'l Jennifer witness from Charles County.

545-546. John L. Summers recorded 6 August 1799, from John Bealmear, deed of trust for £24..1..1.. On account of Archibald Mullican, sells Negro Eve, 22 years old. Signed before J. H. McPherson.

546-548. William Benton recorded 8 August 1799, from Joseph Benton, deed made same day, for £200 for 59 acres, tract called *Grubby Thickett,* signed by mark "B" before John L. Summers, J. H. McPherson. Rachel Benton came and released dower rights.

548-549. James Pierce recorded 10 August 1799, form Joseph Jackson, for £27, deed for tract called *Addition,* being a part of *Good Luck,* adjacent to *Discovery.* Containing 3 acres, 47 perches. Signed.

549-551. James Pierce recorded 10 August 1799, from Evan Thomas deed made 12th day, 2nd month called February, 1799 for £11..17..6, for tract called *Angles,* part of *Two Farms,* beginning at a tract called *Connolly's Lot,* in 2nd line of *Saint Winexburgh,* containing 2 acres, 67 perches. Signed Evan Thomas before Allen Bowie, J. F. Beall. Rachel Thomas released dower.

551-553. James Pierce recorded 10 August 1799, made 12th day 2nd month called Feb. 1799, from Evan Thomas for £7..4..4, tract called *Surplus,* a part of *Poplar Point,* 10 perches from Joseph Jackson's tract, *Discovery,* 140 sq. perches. Acknowledged as above.

553-555. Archibald Mobley recorded 10 August 1799, from Samuel Phillips of Frederick County, deed made 2 July, for £100 tract called *Blandford,* with the Resurvey thereunto for 146 acres. Signed before Wm Luckett, Pat M'Gile. Ann Phillips released dower.

555-557. Joseph Blake recorded 12 August 1799,from James H. Blake, deed. Whereas Joseph Blake, in 1795, then of Calvert County entered into security with James H. Blake to a certain Leonard Mackall in a bond of £5000 and since executor of said bond, Joseph Blake has died and the property and estate may be liable to performance, to indemnify them, I James Blake and James Hugh of Calvert County in trust for Betty H. Blake, wife of me the said James H. Blake, to settle personal property of £750 the amount before remarriage unsecured on younger son James H. Blake ...

557-558. Elizabeth Soper recorded 12 August 1799, from Edward Vollman, bill of sale fir £100, one sorrel mare 4 years old, one bed and furniture, one table, one chest, half dozen chairs, frying pan, crop of corn growing in the field, all plantation utensils. Signed before Elemelech Swearingen.

558-559. Charles Decandry recorded 12 August 1799, from Samuel Gatton, deed. Whereas William Cummins and James Edmonstone, did by indenture of lease, let to Thomas Gatton 200 acres, part of

Preston's March lying then in Prince George's County, but now in Montgomery County for term of 99 years from 20 March 1736, as by lease recorded in Liber Y:318-319, and he conveyed 100 acres to James Gatton for remainder of lease, Samuel conveys the remaining part of 99 year lease. Signed before Aeneas Campbell, Thos B. Beall

559-561. Charles Decandry recorded 12 August 1799 from Samuel Gatton, for £400 deed for part of tract called *Cyder and Ginger,* adjacent to *Preston March,* which separates William Hickman's lease of said *Preston's March,* from Benjamin Gatton's lease of the same, containing according to Richard Henderson's deed to Benjamin Gatton, 73 acres of land, but now by an accurate survey thereof, 59 acres; part of a tract called *Indulgence,* beginning at 3d line of *Edloe's Adventure,* at west fork of Cabbin branch, 58 acres of a tract called *Welfare;* beginning at 30th line of *Resurvey on Brandy;* to a tract called *Farewell.* Signed Samuel Gatton before Ans Campbell, Thos B. Beall.

562. Charles Rogers recorded 13 August 1799, from James Wimsatt, bill of sale for heifer, bed and furniture. Signed before Wm Smith.

562-564. Samuel Clagett recorded 13 August 1799, made 22 June from Archibald Orme, for $850. deed for part of *Piney Grove,* on 10th line of *Eleanor's Green.* Dower release by Elizabeth Orme.

564-566. Zadock Wilson recorded 13 August 1799, from Notley Young, deed Conveyance. Whereas Daniel Carroll Sr., late of Rock Creek, did on 14 May 1794 convey to Notley Young in trust for paying debts of his son, Daniel Carroll Jr., part of *Labyrinth*, and *Joseph's Park*, for £221.

566. Daniel Young of Virginia recorded 13 August 1799, from Adam Young, bill of sale for £196, cow, yearling bay mare, and bay horse, household stuff and farm implements. Signed Adam Young. Witness: Valentine Bogenreiff.

566-567. William Prather recorded 13 August 1799, from Honore Martin, for £100 bill of sale for Negro woman named Lucy and her three children: Ary, Mary and Andrew. Signed Honore Martin before John L. Summers.

567-568. Elijah Walker recorded 14 August 1799, from John Krousz of Georgetown,, bill of sale for $180. One Negro woman, Bet about 17 years old. Acknowledged before Chas A. Beatty

568-570. John Laten recorded 14 August 1799 from James Hinton, for £15..7..6 part of *Moneysworth,* in Clarksburgh on northeast side of road. Signed before Greenberry Howard, John Clarke, Catherine Hinton, released dower.

570-572. John Lodge of Virginia recorded 14 August 1799, from John Bennett, for £113..1..10 ½ deed of bargain & sale for the following parcels: *Self Defense,* 117 acres; *Resurvey on Happy Choice,* 65 1/4 acres; Signed by mark. Mary wife of John Bennett released dower.

573-574. John Beard from James Gatton Senr., deed recorded 14 August 1799, made 10 August for £7..10 tract called *Gatton's Good Luck,* containing 37 acres. Signed before Aeneas Campbell, Thos B. Beall. Elizabeth Gatton wife of James released dower rights.

575-576. Nathan Cooke recorded 15 August 1799, from Walter Brooke of Anne Arundel Co., for £8 sells tract *Cage Harm,* adjacent to *Resurvey on Small Purchase, Grey's Neck,* and *Greys Meadows,* containing 8 acres. Signed before Daniel Reintzel and Henry Brookes. Susannah wife of Walter Brookes released dower.

576-578. James Barnes recorded 15 August 1799, from Vachel Hall for £9, deed for part of *Resurvey on Jeremiah's Park,* containing 2 acres. Signed before Greenbury Howard, John Clarke. Margaret Hall released dower rights.

578. Robert Smith recorded 15 August 1799, a list of four Negroes brought from Virginia in this state, the title to them derived from his wife Elizabeth, namely Nick 20, Beck 16, Alice 12 and Polly age 4 years, which was bought by me of Col. Rawly Dowman.

578-579. Samuel McFarland recorded 17 August 1799, from James Wimsett, bond, for the third part of the Indian Corn growing on the plantation whereon he now dwells.

579-580. Thomas Beall of George recorded 19 August 1799, from David Parker, mortgage for a debt due to Gabriel Greenfield, assigned to Thomas Brooke Beall, assigns one Negro man, Richard; if suit is settled in full, then bill of sale is void.
580-584. Jasper M. Jackson of Georgetown from Doct. James H. Blake of Georgetown, mortgage on one Negro man, Abraham, 27 years old.
584-585. John Busey Junr. Recorded 21 August 1799 from John Busy Senr., bill of sale for services rendered by John Bucy Jr., and he is also to pay all rents due on farm, and debts due to William Wallace, for which he assigns all crops on the farm.
585. Brice Litton Qualification as deputy Sheriff recorded 26 August 1799 before Benjamin W. Jones.
585-587. Kinsey Gittings of Benjamin recorded 26 August 1799, from Aron Gittings, for £225 deed for parcel which was willed to him by deceased father, Benjamin Gittings, an undivided 1/3 part. Signed before John L. Summers, J. H. McPherson. Eliza, wife of Aron Gittings released dower.
587-589. Aaron Gartrell recorded 26 August 1799 from Ephraim Davis of Frederick County, for $1920 deed for *Benjamin's Lott,* whereon Betsy Welsh lately resided and which was devised by the late Elizabeth Brown to her daughter Betsy, and entailed to Amos Davis and his heirs. Reference to Elizabeth Brown's will. Containing 160 acres. Signed Ephraim Davis before Richard Green, Thomas Davis.
589-590. John Young recorded 28 August 1799 for £10, from Carlton Belt, senior part of tract *Whole Included,* on south side of John Young's spring, with 24th line of *Wilson's Delay,* to the *Resurvey on Allison's Adventure,* to a tract called *Goodwill,* for 26 1/8 acres. Signed before Aeneas Campbell, Laurence O'Neale. Ann Belt released dower.
590. Solomon Holland & others to State of Maryland, bond as Collector of the Levy Court. Signed by Solomon Holland, Benjamin W. Jones, Honore Martin on 28 August 1799.
590-591. Kenelon B. Gray, recorded 28 August 1799, qualification as deputy sheriff at the request of Benjamin W. Jones.
591-592. Laurence Neale, William Veirs Senr. and John Veirs of Daniel, from John Bealmear, for £60, deed for 100 acres of *String about,* purchased of John Gaskin for 55 acres. Also equity in Negro slaves: Jacob, Eve, Beney, Nace and increase; all stock of cattle & sheep; plantation utensils and goods.
592. John Suter Junr. of Georgetown, recorded 30 August 1799, from John Huff of Mifflin Co, PA, deed. Whereas Suter is one of the legal reps of Samuel Huff, dec'd formerly of Georgetown, John Huff for $200 grants all his right to said estate. Signed by mark before Chas. A. Beatty and Edward Lloyd.
593-595. John Saml Peters recorded 31 August 1799, from John Snowden of Anne Arundel County, deed for £100 sells *Sapling Ridge,* for 100 acres. Signed before Rd Cramphin, Robert Brent. Anne released dower rights.
595-596. Adam Robb recorded 2 September 1799, from William Prather Williams, deed for £40, for lot #3 & 4, in town of Williamsburgh, containing 1 acre.
596-598. Adam Robb recorded 2 September 1799, from Thomas Perry Willson, for £38 deed for lots 78 & 79 in town of Williamsburgh.
598. Thomas Willson recorded 2 September 1799, from William P. Williams, deed for £40, assigns lots 78 & 79. Signed before John L. Summers, Daniel Reintzel.
599-600. Thomas Perry Willson recorded 2 September 1799, made 1 August, from Adam Robb, deed for £105, lot #3 in Williamsburgh as laid out by Col. Archibald Orme, on *Exchange and New Exchange Enlarged.* ½ acres. Signed before John L. Summers, J.H. McPherson. Receipt. Acknowledgment & Elizabeth Robb released dower rights.
600-601. Thomas Perry Willson recorded 2 September 1799, from John Rawlings, for £40..5..6, bill of sale for one Negro girl Milly. Signed before J. H. McPherson.
601. Joshua Chilton recorded 6 September 1799, from Charles Ogden, for £55, bill of sale for brown mare and colt, red cow, bed, furniture, etc. Signed before Joshua Hickman, William Dison by his mark.

602. Jacob Swomley recorded 7 September 1799, lease from Valentine Linganfelder of Fayette County, Kentucky. For £68, lets lot in Lot Town or Germansburgh, beginning north west of dwelling house where the said Valentine Linganfelter lately lived, which premises were devised 10 October 1793 by William Fulks, called *Resurvey on Robert Delight,* and *Deer Park,* for the term of 99 years beginning 12 May 1790. Signed Valentine Linganfelter and Margaret Linganfelter by mark.
603-604. Charles Decandry recorded 10 September 1799, made 18 June, from Walter Williams, for £55, deed for part of *Mount Pleasant,* 20 acres. Ann wife of Walter Williams released dower rights. Witnesses William Smith, Thos B. Beall.
604-605. Henry Poole recorded 10 September 1799, from John G. Hobbs for £70, bill of sale for all stock, and furniture herein mentioned. Signed before Edward Burgess Jr.
605-606. Robert Peter recorded 11 September 1799, from William Smith, for £140, bill of sale for bay gelding, 16 hands. Signed before J. Lackland.
606-607. John B. Dyson recorded 12 September 1799, from Edward Vears, for £60, deed for part of *Mary,* adjacent to *Resurvey on Non-Eaten,* as formerly conveyed by Daniel Viers to George Dyson for 150 acres, containing 16 ½ acres. Signed Edward Viers before Lawrence O'Neale, Greenberry Howard.
607-608. William Veirs, recorded 12 September 1799, from Lyddia Dyson, John B. Dyson, Basil Dyson and Samuel Dyson, for 20 shillings, deed of confirmation on part of *Non Eaton,* beginning at a line on the heirs of Samuel Dyson's part of a tract called *Thomas Discovery,* to a part formerly conveyed by Daniel Viers to George Dyson for 150 acres. Containing 11 acres. Signed Lyddia Dyson by mark, John B. Dyson, Basil Dyson, Samuel Dyson. Receipt. Acknowledgment.
608-610. James Gatton & others recorded 12 September 1799, from James Gatton Senr., for £187 paid by James Gatton, Jr., Elizabeth Gatton and Verlinda Gatton, bill of sale for all Negroes, stock of horses, cattle and hogs, household and kitchen furniture. That is to say Negroes Swain, Cate, Amy, Gin, Abraham, Charles and Nora; 6 horses, etc. Signed James Gatton before Thomas Gatton, Jeremiah Gatton by mark. Acknowledgment before Aeneas Campbell.
610. William Viers and John B. Dyson and Basil Dyson, recorded Agreement 12 September 1799, regarding boundary line of *Mary.* Signed before Eden Viers, Solomon Viers.
610-613. Thomas Gatton recorded 12 September 1791, from James Gatton Senr., for £791 deed for tracts *Hickman's Discovery, Pheasant's Nest, Gatton's Good Luck,* and *Resurvey on Gatton's Good Luck,* adjacent to 16 ½ acres conveyed to Jesse Phillips. Four separate parcels containing 197 3/4 acres in all. Signed before Ens Campbell, Thos B. Beall. Elizabeth, wife of James Gatton Sr., relinquished dower.
613. Philip Sinn recorded 4 September 1799, from John Davidson, deed. Whereas Phillip Sinn is possessed of lot #58 in Georgetown; and a legal fee simple estate is vested in John Davidson of Annapolis, deed made 3 June 1799 for £20 for the lot in *Beatty and Hawkins Addition to Georgetown.* Signed before John Done. Maria Davidson released dower rights.
614-616. Henry Poole recorded 14 September 1799, made 7 September, from Jesse Hyatt, for £10, deed for tract *Ivey Reach,* part of land formerly called *Bucklands,* but now called *Principal,* adjacent to part conveyed by Jesse Hyatt to Adam Ramsburgh to north side of Bennet's Creek, containing 1 1/8 acres. Signed before Edward Burgess Jr., John Clarke. Receipt. Acknowledgment.
616-617. Richard Dunn & others recorded 16 September 1799. Whereas Mary Regney a single woman appeared before the Justices of the Peace of Montgomery County and made oath that a baseborn female child begot of her body was begot by Richard Dunn, he files bond of recognizance to state of Maryland, by Richard Dunn, Archibald Dunn and John Manley for £30 to keep said child. Signed 14 June 1799.
617-618. Fielder Parker recorded 16 September 1799, from Roby Penn, for £31..10, 10 ½ acres of *Penn's Inheritance.* Signed before Edward Burgess Jr., John Clarke. Acknowledgment. Lucrasia wife of Roby Penn released dower.

618-619. Elizabeth McDavit recorded 17 September 1799, from James Smith, taylor, for £17..10, bill of sale for one sorrel mare, one brown cow and calf; one feather bed & furniture; one walnut chest with drawers. Signed before William Willson, Els. Demorn by mark. Acknowledged before John Clarke.
619-621. Joseph Slater & Sarah his wife recorded 20 September 1799, from William Prout & Sarah his wife, for 5 shillings paid by Joseph Slater, Sarah his wife; Henry Slater, Charles Slater, David Harris Slater, Ann Slater, Sarah Slater and Jonathan Slater, children of them the said Joseph Slater and Sarah Slater of Munro County, Virginia, sell to Joseph Slater and Sarah his wife during their natural lives and the survivor of them, and after their death then to said Henry Slater, Charles Slater, David Harris Slater, Anna Slater, Sarah Slater, Jonathan Slater as tenants in common the following Negroes: Romeo, Henny and her children, and also all others of said William Prout and Sarah Prout's right of any kind, which he the said Jonathan Slater died possessed, excepting one Negro woman called Sally, daughter of Negro Milley. Signed William Prout, Sarah Prout; before Cornelius Cunningham, John Addison, justices of the peace of Prince George's County, and John R. Magruder, Clerk of Court, Prince George's County.
621-623. Joseph Slater & Sarah his wife recorded 20 September 1799, from William Prout & Sarah his wife, of the City of Washington, Prince George's County, deed for 5 shillings, from Henry, Charles, David Harris, Anna, Sarah and Jonathan Slater, sells land late property of Jonathan Slater deceased purchased of Thomas Plater and William Robertson, whereon Anna Slater now lives. Signed William Prout and Sarah Prout before same witnesses as above.
623-624. Ignatius Drury recorded 20 September 1799 from John Lenman of Prince George's County, for £20, bill of sale for Negro Priss about 35 years old and boy Humphrey 2 yrs. 4 months. Signed before John Mountz, Junr.
624-625. Caleb Bently recorded 24 September 1799, from Henry Bowen, for £25, bill of sale for all my crop of corn and tobacco, now growing, 6 pewter plates, one feather bed, iron pot, dozen pewter plates, etc. Signed Henry Bowen before Thomas Davis.
625-627. Robert Briggs recorded 27 September 1799, from Jane Threlkeld & Samuel Williams, for £45..2..8, bill of sale for one Negro lad named Elisha. Signed before Wm Smith. However, intent is that when above sum is paid this sale is void.
627-628. Walter Mackall recorded 20 September 1799, from Leonard Mackall, for $2000 and the assumption of sundry debts, bill of sale for the following Negroes: Ciss, Luke, Fern, Murray, Ben, Priscilla, Nell, Doll, Phill, Alexander, Deliver, Abel, Anna, David, Jacob, Flora, Pompey and all household and kitchen furniture, stock of cattle and horses, tobacco, corn and wheat. Signed before Upton Beall, J.H. McPherson.
628-628#2. Joseph Slater of Munro County, Virginia recorded 1 October 1799 from David Slater of Prince George's County, for 5 shillings, all my interest of property of Jonathan Slater late of Montgomery County. Signed David Slater before Thos Contee, John R. Magruder Jr., Clerk Prince George's County.
628#2. Samuel Clagett recorded 3 October 1799, from Daniel Carroll of *Duddington Manor*, release of mortgage on land called *Treble Troubles.*
628-629. Green & English recorded 7 October 1799, from Ignatius Newton & Clement Newton of Georgetown, for $90. bill of sale for black horse 8 years bought from Mathew Kennedy, providing the true meaning is that they will pay $90 in the amount of $17 out of this quarter's wages for riding at posts, and the further sum of $73. during the course of next years' wages for riding a post, ending 18 March, then the sale is void. Signed Ignatius Newton, Clement Newton, before Thomas Barclay, George Brome, Patrick Magruder, receipt.
629-630. Ninian Magruder of Samuel Brewer Magruder, recorded 7 October 1799, from Patrick Lynch, for £120, bill of sale for Negro Betty age 20 and her two children Harriet 2 years old and Eliza 7 months. Signed before Saml B. Magruder, Walter Magruder.
630-633. Saml McFarland from Thos Beall of George, William Smith and Samuel Williams, for £75, sells tract called *Seneca Ford,* west of coopers shop. Two lots. Signed before John L. Summers, J. McPherson. Nancy Beall released dower, Octavia Smith released dower and Elizabeth Williams released dower rights.

633-635. Reason Johnson recorded 9 October 1799, from John Belt, for £415..6..3, deed for part of tract *Woodport,* and *Richland,* adjacent to part conveyed by Nathan Thompson, and tract called *Crow's Beginning,* to *Resurvey on Sapling Ridge.* Signed before John L. Summers, John Clarke. Acknowledgment, receipt.

635-637. Basil Brooke recorded 11 October 1799, made 23rd day, 7th month, from Richard Thomas deed for *Addition to Charley Forest,* on south side of road from Sandy Spring Meeting House to Basil Brookes. Signed Richard Thomas before Thomas Davis, Elemelech Swearingen.

637-638. Jonathan Browning Senr. recorded 12 December 1798, made 2 July, From Jonathan Browning Junr. for £50, one lot in Clarksburg, ½ acre. Signed before Greenberry Howard, John Clarke. Margaret Browning released dower rights.

638-639. Edward James (or Iames) recorded 14 October 1799, from Robert Peter Sr. and John Threlkeld and David Peter, bond.. Whereas above Edward James is now confined in prison and has petitioned John L. Summers, J. H. McPherson and Thomas Corcoran for his discharge, for relief of insolvent debtors; this bond is for those objecting to release to indemnify them. Signed in presence of Alexr. Peter, John Thompson.

639-640. Robert Peter recorded 14 October 1799, from Joseph Redman, for 2994 lbs. tobacco, bill of sale for one roan mare, one colt, other livestock, furniture and dishes. Signed before Jas. P. Morsell. Acknowledged.

640-641. Solomon Veirs recorded 14 October 1799, from Edward Veirs, power of attorney. Whereas Edward is seized of land in Huntington County, Pennsylvania on Warring Ridge, 4 miles from warm springs containing 172 acres, this appoints Solomon Viers attorney to sell same. Signed before John L. Summers, J. H. McPherson.

641-643. Ninian Magruder recorded 16 October 1799 from Catharine Magruder, executrix of Joseph Magruder, deceased. Deed made 15 October for £40..3, for tracts: *Resurvey on Addition to Magruder's Purchase,* adjacent to *Friendship,* and *Pritchett's Purchase.* Containing 9 acres. Signed before Elemelech Swearingen, J.H. McPherson.

643-645. John Linthicum recorded 19 October 1799, made same date from Zachariah Linthicum, deed for 5 shillings, part of tracts, *Resurvey on Wolf Pitt,* and the *Pig Pen,* beginning at a later resurvey called *Vienna,* and part of tract *Partnership,* resurveyed for Hardage Lane, Zachariah Offutt and Benjamin Edwards, and Alexander Catlet, and part of a tract called *Mount Airy,* resurveyed for John W. Warfield, containing 200 acres. Signed Zachariah Linthicum by mark before John L. Summers, J.H. McPherson. Acknowledgment.

645-649. Thomas Linthicum recorded 19 October 1799, from Zachariah Linthicum, deed made same date, for 5 shillings, part of tracts *Resurvey on Friend in Need,* part of that tract conveyed to Ninian Beall by Thomas Birdwhistle for 116 acres, beginning at 57th line of *Partnership,* 26 2/3 acres; another part conveyed to Zachariah Linthicum by Benjamin Edwards, added together makes up quantity of 200 acres. Signed as above, acknowledgment.

649-651. Zachariah Linthicum recorded 19 October 1799, made 28 May 1799, from Benjamin Edwards, for £438, part of *Partnership,* in 2 parts of 168 acres, and 26 2/3 acres. Signed before Wm Smith, J. Lackland. Receipt & acknowledgment. Margaret Edwards released dower.

651-652. Negro Solomon recorded 22 October 1799, from William Cranch & Nancy Cranch his wife, for $100. Manumission of Solomon, aged about 30 years, on condition that said Solomon serve Mr. Washington Bowie for term of 18 months from this day. Signed before Sam Elliot Junr., Thos Corcoran.

652-653. Nehemiah Lowes to Benjamin W. Jones, Sheriff of Montgomery County schedule of all property including accounts due from James Redmond, John Fitzgerald, and tobacco in the hands of Henry Warring. Signed before John L. Summers, J.H. McPherson.

653-654. Francis Mantz recorded 24 October 1799, from Thomas Gatton son of James, for 5 shillings, mortgage on of part of *Resurvey on Gattons Good Luck.* Signed before Ans Campbell, Thos B. Beall.

654. John Ward recorded 24 October 1799, from John Hoggins, for £25 bill of sale for 2 may mares, a white horse, however, provided if sum is paid, then this is void. Signed before Wm Smith.

655-657. John Orme recorded 26 October 1799, made 6 October, from Richard Orme for £7..10, all his part of *Rich Meadow,* on west of Muddy Branch, adjacent to *Hamilton's Lott,* late property of Richard Ricketts; *Lucas Adventure, Hartley Hall, Maiden's Bower, Cornelius Chance,* and *Deakin's Range.* 155 acres of land. Signed Richard J. Orme before Elemelech Swearingen, J.H. McPherson.
657-659. Caleb Bentley, Isaac Briggs and Roger Brookes, trustees for and chosen by the people called Quakers, belonging to the Sandy Spring Meeting, recorded 26 October 1799, made 23rd day, 7th month (called July) 1799, between Basil Brookes, for 5 shillings, part of *Charley Forest,* 3/8 acres for use of the meeting. Signed before Thomas Davis, Elemelech Swearingen. Acknowledgment, Mary Brookes released dower.
659. John Orme recorded 26 October 1799, from Archibald Orme, for £185 bill of sale for all property sold by John Orme on 30 October 1787, excepting Negro woman, Lett about 27 years old and her issue. Signed by Archibald Orme before Benjamin Gaither.
660-661. Honore Martin recorded 28 October 1799, from Zachariah Allison, for £27, deed for all his right to the real estate of his father, John Allison, late of Montgomery County, deceased. Signed before Ans Campbell, Greenberry Howard. Acknowledgment.
661-663. [Marginal note: Delivered to your son in law, Mr. Simpson, 17 June 1803]. Nicholas Pegno recorded 28 October 1799, from Joseph Burnes, for £100 deed for tract *Inspection,* 150 acres. Signed before Greenberry Howard, John Clarke. Receipt, Acknowledgment.
663. John Scrivener's schedule delivered to the sheriff on 1 November 1799, included one straw bed, one saddle. Signed before Benjamin Gaither, J.H. McPherson.
663-665. Henry Brookes recorded 3 November 1799, made 26 October, from Peter Wilcoxon, for £500, deed for part of *Deer Park,* 229 acres. Signed before Greenberry Howard, Thos B. Beall. Elizabeth Wilcoxon released dower rights.
665-666. Thomas Beall of George recorded 4 November 1799, from Thomas Plater for £1125, sells part of *Zoar,* above the courthouse on the main road to Frederick town adjoining Logg Town, bounded by John Rawling's land and on the west, land where Robert P. Magruder resides on the south William Holme's land on the east, and James M. Lingan's land on the north, containing 300 acres, originally the property of Robert Briscoe and Edward Burgess, deeded to Plater in 1792, and by Edward Burgess, Sheriff in 1793 to Thomas Beall of George. Signed before Patrick Magruder, Thomas Corcoran. Martha wife of Thomas Plater released dower.
667-668. Thomas Beall of George recorded 4 November 1799, from William H. Dorsey & Ann Dorsey, his wife, for £1455..15, part of tract assigned Ann Dorsey for her part of real estate of her deceased grandfather, James Brooke, on west side of Busy's road, 323 ½ acres. Signed before Thomas Plater.
668-669. James Norwood recorded 4 November 1799, from John Poole for £75, bill of sale for his tobacco, corn, a dun mare. Signed by mark before Edward Burgess Junr.
669-672. James Dunlap of Georgetown recorded 4 November 1799, from Samuel Busey, for £566..5, deed for part of *Jones Hope,* and *Labyrinth,* between tracts *Clean Drinking,* and *Charles and Thomas,* granted from John Busey to Samuel Busey. Signed before Joseph Ford and Thomas Corcoran. Ann Busey wife of Samuel released dower rights.
673-675. Benjamin Waters recorded 4 November 1799, from Francis Lowndes of Georgetown, for £393..3..11, deed for part of *Charles and Jane,* beginning at tract which Charles Davis purchased called *Beall's Manor,* 100 acres. Also a 22 ½ acre part of *Beall's Manor,* alias *Three Bealls Manor,* which remained to John Davis after his deed to Charles Davis; also part of *Edmonston's Good Will,* beginning at the tract, *Charles and Jane,* for 163 acres. Signed by Francis Lowndes before Patrick Magruder, Thos Corcoran. Jane Lowndes released dower rights.
675-677. Lenox Martin and others recorded 4 November 1799, from Samuel Williams. Deed made 5 October, between Lenox Martin, Hardage Lane and Thomas Martin. Samuel Williams indebted to diverse persons sells property in consideration of paying and satisfying his debts as trustee of all his property. Signed before John L. Summers, J.H. McPherson. Elizabeth wife of Samuel Williams released dower rights.

Montgomery County Liber I, Land Record Abstracts

1. William Orr and John Wayman, recorded on 5 November 1799, recognizance to State of Maryland, in sum of £30, to keep the county free from charges in maintenance of a male bastard child of Polly Preston, alias Martha Blake, which William Orr fathered. Acknowledged 6 June 1799, before John L. Summers.

1. George Wilson and William Kelly, recorded on 5 November 1799, recognizance bond, State of Maryland. For £30 for maintenance of child of Elizabeth Oden, gotten of George Wilson. Acknowledged 10 May 1799.

1-2. John M. Gantt recorded 5 November 1799, from James H. Blake, mortgage. Whereas I, Doctor James H. Blake of Georgetown, am indebted to Samuel Davidson for $270.59, mortgages Negro man called Natt, 14 years of age, if I do not pay the sum by 1 Jan. 1803, then he is to be sold at public sale. /s/ James H. Blake, before Thos Corcoran.

3-4. John Beall recorded 6 November 1799, from Jacob Lazier, for £40, two pied cows, etc. Signed 6 Nov. 1799, by mark before John L. Summers.

4-5. John Reed recorded 6 Nov. 1799, from Michael Tully, bill of sale. For £60, sells one brown or black mare, about 11 years old, other items, also parcel of tobacco now hanging in the house of Henry Dorsey on the place where I live. Signed by mark, before John Clarke.

5-6. Ashford & Uriah Leaton recorded 6 November 1799, from Jeremiah Gray of Pittsylvania Co., Va., for £250, sells two parcels, *Double Trouble,* and the other *Long Tract,* lying on Little Bennets Creek – a grist mill stands at end of 49th line called *Friendship,* 12 acres. The second tract begins at *Resurvey on Content.* Signed before John Clarke, Greenberry Howard.

6-7. Thomas Plater recorded 6 November 1799, from Gerrard Briscoe, of Frederick Co., Virginia, deed for 5 shillings, part of *Zoar,* whereon Jones resided, for 35 acres, and was bought at sheriff's sale, by Thomas Plater, at suit of Samuel Beall against Edward Burgess. Signed before Charles A. Beatty. Acknowledgment.

7-8. Isaac Dawes from Aaron Dyer, bill of sale for £60 for one mahogany desk, mahogany table, one cherry table, one walnut table, one cupboard, one trunk, three beds, bedsteads, one black mare, two pied cows, 4 chairs, 11 pewter basins and one framed houses. Signed before Abraham Dawes.

8-9. John Poole Jr. recorded 7 Nov. 1799, from William Willcoxon, bill of sale. Made 1 October for £300, Tract called *Prospect Hills,* for 150 acres. Signed before Aeneas Campbell, Thos B. Beall.

9. Hezekiah Thomas from Robert B. Beall & Robert E. Yates, bill of sale recorded 7 Nov. 1799. We, in consideration of being exonerated in a suit removed to court of appeals for William G. Pierce, and for indemnification, we had a bill of sale for Negro man Arch, property of said Pierce, we now release all claim unto Hezekiah Thomas. Acknowledged before Patrick Magruder.

9-10. Lloyd Frizzell from Edward Iglehart, deed recorded 7 Nov. 1799, an agreement to farm and let part of *Mount Radnor,* 91 acres, from 20 Nov. 1798 for 11 years. Iglehart agrees to furnish plank and nails to finish a dwelling house, to plant 100 apple trees, and to build a tobacco house. Signed before Edward Burgess Jr., John Clarke.

10-11. Shadrock Newton from Richard Fenwick, B/S. recorded 8 Nov. 1799 for £60, crop of corn in the field, and crop of wheat, and 2000 weight of tobacco now hanging in the house. Signed Richard Fenwick.

11-12. Upton and Margaret Beall recorded 9 November 1799, bill of sale. I Thomas Nicholls of Simon, of Montgomery County for £134, sell Negro man, Anthony, 45, woman Peg, 25, boy Charley 9, girl Sophia 7 years old, boy Ben 5 years; boy Bill 2 years. If Thomas Nicholls pays same before 10 December then sale void. Signed before J.H. McPherson. Marginal note: I have received satisfaction of Mr. Thos Nichols of Simon for the foregoing bill of sale.

12-16. Leonard M. Deakins of Prince George's County, recorded 9 November 1799, from James Gatton, Elizabeth his wife and Thomas Gatton, their son, mortgage for £6..2..4 and the quantity of 63,000 lbs. Of tobacco, on tracts *Hickman's Discovery, Pheasant's Neck.* Dower release Elizabeth Gatton. Detailed summary of debt, original 45,000 lbs. Tobacco with interest & court costs.

16-18. Leonard M. Deakins from James Gatton Senior, James Gatton Junior, Elizabeth Gatton and Verlinda Gatton, mortgage, premises as above and also Negro slaves: Susanna, Cate, Amy, Gin, Abraham and Nan, and six horses, 5 cows, 19 hogs and all the plantation and kitchen furniture.

19-20. Ephraim Gaither recorded November 1799, made 21 Oct. 1799, from Richard Weaver Jones of Loudoun County, Virginia who mortgaged three Negroes, Shrewsbury, Bristol and Priscilla, to secure payment, and Priscilla's two children born since the mortgage. Signed before Thomas Davis, Nathan Musgrove.

20. Alice Russell recorded 12 November 1799, from Isaac Russell, for £25, bill of sale for 2 beds, bedsteads, household furniture, 2 sows and hogs, one calf. Signed by mark.

20-21. Joseph Compton recorded 13 November 1799, and Monica Tenley, agreement. Whereas they are contemplating the state of wedlock, within a few days, and each party possesses property, to go to their respective children of former marriages, it is agreed to maintain separate estates. Signed 18 November 1799. Acknowledged before Wm Smith, Michael Whelan.

22. Michael Hefner of Frederick County, MD., recorded 13 November 1799, from Hugh Couplund, mortgage made 5 Oct. 1799, for £21..3..6 undivided part of *Moneysworth,* in Clarksburgh on SE side of road marked #8, for 96 perches of land, unless sum is paid by 6 March 1801. Signed by Hugh Coupland before John Clarke, Greenbury Howard. Ack.

23-24. Daniel Candler recorded 15 Nov. 1799, from Joshua Owens, deed for £100, part of tract called *Owens Conclusion,* containing 37 acres. Signed before Henry Brookes, Benjamin Gaither. Mary Owens, wife of Joshua released dower rights.

24-25. Daniel Candler recorded 15 Nov. 1799, from William Candler, deed for £100 for part of tract called *Pleasant Plains of Damascus,* metes and bounds given for 100 acres. Signed William Candler before Henry Brookes, Benjamin Gaither.

26-28. John Clagett of Thos. Recorded deed 16 November 1799, made 13 November from Daniel Candler, for £378..15, several tracts, part of *Pleasant Plains of Damascus,* taken up by Matthew Pigman, containing 166 acres; and a second part containing 100 acres and also one other parcel called *Owen's Conclusion,* containing 37 acres. Signed by Daniel Candler, before Henry Brookes and Benjamin Gaither.

28-29. Jacob Stires Sr., recorded bill of sale 18 Nov. 1799 made 24 May 1799 between Basil Beckwith for £16, sells tract, part of *Resurvey on Brandy,* formerly conveyed to Rezin Spates by John and Elizabeth Scrivener, and by Spates to Beckwith, containing 1 acre and 6/10. Signed Basil Beckwith before Wm Smith, Thos B. Beall. Receipt. Acknowledgment.

30-32. William Viers Senior recorded 20 Nov. 1799, made 2 November, from Zadock Magruder Junior, part of *Resurvey on Noneaten,* called *Mary,* being in three parts, together with tract *William and Mary,* and *Daniel's Inheritance,* part formerly conveyed to Mary and Maddox Dyson for 225 acres, also second part of 1 ½ acres. Signed Zadock Magruder before Thos B. Beall and Lawrence O'Neale. Martha Magruder wife of Zadock released dower.

32-34. Zadock Magruder recorded 20 November 1799, from William Veirs Senior, for £140, deed for part of *William and Mary,* and part of *Daniel's Inheritance;* 17 ½ acres and another part of *Resurvey on Noneaten,* beginning at 2nd line of *Liver's Good Luck,* adjacent to part formerly conveyed to Mary and Maddox Dyson, 4 acres, to a deed conveyed by John and William Veirs to Mary and Maddox Dyson for 225 acres; and that the tract *Accident,* is not mentioned in either conveyance but may be in part, included in those lines. Signed and witnessed as deed above. Mary wife of William Veirs released dower.

34-37. William Willson, Samuel Willson, Susanna Magruder of Frederick County, Virginia, Charity Magruder and Margaret and Martha Willson recorded 22 November 1799, from Jacob Waters of Anne Arundel County. Whereas Jacob Waters on 20 November 1793, by instrument of writing did convey to John Willson, of Montgomery County, two parcels, *Susannah,* and one called *Resurvey on William and John,* and whereas he died intestate and without issue, it descended to his brothers and sisters; and upon examination

of the deed recorded in Liber E, errors were made, this indenture is to correct same. Signed by Jacob Waters, before Samuel Godman and Brice T. Worthington. Elizabeth, wife of Jacob Waters released dower rights.
37-38. Benjamin Loveless recorded 22 November 1799 from John Yates for £50, all that tract adjoins tract granted to Henry McGlocklin by John Knobbs, also tract *Twice Gott,* Signed by John Yates. Eleanor Yates released dower.
38-40. Mathew Reid recorded 23 November 1799, from Laurence O. Neale, William Viers Sr., John Veirs of Daniel and John Bealmear for £43..13, deed for tract *Scanackety* on third line of *Holding Spring,* containing 6 7/8 acres. Signed. Acknowledgment.
40-42. Matthew Read recorded 23 Nov. 1799, made 4 Sept. from James Riggs of Bedford County, Pennsylvania, executor of Edmund Riggs of Montgomery County. For £354, part of tract called *Resurvey on Albany,* adjacent to *Holding Spring,* 100 acres. Signed. Receipt. Acknowledgment.
42-43. Samuel Phillips of Prince George's County, recorded 26 November 1799, from Basil Perry, deed made 25 Nov. for £405 for three pieces of land, part of *Ray's Adventure,* and part of tract called *Trouble Enough,* running along lines of *Hope Improved,* to 5th line of deed from James Perry to William H. Gartrell for 125 acres; this parcel containing 135 acres. Signed by mark before Greenbury Howard, John Clark. Acknowledgment.
43-45. John Wilson recorded 28 Nov. 1799, from Joseph Jones, deed made 18 Nov. for £330 called *Labyrinth,* also part of *Resurvey on Happy Choice,* also to 12th line of tract called *Mackey's Chance* for 105 3/4 acres, second part also *Resurvey on Happy Choice,* for 4 ½ acres. Signed Joseph Jones, before witnesses as above. Receipt. Ack.
45-46. Benjamin Edwards recorded 25 November 1799, from John Wayman, for £30..12, bill of sale for mulatto woman, Betsy and her child, Lucy. Signed before J. H. McPherson.
46-48. Joseph Jones recorded 28 Nov. 1799, from Phillip Hammond Hopkins of Ann Arundel Co., made 22 August 1799 for £100, part of tract called *Labyrinth,* lying partly in Frederick and partly in Montgomery County, starting at 2nd line of *Resurvey on Happy Choice,* 110 acres. Signed before Edward Hall & Phillip Hammond. Acknowledged in Ann Arundel County.
48-50. Hardage Lane and Miss. Mary Greenfield recorded 30 November 1799, who plan to marry soon, record marriage contract. Miss Mary Greenfield agrees to receive in lieu of her dower, should she outlive Hardage Lane, part of tract called *Fortune,* 56 acres, and part of tract *Mill Road,* containing 100 acres; and the following personal property, one Negro slave called Eliza, and a choice of feather beds, furniture, horse and two cows. Signed Hardage Lane, Mary Greenfield, in the presence of Wm Smith, J. Lackland, John Smith, James Smith, Joh. Moore, Jos. Atlin, Benj. Thomas, Charles Rogers, and Weathers Smith. Acknowledged before Wm. Smith, J. Lackland, 23 November 1799.
50. Edward Beall, recorded qualification as deputy sheriff, 29 November 1799.
50-51. Frederick Duvall recorded 2 December 1799, from Edward Crow, deed of trust made 6 June 1799, whereas Richard Morgan and Eleanor his wife, did about 8 Oct. 1788, by indenture of bargain and sale make over their undivided fifth part of land, *Hold Fast What You Have Got,* containing 45 acres recorded in D:128-129; and the undivided fifth part of aforesaid tract; the above named Frederick Duvall has agreed to purchase for £89..5. Signed Edward Crow before Wm Smith, John Clarke.
51-53. Ninian Magruder recorded 4 December 1799, from Nathan Cooke, deed made 4 Dec. 1799 for £171..16..10, an undivided moiety of two tracts, one called *Owens Resurvey,* 136 1/4 acres; the other *Abel's Levels,* 16 ½ acres, which were conveyed to Ninian Magruder and Nathan Cooke by William Leach, 25 Sept. 1798. Signed Nathan Cooke, before John L. Summers, J. H. McPherson. Rachel Cooke, wife of Nathan released dower rights.
53-54. Zachariah Dowden from Samuel Offutt, deed, recorded 4 December 1799 for £40, *Bad Luck,* and *Hunting Hill,* 10 1/4 acres. Elizabeth wife of Samuel Offutt released dower rights.

54-55. Thomas Alexander Brooke recorded 5 December 1799 from Wm Dent Beall, for £1000 debt, I have had for several years. Bill of sale for Lucille 40 years; Sylvanus 20 years; girl Alley, 10 years; Molly 35 years old. Signed before Thos Corcoran, Lloyd Beall.

55. Richard Hoggins recorded 16 Dec. 1799, from Richard Hoggins, Jr., for £140, bill of sale for one Negro woman, Darcus about 24 years old, one Negro girl Henny, 3 years old and one Negro boy, Benson about 3 months old, 2 feather beds, bedsteads, one black mare, one sorrel mare, two cows, other livestock, signed Richard Hoggins Jr., before Greenbury Howard.

56. Susannah Edenburgh recorded 7 Dec. 1799, from Banford Jewell for £210, bill of sale for one Negro man, Dick, one wagon and two horses. Signed before Thomas B. Beall

56-57. Jane Edenburgh recorded 7 Dec. 1799, from Banford Sewell for £160, one Negro Bob and one dunn mare and colt. Signed by Banford Sewell.

57. Joshua Owings recorded 9 Dec. 1799, from William M. Stewart, for £8, bill of sale for one bay mare, 15 years old; 2 tables, 3 chairs, one feather bed, two sheep, other items. Signed by mark before B. Gaither.

57-58. Samuel Clagett recorded 9 December 1799, from Daniel Carroll of Duddington Manor, in Prince Georges County, for £1370, being the principal and interest due for the redemption of the tract called *Trouble, Trouble,* mortgaged by Samuel Clagett 16 March 1791. Signed before Thos Corcoran, Dan'l Reintzel.

58-59. Harriott White recorded 10 December 1799, from James White of Georgetown, for the love and affection I bear to my daughter and 5 shillings, grant one Negro woman Betty, but if the said James White have another child or children, then the increase of said Negro is to be divided among them. Signed 4 December 1799 before Jonathan Morrow.

59-60. William & Mary Monro recorded 10 December 1799, from Jonathan Monro, of Georgetown, bill of sale for the love and affection towards my children, one frame house whereon I now live; with furniture, one Negro woman, other items. Signed before James White, John Pringle.

60-61. John Adamson recorded 12 December 1799, from William Kelly, deed made 16 August for £150, part of *Clean Shaving,* beginning at 5th line of *Resurvey on Addition to Susannah and Elizabeth,* containing 158 acres. Signed before Laurence O'Neale, Dan'l Reintzel. Ack.

61-63. William Dickson recorded 12 December 1799, from Jonathan Browning Jr., deed made 17 July, for £18..15 one lot or part of *Moneysworth*, on NE side of road in Clarksburgh, lot #12, Signed before John Clarke, Greenbury Howard. Receipt. Ack. Margaret Browning wife of Jonathan, released dower rights.

63-64. John Belt recorded 16 December 1799, from Samuel Hobbs and Priscilla Hobbs his wife, for £150 deed for part of *Hinton's Care,* conveyed by John Hinton to Samuel Busy, 34 acres; also part of *Hazard,* to the 6th line of *Rich Land*, 33 ½ acres. Signed before Greenbury Howard, John Clarke.

64. Thomas C. Nicholls qualified as deputy sheriff 18 December 1799 at the request of Benjamin W. Jones. Sworn before John L. Summers.

64-65. William O'Neale Senior recorded 21 December 1799, from Hezekiah Allison, of back [?] County, and State of Maryland, deed made 5 Oct., for all his right to the real estate of his father John Allison, late of Montgomery County, deceased, from his last will and testament. Signed by mark before John L. Summers.

65-66. Samuel Shaw recorded 23 December 1799, from Thomas Davis, for £750, bill of sale for 3 pris of bellows, 3 vises, 3 anvils, 4 sledges, 6 hand hammers, chisels, files and other tools named; iron; bed, bedstead and other furniture, ten plate stove, etc. Signed before Thomas Corcoran.

66-67. Caleb Bentley recorded 23 December 1799, from Thomas Wright, mortgage made 19 Dec. 1799, for part of tract called *Pigman's Inheritance,* on line of *Charley's Forest,* 50 acres. If sum of £170 paid with interest sale is void. Signed Thomas Wright before Thos Corcoran, Jos Forest.

67-68. Leonard Hoyle recorded 23 December 1799, from George Heeter, blacksmith, deed of sale, for 5 shillings, part of *Dabster's Tryal,* adjacent to *Dry Spring,* granted to Daniel Carroll, to the *Resurvey on*

Friend's Advise to tract called *Mary,* 13 ½ acres. Signed George Heeter before Wm Smith, John L. Summers, acknowledgment.
68. Henry Forrest recorded list of Negroes brought from Virginia 24 Dec. 1799, derived from his marriage with Jane Lowe of Virginia. Negroes Sally, 35 years; Violet 26 years; Ann 7 years. Witness, Joseph Forrest.
68. Benjamin W. Jones and Allen Bowie recorded 24 December 1799. I Gerrard Johnson, for £53..4.. Negro man John 28 years ld; a gray mare and other livestock. Signed 14 Dec. 1799, wit. By John L. Summers.
69-70. John B. Allison from James B. Crawford and Anne Crawford, his wife, recorded 28 Dec. 1799, made 8 Dec. for 5 shillings, and in consideration that Elisha Allison, late of Montgomery County, former husband of said Anne, did by his last will and testament bearing date 28 June 1796, did appoint that ½ of his estate should be returned unto his fathers' family after the death of her the said Anne, her undivided half share in *Rock Spring,* 83 acres; and also *Addition to Alexandria,* 6 ½ acres; and one lot in *Williamsburgh*; after the death of Ann. Signed James B. Crafford, Ann Crafford. Dower released.
70-71. James and Anne Crawford from John B. Allison, recorded 28 Dec. 1799. Tracts, *Cool Spring,* and *Addition to Alexandria.*
71-72. Lawrence O. Holt recorded 28 December 1799, from James and Anne Crawford, deed for 5 shillings, tract called *Addition to Alexandria* for 6 acres; lot in town of *Williamsburgh* #30, nevertheless, for the use and interest hereafter stated, the aforesaid Lawrence O. Holt is to proceed without delay to the sale of lands and estate aforesaid on terms that will benefit all interested parties. He is to pay and discharge all debts due from Elisha Allison, late of Montgomery County, and all debts of the aforesaid James B. and Ann Crawford, and any remainder to be paid to them after sale. Signed James B. Crawford, Ann Crawford.
72. Benjamin W. Jones recorded 30 Dec. 1799. Bond of Benjamin W. Jones, Henry Jones, Richard Jones of Edw., John Harwood and Solomon Holland of Montgomery County, bond of £10,000 for his performance as Sheriff. Signed before Charles A. Beatty, John L. Summers, J. H. McPherson.
72-73. Upton Beall from Leonard Mackall & Catherine, his wife, deed recorded 1 Jan. 1800, made 1 Oct. 1799, for £5000, sell all their part of the estate of Brooke Beall. Signed before Patrick Magruder, Thos Corcoran.
74. Isaac Russell to Sheriff of Montgomery County, schedule of property recorded 2 January 1800, listed credits due from Benjamin Holland Sr. and Basil Leach.
74. Michael Tully to Sheriff of Montgomery County, schedule recorded 2 Jan. 1800, listed 3 old weeding hoes, one looking glass, 3 empty barrels; one bar shear plough; a parcel of cabbages and parsnips, one pair of tongs. Signed by mark.
74-75. Solomon Glissan of Frederick County, recorded deed 3 Jan. 1800, from Joseph Jones of Montgomery Co., made 18 Nov. 1799. For £12, sells part of *Labyrinth,* beginning at end of 8 perches on the given line of tract called *Resurvey on Williams' Chance,* metes and bounds given for 4 1/4 acres. Signed before Greenberry Howard, John Clarke.
75-77. Solomon Glissan recorded 8 January 1800, from Thomas Kirk Senior and Thomas Kirk Jr., deed made 8 August 1799, for £227..5, part of tract, *Williams Chance,* also part of *Resurvey on Williams Chance,* and *Resurvey on Strife,* partly in Montgomery Co. and partly in Frederick County, contiguous to each other, beginning at end of 6 perches on a line drawn 47 deg. East from end of 26 ½ perches on 1st line of *William's Chance,* adjacent to *Mackey's Chance,* containing 75 3/4 acres. Signed Thomas Kirk, Thomas Kirk Jr., before Jacob Young, G. Kennedy, J.P. of Frederick County. Elizabeth Kirk, wife of Thomas Kirk Sr., released dower rights. Wm. Ritchie, Clerk of Frederick Co. sent copy.
77. Elizabeth Townsend & others from Henry Townsend, of Georgetown, Montgomery County. Whereas the said Henry Townsend has the bond of Isaac Pierce, Jesse Bayley, and Thomas B. Offutt, for conveyance of all their, as well as Samuel Evans, Hadley Baldwin, Ann Cloud, Joseph Cloud and Abner Cloud's interest in four lots, #1, 2, 3 & 4, containing 39 acres of land in a tract called *Whitehaven,* conveyed by Benjamin ____ to a certain Amos Cloud, now deceased; and Henry Townsend wishes to convey the same to his four children, as tenants in common, for the natural love he bears to them, the said Elizabeth Chesley Townsend,

Rebecca Townsend, Sharlotte Augustus Townsend, and George Frederick Augustus Townsend; and for five shillings, he sells his interest. Signed Henry Townsend, before James P. Morsell. Acknowledged before Thos Plater.

78. Elizabeth Townsend & others, from Henry Townsend, recorded 4 January 1800. Same parties as above, for 5 shillings, gives personal property, Negroes called Bob, Dick, Daniel, Kate, Nan and Hester, together with their increase and all household furniture. Signed 19 Dec. 1799, before J. P. Morsell. Receipt and ack. Before Thos. Plater.

78-79. John L. Summers recorded 4 Jan. 1800, from Hezekiah Veirs, bill of sale for £200, for Negroes Jane, Lab and Moriah. Signed before J. H. McPherson.

79-80. John C. Summers recorded 4 Jan. 1800, from David O'Neale, deed for tract, a part of *Wheel of Fortune,* including the house where he now lives, and 10 acres, which came to him at the decease of his father, William O'Neal. Signed David O'Neale before J. H. McPherson, and Patrick Magruder. Acknowledgment.

80-81. Mulatto Betsy and children from John Green, manumission recorded 7 January 1800. In consideration of the natural love and affection I have for my wife, Betsy, a mulatto woman and her two children, Letty and Eliza, lately purchased by me from William A. Needham, Betsy, aged 24 years, and said two children about 2 months, each. Betsy to be free immediately, and the children after they arrive at 12 years of age. Signed John Green by mark, before Jno. L. Morsell.

81-82. Samuel McFarland recorded 7 January 1800, from Hezekiah Thomas, bill of sale for £80, a Negro boy, named Bob White. Signed by mark before John Morris and Thomas Waters.

81-82. Thomas Davis recorded 7 January 1800, from Zadock Duvall, bill of sale made for £14..8, sells black cow and yearling, 1 sow, feather beds, etc., including shoemakers tools. Signed. Acknowledged 23 Dec. 1799 before Richard Green, J.P.

82-84. John Mason from Washington Bowie, agreement regarding cargo aboard Schooner Peggy sent to islands in 1799. Named in document, John Thompson and Ebenezer Evleth, Captain.

84. The Sheriff of Montgomery County, Benjamin Jones, recorded 8 January 1800, from William Cox, schedule of debts owing him from Zachariah Gray, and Nicholas Hocker. Sworn before John L. Summers, J. H. McPherson.

84-85. John Oliver of the City of Baltimore recorded 8 Jan. 1800, from Walter Rice of Fredericksburg, Virginia, deed made 23 July 1799 for 5 shillings, sells part of *Addition,* to part of *Conclusion,* beginning at a tract called *John's Lott,* to 6th line of tract *Pork and Potatoes,* for 236 acres. Tract conveyed to Walter Rice by the late William Deakins on 3 July 1781. Deed signed before W. Winchester. On 2 Oct. 1799, in the Virginia Supreme Court, Sarah, wife of Walter Rice, examined and released dower rights.

85-86. Hezekiah Thomas recorded 8 January 1800, from Hezekiah Veirs, for £45, bill of sale for one Negro, Rachel, 8 years old. If sum paid by September next with interest, then sale is void. Signed by Hezekiah Veirs before John L. Summers.

86. Joseph Clagett recorded 9 Jan. 1800, from Basil Leach, bill of sale for set of blacksmith tools, now in said Clagett's shop, for £21..14, which Basil Leach can redeem for said sum. Signed by Basil Leach before J. Lackland.

86-88. Hugh Thompson of Baltimore, Recorded 10 Jan. 1800, from James Ellis Sr. of Washington Co., Pa., and Jeremiah Ellis of Brooke Co., Va., bill of sale. James Ellis by letter of attorney, and signed by Mary his wife, approved said Jeremiah his attorney at law. For £16..8..1, part of *Woodstock,* and part of *James Delight.* Signed by Jeremiah Ellis before Aeneas Campbell, Thos B. Beall.

88. Jeremiah Ellis from James Ellis, power of attorney. Recorded same date as above.

88-89. Benjamin Benton recorded 11 Jan. 1800, made 23 Nov., from Joshua Owen, for £40, deed for part of *Owen's Contrivance,* and all his rights to *Owen's Conclusion,* metes & bounds given. Joshua Owen signed and Mary his wife released dower.

89. Erasmus Perry recorded release 12 Jan. 1800. I Thomas Cramphin for 5 shillings assign the following Negroes: Abraham 48, Sal 32, Thomas 25, Millie 28, Fanny 18, James 9 years, Simon 10 years; which Negroes Basil Harding sold me 13 May 1793, recorded in E: 338-339.
89-90. Samuel Bealmear recorded 13 January 1800, made 29 Oct., 1799, from George Riley, for £150, deed for part of *Two Brothers*. Sarah Riley released dower.
90-91. Benjamin W. Jones recorded 15 Jan. 1800. Schedule of goods and credits of William Stewart. Included farm tools, plates, iron pots, knives and forks.
91. Clement Sewell recorded Negro boy Jacob imported from Virginia to work for himself, 13 January 1800.
91. Alexander Chesley of Georgetown recorded from Miranda Chesley, bill of sale. For the love and affection I have to my children: Clagett Chesley, Sarah Chesley, Elizabeth Chesley, John Thomas Chesley and Alexander Chesley Jr., assigns Negroes in common, viz: Sam, 50 years; a man [Name ?] age 34 years; Jim 32; Nace 30, woman [Kaba ?] 45 years, girl Nan 16, Charles 9 years and Harry 3 years old. . 17 Jan. 1800. Signed Alexander Chesley before Peter Light, Wm Bansil by mark.
91-92. Zachariah Knott recorded 17 Jan. 1800, from Basil Carlisle, bill of sale. For £66..15, sells one bay mare, one black mare, colt.
92. Thomas Nicholls of Jno. Recorded qualification as deputy sheriff, 17 Jan. 1800.
92. Thomas Turner recorded 18 Jan. 1800, from Benjamin Ricketts of Wm for £2..16, bill of sale for a horse. Signed by mark before James Lackland.
92. Francis Davis, John L. Summer, John Clark, Charles Wayman, James Lackland and Thomas B. Beall, recorded 20 January 1800, levy commissioners bond.
93-94. Joseph Slater of Monroe County, Virginia, recorded deed Jan. 1800 from David Slater of Prince George's County. All his right, and claim to tract *Bradford's Rest,* purchased by Jonathan Slater from Thomas Plater and William Robertson, which said Jonathan is dead. Signed David Slater before Rob't Bowie and Thos Contee. Sarah Slater released dower. Attested to in Prince George's County.
94-95. Joseph Sims recorded mortgage 24 Jan. 1800 from William D. Beall for $415. The said William Beall entered into notes to James P. Morsell, trustee for his creditors. Signed William D. Beall before Patrick Magruder. A schedule of Beall's personal belongings was recorded following assignment. No slaves or real property or debts due were listed. Personal property included one bay horse, one brown horse, 5 head cattle, 7 head sheep, 4 sows and pigs, 10 geese, 7 turkeys, several dunghill fowls; 10 small chickens, 8 ducks, 1100 wt. Pork, 150 wt. Beef; one pair cart wheels, one old sulkey, saddle & bridle; 1 small sworth; 6 razors & strope & case, 1 silver watch; 1 desk & case, a parcel of old books, 3 barshear ploughs, 2 shovels, 6 weeding hoes, 2 grubbing hoes, 2 matoxes, 1 adze, 1 hand saw, [other tools were listed] 14 towels, 8 tea clothes, 8 table clothes, 3 oznab. Mill bags, 5 beds and furniture, 3 mattresses, cradle furniture, 2 dining tables, 2 tea tables, 1 side table, 1 dressing table, 21 chairs & frames, 1 small looking glass, 7 trunks, 1 cupboard, 1 pepper box, 1 candle box, 2 brass candlesticks, 2 candle moulds, 1 tea strainer, 1 funnell, ½ doz. Cups, saucers, tea pot, cream pot, 2 Queens ware pitchers [many more kitchen items] 1 pair hand mill stones, 100 ft. plank, some dried herring.
95-96. Solomon Holland recorded 27 Jan. 1800, from John Harding, for £40, bill of sale for one Negro boy Jack, age 9 years and one black mare 8 years old. If sum paid before 1 May sale is redeemed. Signed by John Harding before John L. Summers.
96. John Clarke recorded 28 Jan. 1800, from Henry Wathen, for £59..4..10, bill of sale for Negro William aged 18 years. Signed before Greenbury Howard.
96-97. William Magrath recorded 28 Jany 1800, from Phillip O. Connell, for £30, bill of sale for one cow, 3 tables, 6 green windsor chairs, 6 flagg bottom chairs, 3 iron pots, one Dutch oven, 2 chests. Signed Phillip Connell before J. H. McPherson.
97. Mathias Martin recorded 30 January 1800, from John Suter, Junr. of Georgetown, for £100, bill of sale for one Negro slave, Jack, 25 years old. Signed before James Simpson, Rob't McClan.

97. Lewis Marthen [or Martler] recorded 30 January 1800, from Charles D. Green & David English, of Georgetown, for £52..10, sells one Negro slave girl, "China" aged about 12 years. Signed Green & English, before Jacob Snyder, C. Flaut.
98. Isaac Polock of the City of Washington, Prince George's County, recorded 4 February 1800, from Thomas Johnson, Esq., of Frederick Co., Md., for £2035, deed for part of two tracts, *Magruder's Choice,* and *Addition to Magruder's Purchase.* On 4 Dec. 1794, conveyed by Edward Magruder and Archibald Magruder, containing 295 ½ acres. Signed before John McPherson. Acknowledged before Wm Ritchie, clerk of Frederick County.
98-99. Josias T. Beall recorded 6 February 1800, bond from Sylvester Jones, Samuel Jones and Moses Jones, in consideration that Josias T. Beall paid to Nathaniel Beall 3000 lbs. tobacco for rent at Bladensburg. Signed before Allen Bowie, Rebecca Jones.
99-101. James Perry recorded 6 February 1800, from Thomas Nicholls of Simon for £106..7, land called *Little Park,* on the 31st line of tract called *Piney Grove,* originally sold 20 March 1777 to Thomas Johns for 1543 acres, to tract called *The Pines,* at end of the last line of *Wickham and Pottinger's Discovery.* Signed before John L. Summers, J. H. McPherson. Receipt. Acknowledgment. Cassandra Nicholls, wife of said Thomas released dower.
101. The State of Maryland to Thomas Davis, Allen Bowie, John L. Summers, John Clark, James Lackland and Thomas B. Beall of George are appointed and assigned Justices of the Levy Court of Montgomery County. Signed February 1800.
101-102. [Marginal note. Examined & Delivered to Hezekiah Baggerly 4th March 1802] Hezekiah Baggerly recorded 8 February 1800, from Henry Baggerly for £5, deed made 25 November 1799 for part of tract, *Beal and Edmonstons Discovery,* beginning at 8th line, containing 138 acres. Signed and acknowledged before John L. Summers, Allen Bowie. Mary Baggerly wife of Henry released dower rights..
102-103. Caleb Bentley recorded 11 Feb. 1800, from John Kirby for £37..10, bill of sale for one black horse, one bay horse, one red & white cow, one walnut clothes press in possession of Wm Elliott near New Market; one corner cupboard painted blue, one poplar chest, two sets china with green edged plates; 7 pewter plates, sells all his possessions, signified by delivery of black horse. 28 January 1800 before Thomas Davis.
103-104. Caleb Bentley recorded 11 Feb. 1800, from Christopher Sipes, for £20..5, bill of sale for one pair of bellows, two anvils & other items. Signed before Thomas Davis.
104. Benjamin W. Jones, sheriff, recorded 11 Feb. 1800, schedule of goods and credits of Banford Sewell delivered to him as of 7 Feb. 1800: Accounts or judgments on Lewis Taney, James Reed, William Keitch, Jacob Wolfe, John Burekman and John Smith. Signed before John L. Summers, J. H. McPherson.
104-105. Samuel Craig [or Craik] of Alexandria, Va., recorded 15 Feb. 1800, from Thomas Frederick Brooke, of Prince George's Co., deed made 17 August 1799, for £198, part of tract called *Dann,* beginning at line of part conveyed by Clement Brooke to Richard Forrest, containing 66 acres. Signed before Robt Bowie, Thos Contee. Receipt. Ack. Ann, wife of the said Thomas Brooke released dower rights.
105-106. Benjamin Ray Jr. and William Lodge recorded 18 Feb. 1800, from William Prather Williams, for £300, deed for lot #23 in town of Williamsburgh, on part of *Exchange and New Exchange,* containing 1/4 + half of 1/4 acres. Signed before John L. Summers, J.H. McPherson.
106. George B. Magruder, Elisha O. Williams and Thomas B. Beall, bond to state of Maryland for £1000 to serve as tobacco inspectors at warehouse.
106-107. Elisha O. Williams & others, bond to state of Maryland for £1000. Dated 12 Feb. 1800. Walter Clagett, George B. Magruder and Elisha O. Williams bondsmen. Bonded to examine all tobacco brought to the warehouse.
107-108. Hardage Lane certificate of a Negro brought from the state of Virginia, 21 Feb. 1800. Negro John about 18 years old, his mother Betty Duncan, whom I bought in Virginia in 1771 or 1772, and he was born on my property and been employed cultivating my farm in Fairfax County and is now removed to my farm in Montgomery County.

108. Francis Deakins Wayman recorded 24 Feb. 1800, from Samuel Hepburn of Prince Georges Co., for $100. bill of sale for Negro girl, Page. Signed before Thos Corcoran.
108-109. Jeremiah Crabb recorded 24 Feb. 1800, from George Riley, for $620. deed made 13 Jan. 1800 for two tracts on main road from Georgetown to Frederick Town, east of Samuel Bealmar's land, called *Two Brothers,* and *Valentine's Garden.* 62 acres. Signed George Riley before John L. Summers, Elemelech Swearingen. Sarah, wife of George Riley released dower.
109-110. Jeremiah Crabb recorded 24 Feb. 1800, from Benjamin W. Jones, sheriff. deed. Whereas a judgment was obtained against Lawrence O'Neale, against the tenement of Thomas Dyson, and by a writ of Fieri Facias, tract *Lost Knife,* was sold to the highest bidder for £442..2..11, containing 150 acres. Signed Benjamin W. Jones before John L. Summers, J. H. McPherson.
110-111. Joseph Sprigg Belt, trustee, recorded 17 January 1800, schedule of Francis Valdener made 10 January, to sell property for the benefit of his creditors. Before Thos Corcoran, Daniel Reintzel.
111. Act of the Assembly recorded 28th February 1800. To Aneas Campbell, William Smith, Lawrence O'Neale, Richard Green, Daniel Reintzel, Henry Brookes, Thomas Davis, Allen Bowie, George Ham. Offutt, Thomas Corcoran, Solomon Holland, John L. Summers, Greenbury Howard, Edward Burgess Jr., Joseph T. Belt, Thomas B. Beall, Josias Fendall Beall, Elemelech Swearingen, Benjamin Gaither, Joseph Forrest, Charles Wayman, Patrick Magruder, James Lackland, Archibald A. Beall and Thomas Beall of George, all appointed Justices of the Peace for Montgomery County.
111-113. John Burgess recorded 3 March 1800, from Samuel Thomas of Ann Arundel Co., deed made 14 Oct. 1799, for $295. money of the United States, part of *Rich and Level,* and *Gaithers' Forrest,* metes & bounds given for 36 acres. Signed Samuel Thomas before Charles Alexander Warfield and Thomas Hobbs. Receipt. Acknowledgment. Anne Thomas, wife of Samuel released dower rights.
113. John Poole Junr. recorded 3 March 1800, I Thomas B. Beall for £125 sell Negro woman Nan, and children Sol and Adam. Signed before Aeneas Campbell.
113. Archibald A. Beal recorded 3 March 1800, l from David Turner Davis, for £25 bill of sale for a dun mare and other personalty.
113-114. Samuel Clements recorded 3 March 1800, from Henry Clemens, for £99, bill of sale for bay horse & livestock.
114-115. Charles Penn, recorded 4 March 1800, from Roby Penn for £180..17..3, part of *Addition to Rays Adventure,* formerly conveyed to John Wynn Penn, 226 acres. Signed Roby Penn before Edward Burgess, Thomas Davis.
115-116. Zacheus Penn recorded 4 March 1800, from Roby Penn for $549. Tract *Penns Inheritance.* Except for part deed to Field Parker some time past. Signed Roby Penn before Edward Burgess, Thomas Davis.
116-117. William Wilson recorded 4 March 1800, from Edward Crow, for £187..10, bill of sale for one Negro woman Kate, Negro child Henry and Negro boy Frederick, the child of Kate; also 8000 weight crop tobacco, now on the place sold Hezekiah Thomas. Signed 20 February 1800, Edward Crow, before John Clark.
117. Francis Deakins recorded 6 March 1800, from John Wayman, for £60 specie, bill of sale for 5 feather beds and furnishings, 3 large walnut tables, one walnut desk, 2 large looking glasses, 2 dozen chairs. Signed John Wayman, before J. H. McPherson.
117-118. William Price recorded 6 March 1800. I Nathan Neighbors for £20 sells one bay horse, 10 years old, a cow, feather bed and other furniture and personalty. Signed 11 Feb. 1800 before Greenbury Howard.
118. Archibald Trail recorded agreement 6 March 1800. Whereas James Trail Senr. deceased did in his lifetime, viz on 11 March 1783, make a last will and testament, and devised to his son Archibald several tracts of land, among them part of a tract *The Younger Brother,* which extended into a part of the plantation of Henry Brooke. In order to accommodate his neighbor and himself, by laying both their lands in a more regular form, he exchanged 17 acres of said land laying contiguous to each other, said exchange to remain

the property of Archibald Trail. Signed 16 Oct. 1799, James Trail, Ozburn Trail and Rachel Seybert (signed by mark) before Benjamin Gaither.

118-124. William Waters and others, on *Maiden's Fancy*, Land commission. Recorded 6 March 1800, made 9 March 1799 by petition of William Waters, Plummer Waters and Thomas Waters, son of Plummer, to mark and bound a tract of land called *Maiden's Fancy,* lying partly in Prince Georges and partly in Montgomery County, now held in fee by said Waters. Commission is directed to William Holmes, Jonas F. Beall, Richard Thomas, William Culver and Absolom Beddle. Commission met May 6, 1799. Deposed Arnold Waters, age 58 years, a Quaker, who solemnly affirmed testimony. He states he was at the bound tree 28 years ago when Thomas Ijams told him, that Richard Snowden and Richard Ijames said that that white oak was the beginning tree. Edward Browning Sr., age 76 years sworn and deposed that about 20 years ago he was shown a white oak tree by Thomas Ijams as the bound tree. Thomas Richardson, age 55 years, sworn and deposed that 26 years ago he was shown the boundary. May 15, 1799, William Stabler appointed surveyor for tract. Basil Burton and Robert Mack as chain carriers and William Brookes as pole carrier.

Tuesday, June 4, 1799, with commissioners for John Beall of Prince George's County and Thomas Orme of Montgomery County. Deposed Thomas Orme, surveyor, about 30 years. Some years ago he was employed by Mr. James Ray to survey tracts. Jeremiah Turner aged 58 deposed that 33 years ago, being at the house of Samuel Waters, he shows them the boundaries, and Samuel Waters asked an old man in their company, Thomas Iiams, regarding bound tree. John Beall, being unable to attend the meeting from indisposition, his deposition was taken at his own house. John Beall, aged 70 years, made oath that 21 years ago, he was employed by Mister Samuel Waters, William Thomas Waters and Arnold Waters to make a division of the land *Maiden's Fancy,* and part of tract called *Waters Purchase.* Richard Thomas, a Quaker, qualified by affirmation,. Commissioners met regarding bounds of *Welsh's Discovery,* lying next to *Maiden's Fancy.* Description given from the banks of the Patuxent, including lines adjacent to Benjamin Owen's part of *Maiden's Fancy,* and plat recorded in page 122.

124-125. Samuel Hobbs recorded 7 March 1800, from John Bell, deed made 7 December 1799, in consideration of an agreement made, he assigns part of tract *Rich Land,* and part of tract *Wood,* for 22 3/4 acres. Signed before George Hawkins, John Clark.

125. Thomas Stonestreet recorded 8 March 1800, from Edward Metcalf, for £20, assigns two cows, one feather bed, 500 weight tobacco. Signed before John L. Summers.

125. John Poole Junior recorded 10 March 1800, from Jesse Wade, for £60, bill of sale for one Negro girl Sophia. Signed before Thos B. Beall. Acknowledgment.

126. Thomas Iames of Frederick County, recorded 10 Mach 1800, from Lewis Duvall, for £150. bill of sale. Whereas said James hath released Duvall of a debt due to Frances Mantz for the above sum paid to Mantz, Duvall grants Negroes Rachel, Nance, Emilia and Carry together with all personal property now in his possession. Signed Lewis Duvall before Isaac Iiams, and John Iiams. Acknowledged before John L. Summers.

126-127. Charles Gassaway recorded bond for performance as Coroner 10 March 1800. Signed Charles Gassaway, Hezekiah Thomas, Caleb Dorsey before Richard Potts, Upton Beall.

127. Ashford Leaton recorded 12 March 1800, from Elizabeth Flemming and John Flemming, executors of James Flemming, deceased. For £89, deed for part of tract *Resurvey on Content,* 56 acres; also tract *Here I Am*, containing 6 acres. Signed before Edward Burgess Junr., John L. Summers.

128-129. Clement McDermott recorded 13 March 1800, from Patrick Dempsey, for £50, bill of sale for one dark bay horse, 1 milch cow, 2 feather beds, other items listed. Signed before J. H. McPherson.

129. Richard Ricketts recorded 13 March 1800, from James Stewart, for £30 bill of sale for a horse, cows ... Signed by mark before John Clarke.

129-131. Walter & Elizabeth Lanham, executors of the will of Aaron Lanham, recorded 18 March 1800 from Benjamin Ray & Eleanor Ray his wife. Whereas Eleanor Ray is one of the daughters of Aaron Lanham, and is entitled to one Negro woman, and also a devise to Eleanor Ray, together with Elizabeth, Lethe and Mary

Ann Lanham, a tract called *Little Worth,* near South Mountain containing 25 acres; and another tract called *Chestnut Level,* 250 acres in Loudoun and Frederick Counties in Virginia; and whereas Walter and Elizabeth Lanham have satisfied Benjamin Ray with the sum of £367..6, for her legacy tract sold to executors. Signed before John L. Summers, J. H. McPherson. Eleanor Ray was examined and is of full age, released dower before Richard Potts, Chief Justice of the Montgomery County Court.

131-134. Richard Thomas & John Clark recorded 15 March 1800, instrument of writing from Edward Crow.

134-135. Samuel H. Wheeler, recorded 17 March 1800, list of Negroes brought into this state from Virginia, left him by his father Clement Wheeler in his will recorded in Prince Georges Co., Md., 21 March 1788. Negro Ball, age 45; Negro Abraham 6 years; Negro David 5 years; Negro Minty (female) age 40; Negro Milly 12 years old and Ann 10 years. Also list of Negroes willed to the Children of Samuel H. Wheeler by the will of Clement Wheeler, Samuel H. Wheeler acting as their agent. Negro Ginny a male 22 years willed to Sarah Wheeler; Negro Sam a male aged 15 willed to _____ Wheeler; Negro John, a male 14 years old willed to Clement Wheeler. Negroes were moved by me from my farm in Loudoun Co., Va. to Montgomery Co., Md. Samuel H. Wheeler.

135. John L. Summers recorded 18 March 1800. I, Hezekiah Veirs, for £30, bill of sale for one Negro lad named Toby, aged 11 years. Signed Hezekiah Veirs before J. H. McPherson.

135. Record for George Town from Mayors order. Request recorded 20 March 1800. To wit: to Upton Beall, Sir: Please deliver to bearer the book of the Record of Georgetown, containing the courses of lots in said town, as well as the plats, said book having been lodged in your office some years ago. Signed Daniel Reintzel, Mayor of Georgetown. 20 March 1800, delivered to book of records mentioned in the foregoing order.

135-136. Gerard Brooke and Caleb Bentley recorded 20 March 1800 bill of sale. I Ezekiel Jackson for £50 paid by Gerard Brooke and £35 paid by Caleb Bentley sell all my crop of tobacco, corn and wheat now seeded on the place; one brown mare, tools and furniture listed. Signed by mark before Thomas Davis.

136-137. Negro, Polly Right recorded manumission 24 March 1800. I Abednego Baker, enfranchise Polly Right, from 1 January 1806; Jenny, daughter of Polly to be free after 1 January 1818 and Rachel, daughter of Polly to be free from 1 January 1821. Signed 18 March 1800. Abednego Baker before John Clarke.

137. William Willson recorded March 1800, from William Wyvill, for £47, bill of sale for livestock and personal property. Signed before John Clarke.

137-138. Thomas Wright recorded 25 March 1800, from Adam King, for £100, deed made 17 December 1799, for part of tract called *Charley's Forrest,* and *Pigman's Inheritance.* Signed before Thomas Corcoran, D. Reintzel. Grace King, wife of Adam released dower rights.

138-139. Negro Vinney aged about 35 years, recorded 25 March 1800, from Arnold Holland, manumission. Signed before Richard Thomas and Caleb Bentley. Acknowledged before Thomas Davis.

139. Joseph D. West recorded 25 March 1800, from Hezekiah Viers, bill of sale. For £45 assigns Negro girl named Maria, about 2 years of age. Signed before J. H. McPherson.

139-140. Bazil Perry recorded bill of sale 1 April 1800. I Francis Perry of Montgomery County, for £45 sells Negro girl Henny, 17 years old. Signed before Edward Burgess Jr.

140-141. Richard Wootton and Robert Pottinger Magruder recorded 1 April 1800, from John Beckwith, for £150, bill of sale for Negro Richard. Signed before John L. Summers.

141-142. Jeremiah Ellis recorded 2 April 1800, from John Harris and wife, of Brook County, Virginia, power of attorney. to recover the residue of a tract of land called *Johns Delight,* sold by John Harris and Elizabeth to Archibald Allen, and further to grant said parcel. Signed John Harris, Elizabeth Harris by mark before Robt Colwell, Polly Griffith. John Connell clerk of county aforesaid certifies James Griffith Esq., before whom power of attorney was acknowledged.

142-143. Thomas Green records deed for *John's Delight,* from John Harris by Jeremiah Ellis, both of Brooke County, Virginia. John Harris with a certain instrument of writing signed by Elizabeth Harris his wife, appointing him her true and lawful attorney, sells the residue of a tract of land called *John's Delight,* part containing 3 1/4 acres. Signed before Aeneas Campbell, Thos B. Beall.

143-144. Thomas Davis recorded 7 April 1800, from Ephraim Davis of Frederick County, Maryland, made 4 November 1799, for $160. That piece of land devised to him by the will of Betsey Welsh, called *Gaither's Meadow,* beginning at a part of the land from where Hinkle had made over to John Johns. Signed before John Leseley, Jacob Young.

144-145. Caleb Bentley recorded 7 April 1800 bill of sale from Greenberry Peddicord, for sum of £60, all m crop of tobacco, a bay horse, one brown horse, other farm items. I Carlton Peddicord, assign to the said Greenbery Peddicord and will warrant the same to Caleb Bentley. Signed before Richard Green.

145. Richard James recorded 8 April 1800, from Philip Tracey, bill of sale for sum of £15, one roan mare and one bay mare. Signed before Thos Simpson, Joel Simpson.

145-146. Martin Sheets recorded power of attorney, 10 April 1800. I Thomas Aldridge of Franklin County, Kentucky, appoint my son-in-law to demand and sue for recovery of the following slaves belonging to me and now supposed to be in Maryland. Negro woman Bet and her increase, supposed to be in possession of Eleanor Penn; Negro woman Sillar & her increased supposed to be in the possession of Samuel Darby; and one other Negro woman. Signed Thomas Aldridge. Sworn before Justices in Kentucky.

146-147. Francis Perry recorded bill of sale 10 April 1800, from Martin Sheats of Franklin County, Kentucky, for £25, sell all the Negroes mentioned and now remaining in Montgomery County; to wit, Negro woman named Bett and her child Anne about three years old; Negro woman named Sillar and her child named James about 5 years old. Signed before Edward Burgess Junr.

147-149. Nathan S. White recorded 10 April 1800, from George Viley of Scott County, Kentucky, deed for £700 sells land called *Wolf Cow,* containing 276 ½ acres, beginning at 17th line of tract, Signed George Viley. Martha Ann Viley released her right and title of dower in state of Kentucky. George H. Offutt and James Beatty, J.P. signed off on deed.

149. Thomas Cramphin, recorded bill of sale. 12 April 1800 from Truman Brashears of Prince George's County, a Negro slave man named Adam, 28 years old. Signed by Truman Brashears before Thomas Corcoran.

150-151. Thomas B. Beall of Georgetown, mortgage from Philip Dougherty, bill of sale for debt of £71..6 sells sorrel mare, black mare. Wagon, 7 head of sheep, other goods and chattels. Sale to be void if debt paid with interest. Acknowledged before Thos Corcoran.

151-152. Nathan Musgrove recorded 1 April 1800, from Joseph Barnes, deed made 26 Oct. 1799. Whereas Richard Weaver Barnes did in 1787 mortgage to Joseph Barnes, 200 acres, *Addition to Snowden's Manor,* for 8000 lbs. Of tobacco, and by deed of conveyance 20 Oct. 1787 sold to Nathaniel Musgrove, to satisfy debt due from Nathaniel Musgrove to Ephraim Gaither, assignees of Usher and Donaldson. Signed Joseph Barnes before Richard Green, Thomas Davis. Acknowledged.

152-153. William Campbell recorded 20 April 1800 from Charles Wayman, assignment, deed of trust for all balances due in the hands of William Murdock of London, from my tobacco shipments after paying any endorsements from George Murdock on bills. Signed before Uriah Forrest. Indenture made 12 April 1800 between Charles Wayman of Georgetown and William Campbell and William Whann, and heirs, all his estate with all bonds, to pay and satisfy William Campbell, George Murdock, Randolph B. Latimer, Uriah Forrest and Thomas Turner, as made over; and whereas Charles Wayman has signed over one half part of the Schooner, *Widows' Son*, which sailed from port of George Baltimore [sic] about 10th March last to Cape Fear under Captain Peter Wickham, master; and he assigned to Thomas Turner, ½ Schooner, *Union*, now laying at Georgetown, and ½ of the Brigg, *Favorite*, now on voyage to West Indies and ½ of 30 hogsheads of tobacco in the *Atlantic* to Spain, assigned to Jesse Dawes and ½ of a debt due from William M. Dickerson, satisfying these claims assigned to Uriah Forrest; and debt to Forrest and Stoddert. Signed before Joseph Forrest by Chas Wayman.

153-154. Robert Peter, Esq. of Georgetown recorded 21 April 1800, from Thomas Offutt Senior, for £745, deed for *James Park.* Beginning at the original tract beginning, metes and bounds for 149 acres. Receipt, ack. Signed before John L. Summers, J.H. McPherson

154-155. John Gatton, schedule of goods recorded by Sheriff Benjamin W. Jones 24 April 1800, included one straw bed and one old blanket, 3 earthen plates and 3 forks and 3 knives. Signed by mark.

155. Honore Martin recorded 26 April 1800, from Josiah Oden, bill of sale for £50 assigns three feather beds, and furniture belonging to him, one horse, one cow, spinning wheel, chests. Signed before J. H. McPherson, Kenelmn T. Gray.

156. Uriah Forrest and Thomas Turner, recorded order 26 April 1800, also from Charles Wayman, bill of sale for interest in the cargo of *Favorite.* Regarding 30 hogsheads of tobacco on board the ship *Atlanta,* Captain Bamberry. Signed Charles Wayman.

156-157. Ann Gaither recorded 26 April 1800 from William Gaither of Frederick County, deed for 5 shillings for two tracts of land on the Hawlings River, *Round About Hills,* and *James Addition,* made 17 February 1800. Signed before Daniel Dorsey, Francis Sappington.

157-158. Rudolph B. Lattimore of Baltimore Town recorded 27 April 1800, from Charles Wayman for $25, his half part and interest in a schooner called the *Indecision,* of Baltimore, which sailed from Baltimore Port under Captain Peter Wickham bound to Cape Frances.

158. Patrick Dempsey to Sheriff Benjamin W. Jones, recorded 28 April 1800, of Montgomery County, schedule as an insolvent debtor including one old razor, one shaving box, one wooden square. Signed before Elemelech Swearingen, J.H. McPherson.

158-160. Chas A. Beatty and John Gozlar recorded 27 April,1800, bill of sale and mortgage from Adam Waggoner for a wagon and team of horses purchased in January 1799 for $100. Mortgage describes horses and wagon in detail. Agreement signed and witnessed by Patrick Magruder, Joseph Forrest.

160. Jesse Bayley recorded bill of sale 27 April 1800 from William Brookes of Georgetown, for $400, sells Negro lad named Lye age 17 years. Signed by mark before Thomas Corcoran.

161-162. George Riley recorded 27 April 1800, from John Beckwith, for $887.50 deed for part of *Hobson's Choice,* adjacent to a tract called *Two Brothers,* Signed before John L. Summers, J. H. McPherson. Martha Beckwith released dower rights.

162-163. William Veirs recorded 2 May 1800, from Edward Veirs, for £50, indenture made 7 December 1799, a tract called the *Mary,* located between the lines of a tract called the *Day Spring,* and a tract of land called *String About,* and a tract called *Swans Good Luck.* Signed Edward Veirs before Ans Campbell, Thos B. Beall. Receipt and acknowledgment.

163-164. Upton Beall recorded 2 May 1800, from William Prather Williams, for £20, deed for lot in town of Williamsburgh, or Montgomery Court House, number 57, being part of a tract called *Exchange and New Exchange.* Signed before Allen Bowie, J.F. Beall. Receipt and acknowledgment.

164-166. Robert Peter recorded 3 May 1800. Between Thomas Plater, for £900 part of *Brightwell's Hunting Quarter,* laid out for 150 acres. Receipt. Acknowledgment. Margaret Plater wife of Thomas Plater released dower rights.

166-167. Richard Wootton recorded 3 May 1800 from Solomon Simpson, for £2,410 deed for part of tracts called *Saint Thomas,* and part of a tract of land called *Friendship,* part of a tract of land called *Simpsons Dwelling Place,* and part of a tract called *Wilsons Delay,* and known by the name of *Ellis' Purchase;* part of a tract called *Chapple Forest,* part of tract *The Apple Orchard,* part of *Johnny and Molly's Conclusion,* and part of land called *The Slipe,* all lying contiguous to each other, and included in the following metes and bounds: given. in all containing 382 acres. Also, a part of *Wilson's Delay,* adjacent to the heirs of William Young, late of Montgomery County, containing 100 acres. Solomon Simpson signed by mark before Thos B. Beall, Lawrence O'Neale. Receipt. Acknowledgment. Dorcas Simpson released dower rights.

168. Robert Peter recorded 3 May 1800, deed made 22 April 1800 from Benjamin W. Jones, sheriff of Montgomery County, sells land obtained by James Dunlap in the county court judgment against William

Gates Pearse, on 5 August 1799, on a tract called *Port wine,* containing 100 acres more or less. William Gates Pearce as one of the join heirs at law of John Baptist Pearce deceased. Robert Peter being the highest bidder in the sum of £18. Signed Benjamin White Jones before Elemelech Swearingen, J.H. McPherson. Receipt. Acknowledgment by sheriff.

169-170. Jane Ayton, widow of Richard Ayton, deceased, recorded 31 May 1800, made 9 April between Jeremiah Berry 3d, for £131 sells tract where on the parties hereto now reside, a part of *Charles and Benjamin,* containing 500 acres. Signed Jeremiah Berry 3d,who released all his right to the estate of the said Jane Ayton, her heirs and assigns, and at the same time, Molly Berry, wife of the said Jeremiah released her rights to dower, before Elemelech Swearingen, John McPherson. Receipt.

170. Benjamin W. Jones, sheriff, recorded 5 May 1800, from Philip O. Cornell [or O'Connell] schedule of all goods and chattels rights and credits, as of May 3, 1800. John Emmerson on note, £20..10..11 1/4; Richard Morgan, 1..14..4 on account; Felix H. Hillaire, 5..0..10; Basil Beall, on acct, 6..15..0; Philip Hackett judgment, 2..5..7; Nathaniel Porter, judgment, 9..0..0; James B. Crawford on acct., 16..0..0. 100 acres of land in the western country, the papers concerning which were lodged in the hands of Clement Green in the year 1799. Philip Cornell before Elemelech Swearingen, J. H. McPherson.

171. Benjamin W. Jones, sheriff recorded 5 May 1800, schedule from James Noland. Lists one old hammer, one old shoe knife and two awls. Due from Leonard Wayman on acct ..5..7 ½, Burnheart, on acct, ..3..4. Signed by mark before Henry Brookes, J H. McPherson. Sworn before Henry Brookes, J.H. McPherson.

171-172. William Gaither recorded 8 May 1800, made 6 May between Philemon Griffith of Frederick County and Joshua Griffith of Montgomery County, executors of Henry Griffith, late of Montgomery County, deceased. Whereas Henry Griffith by his will appointed his executors to sell in fee the land hereinafter described which he had purchased of a certain John Beall Bordley Esq., and Henry Griffith did depart this life before the purchase money was made, but the estate has since paid up the purchase money, and obtained from said Bordley a deed of conveyance, and the property sell at public auction as described herein to William Gaither, on or about 12 December 1800. They sell and confirm to William Gaither a part of tract *Tusculum,* Signed Philemon Griffith Joshua Griffith of Hy before Richard Green, Thomas Davis. Receipt for $714., acknowledgment for deed.

173-174. James McCubbin Lingan recorded 12 May 1800, from Archibald Trail for $200, tract of land willed to Archibald by his father James Trail, called *Trails Addition* containing 23 acres. Signed in the presence of Henry Brookes, Benjamin Gaither. Monica Trail, wife of Archibald released dower rights.

174-176. Edward Veirs recorded 12 May 1800, from William Veirs, deed made 7 Dec. 1799 for £51..9..4 ½ for tract called *William and Mary,* and *Daniel's Inheritance,* 10 3/4 acres, adjacent to *New Years Gift,* surveyed for John Swan, to part of a resurvey called *Mary,* formerly conveyed to Mary and Maddox Dyson for 225 acres, to a resurvey on *NonEaten,* containing 2 7/8 acres with improvements. Signed before Ens Campbell, Thos B. Beall. Acknowledgment.

176-177. John Lucas recorded 17 May 1800 from George Ellicott and Elizabeth Ellicott, his wife, of Baltimore County, for $112.50 deed for part of a tract called *Ludwicks Range,* the same first line of that tract of *Glascow,* reconveyed to George Culp, and by a dividing line between them. Deed signed before Saml Godfrey, John Ellicott. Receipt and dower release.

177-178. Negro William recorded 20 May 1800, from Basil and Caleb Darby, manumission for mulatto William, age 29 years. Signed before William Smith.

178-179. George Culp recorded 20 May 1800 from George Ellicott and Elizabeth Ellicott, his wife, of Baltimore County, for $112.50 deed for part of a tract called *Glasco.* Deed signed before Saml Godfrey, John Ellicott. Receipt and dower release.

179-181. Richard Thomas Junr. Recorded 21 May 1800, from Basil Brooke, deed for 7 shillings, 6 pence, part of *Addition to Brooke Grove,* for 10 ½ acres. Mary Brooke, wife of Basil Brooke released dower.

181-182. Montgomery County Division into Districts. Pursuant to an Act of Assembly (passed at November Session 1799) the following division of Montgomery County was recorded the 21st day of May 1800 to wit:

We the commissioners appointed to lay of Montgomery county aforesaid into districts agreeable to an act of assembly, entitled An Act to alter, abolish and repeal certain parts of the constitution and form of government of this state, as are therein mentioned, and the act of Assembly entitled an act to regulate Elections and Supplement thereto passed at November session 1799, do certify that we have laid off said county into districts, do in the following order to wit:

For the first district, beginning at Parrs Spring and running down Patuxent to the mouth of Hawlings River, then with said River to the mouth of Reedy Branch, then up said branch to the head (Gerard Brooke's spring) then to the pole bridge near Cyrus'es Smith Shop, then with a small road leaving Serrett Dickersons on the right, till it intersects the road passing in front of Col. Magruder's house at the corner of his fence, then with said road leaving John B. Magruder's on the left, Benjamin Ricketts on the right, till it intersects the Bladensburgh road at the lower end of said Rickett's plantation, then with the road through Zadock Ricketts lane to the head of Muddy branch, then down said branch to the George Town Road, then with said road to Benjamin Gaither's shop, then with the road leading by Zachariah Maccubin's Mill, Samuel Simonses, and Richard Hoggins, to the road leading to the mouth of Monocacy to Greens Bridge on the east side of Joshua Perry's plantation, then with the road by John Wilson's to the mouth of the lane, then with the lane to the line of Frederick County; then with said line to the beginning, the Election to be held at Goshen Mill.

For the second district beginning at the Mouth of Monocacy, and running down Potomack, including the islands, to the mouth of Seneca, then up Seneca to Zachariah Maccubin's, then with the line of the first district to Frederick County line, then with said line to the beginning the election to be held at Medley's tavern.

For the third district, beginning at the Mouth of Seneca and running down Potowmack, including the islands, to the line of the territory of Columbia, then with said line to Rock Creek, then up said creek to Robertson's Mill, then up the Bladensburgh road till it intersects the line of the first district at the lower end of Benjamin Ricketts plantation then with the line of said first district to Zachariah Maccubin's Mill, then down Seneca to the beginning. The election to be held at the Courthouse.

For the fourth district, beginning at the mouth of Hawlings River and running down Patuxent to Prince George's County line, then with said line to the territory of Columbia, then with such Territory to Rock Creek, then up Rock Creek to Robertson's Mill, then up the Bladensburg Road till it intersects the line of the first district at the lower end of Benjamin Ricketts plantation, then with the lines of the first district reversed to the beginning. The election to be held at John Thomases stone house near Richard Berry's plantation.

For the fifth district, all that part of Montgomery County lying within the Territory of Columbia, the election to be held at Georgetown.

Given under our hands and seals this twenty first day of May 1800. Dan'l Reintzel, Thomas Fletchall, John Adamson, Thomas Davis.

182-184. Richard West recorded 24 May, 1800, deed from Joseph Beck, and Mary his wife of Montgomery County, William Mordecai Chaney and Anne his wife and John Baptist Robeson and Sarah his wife of Anne Arundel County for 5 shillings, release all their interest in a 100 acre part of *Wickham and Pottinger's Discovery.*

184-186. Benjamin Waters recorded 27 May 1800, from Samuel Snowden, Thomas Snowden & John Snowden, deed for part of *Bealls Manor,* beginning at Francis Edward's part of tract. Signed before Richard T. Lowndes, Richard Cramphin. Acknowledgment.

186-187. Thomas Iiams of Frederick County, miller, recorded 28 May 1800, from Louis Duvall of Hyattstown, six lots for £400.

187-188. Negro woman Venus, aged 34 years, from Sarah Thomas, manumission signed 5th day 5th month, 1800 before Richard Green, Jno Thomas.

188. Negro Harry & others, recorded 30 May 1800, manumission from Sarah Thomas, manumission for Harry age 15 ½, girl Milly age 4, boy Joshua age 2 years; girl Hannah about 9 months, when they shall arrive at age 21 for boys and 18 for girls. Signed 3rd day, 5th month, 1800. Sarah Thomas before Richard Green, Jno Thomas 3d.

188-189. Negro Florah recorded 30 May 1800, from Samuel Thomas, manumission for girl Florah, now 8 years old, when she shall arrive to age 18. Signed by Samuel Thomas before Richard Green, Jno Thomas 3d.

189. Negro William, aged about 25 years, recorded 30 May 1800, from Samuel Thomas, manumission for him after the expiration of 1802. Signed Saml Thomas before Richard Green, Jno Thomas 3rd.

189-190. John Clarke recorded 2 June 1800, from Elisha Walker, for £40, bill of .sale, one black mare about 9 years old; and one bay horse 5 years old; one pyed cow 3 years old. Signed by mark before Greenberry Howard.

190-191. William Willson recorded 2 June 1800, from Adam Ramsour for £75, six lots in Hyattstown, signed before Greenbury Howard, Jno Clark. Receipt, acknowledgment. Mary Ramsour released dower rights.

191-193. Townshend Dade recorded from Benjamin White for £5, deed for part of tract called the *Resurvey on Albany,* beginning in the road leading between the said White and Dade, containing 1/10 of an acre; and for the second part, of tract, adjacent to a *Resurvey on Friends Advice,* and *Liberty,* containing 8+ acres, containing in the whole 8 1/4 acres. Signed Benjamin White before Ans Campbell, Greenbery Howard. Acknowledgment, and Rebeccah White released dower rights.

193-195. Ann Sparrow, relict of Thomas Sparrow; Thomas Baldwin, Margaret Baldwin, Thomas Sparrow, John Ellicott and Ann Ellicott recorded 4 June 1800, from Thomas Drane, Senior, *Hold Fast,* 47 acres. Thomas Sparrow's surviving children, were Margaret Baldwin, Thomas Sparrow and Ann Ellicott. In his will, dated 20 Feb. 1792, Thomas Sparrow left property to his children Margaret Baldwin, Thomas, Ann and Aquilla Sparrow. Ann has since married John Ellicott, and Aquilla has died unmarried and without issue. Whereas Thomas Drane Senior had transferred tract to George H. Offutt, executor of the will of Thomas Sparrow, by omission a part of the land mentioned is left out, so new deed was made. Receipt and acknowledgment.

195-198. John Wade from Ann Sparrow, Thomas Baldwin, Margaret Baldwin, Thomas Sparrow, John Ellicott, and Ann Ellicott, recorded 4 June 1800. For £70..7, 57 acre tract *Hold Fast.* Signed by all parties, and the women, Ann Sparrow, Margaret Baldwin, Ann Ellicott and Ann Sparrow wife of Thomas Sparrow, all examined and released dower rights. Witnesses: Elemelech Swearingen, J.H. McPherson.

198-199. Joseph Sprigg Belt recorded 6 June 1800, from Theophilus Roby, deed made 16 January for $50, lot on east side of road from Georgetown to the courthouse, near the forks of River Rd. At the beginning of Michael Brady's lot. Signed by mark before Dan'l Reintzel and Thomas Corcoran. Ann wife of Theophilus released dower rights.

199-200. Susanna Robertson recorded 9 June 1800, from Samuel Robertson 3rd for £221.8. Possessed of two tracts, part of *Dantzig,* 60 ½ acres, and part of *Boyd's Delay,* conveyed to Thomas Wootton by Abraham Boyd, and bequeathed to Turner S. Wootton by the will of Thomas Sprigg Wootton, and beginning at the tract *Dantzig,* containing 31 3/4 acres. Signed before Elemelech Swearingen, J. H. McPherson. Acknowledgment. Rachel Robertson, wife of Samuel relinquished dower rights.

200-202. George Beall recorded 9 June 1800, from Elizabeth Henry of the City of Baltimore, widow of Daniel Henry, for £100, deed for all interest in *Friendship,* and the *Addition,* and *Resurvey on Chance,* conveyed by a certain Hezekiah Roberts unto Daniel Henry deceased. Signed before W. Winchester.

202. John Fitzgerald to Sheriff of Montgomery County, schedule was recorded 10th June 1800, goods chattels and credits of John Fitzgerald delivered to Benjamin W. Jones. One bed stead, one bed, one fork, one wooden dish, one tin pan; William Fling one note on hand for £2..15; accounts due from Burch Cheshire, Saml Baker, George F. Myers, Doct. Richard Orme, Hezekiah Viers. Signed by mark before J.H. McPherson, J.F. Beall.

202-204. George W. Offutt and Thomas B. Offutt, agreement and division of lands. Includes plat for *Barren Hill,* which was the tract being divided, as devisees of Nathan Offutt, late of the County aforesaid deceased. Surveyed 17 December 1799, Wm Smith, Assistant Surveyor Montgomery County

A: The beginning of *Barron Hill*, containing 42 acres. Line between Thomas B. Offutt and George W. Offutt as follows, begins at the original beginning, follows to B. contains 17 6/10 acres. Done under the direction of Thomas B. Offutt and George W. Offutt, devisees of Nathan Offutt, late of the county deceased. Thomas B. Offutt's part, begins at a bounded rock marked S.O. 1759, it being the beginning of a tract called *Resurvey on Newton.* It contains 24 6/10 acres. Signed by Wm Smith, surveyor, 17 December 1799. Plat from Land Records, between pages 202-204.

204-206. Anthony Reintzel recorded 19 June 1800, from Valentine Reintzel, who is justly indebted unto Anthony Reintzel merchant of Georgetown, for a note of May 31, 1791; for £107..12..6 3/4, and also an open book account for several years back and other notes amounting to £503..17..11, and in the whole for $2204.37. Therefore he assigns all the Negro slaves, goods, household stuff, whatsoever. To wit: Charles aged 27 years; Joe aged 20 years; Jack aged 10 years; Peter aged 8 years; Jacob aged 6; Frederick age 5; Walter aged 3 years; Peck aged 40 years; Henny aged 27 years; Matilda 15 years; Mariah aged 9 years; Jenny aged 5 years; five feather beds with furniture complete, one mahogany side board, four large tables, one desk, one dozen mahogany chairs, looking glasses, one dozen silver table spoons, one plated coffee pot, serving dish, bread toaster, inkstand, irons with brass stops; six decanters, six goblets, one map of the state of Maryland, 3 pair brass candlesticks; 8 wheel barrows, one milch cow, one horse, car with gears, one Negro woman aged 40 years name not known; one ten plate stove, two brick sheds with about 200,000 raw bricks. Signed Valentine Reintzel before Dan'l Reintzel. Acknowledgment.

206-208. Elias Harding recorded 19 June 1800, from Leonard Wayman, deed for £704..5 part of tract called *Elysian Fields,* adjacent to 5th line of tract called *Hobson's Choice,* and *Leonards Conclusion;* containing 134 3/4 acres. Signed before Jno Clark, Greenbury Howard. Receipt. Acknowledgment. Eleanor wife of Leonard Wayman relinquished dower rights.

208-209. Abraham Jones recorded 20 June 1800 from Walter Duvall Mitchell for £15, bill of sale. For one feather bed and furniture, one bedstead, one chest, one chest of tools, one iron pot, one skillet, one Dutch oven, one cow and yearling. Signed before Ans Campbell.

209. Aquila Magruder recorded 23 June 1800, a list of slaves brought into the state. A Negro woman named Sophia, about 13 years old which fell to him by his marriage with Mary Ann Magruder of Virginia.

209. Joseph Slater, recorded 2 July 1800, list of slaves brought into Maryland from Virginia, viz: Florah 28, Daphna 10 years old, Hagar 8 years old, Ben 6 years, Fanny 4 years, Daniel 15 months. Signed 2 July 1800.

210-211. Samuel Thomas of Anne Arundel County, recorded deed 5 July 1800, from Orlando Griffith, Charles Greenberry Griffith and John Howard Griffith, deed made 21 June for $48. Sells part of *Gaither's Forest,* conveyed by Samuel Thomas to them, at Wild Cherry Tree Spring, to part conveyed to Samuel Thomas by William Bell of Philadelphia, 9 acres. Signed by Charles Greenbury Griffith, John Howard Griffith and Orlando Griffith my his mark, before Richard Green, Thomas Davis. Mary Griffith, wife of Benjamin Griffith released dower rights.

212. Samuel Nicholls, list of Negroes brought into the state from Virginia, because of intermarriage with Ann Finch. Negroes Betty age 16 and Cyrus age 11.

212-214. Charles Higbee recorded 13 July 1800, from Josiah Watson and Jane, his wife, of the town of Alexandria, Virginia, bargain & sale, part of tracts called *Chevy Chase,* and *Friendship.* Containing 21 acres, on the main road from George town to Montgomery Court House, adjacent to tract called *Charles and Thomas.* It being the same tract of land on which Michael Cookendorfer lately resided, which was sold to Josiah Watson by an indenture made 26 June 1791. Signed by Josiah Watson, Jane Watson, before Robert Casey, Josiah Watson Junr., John Taylor Jr., James Watson. Deed acknowledged before Robt White one of the Judges of the General Court.

214-216 Thomas King from Upton Beall, deed recorded 15 July 1800. For £30, lot #28 in Williamsburgh. Signed by Upton Beall, Matilda Beall released dower. Witness: John L. Summers, J. H. McPherson

216-218. Lenox Martin recorded 19 July 1800, from Levi Hayes & Eleanor, his wife, deed made 9 June. Whereas the parties agreed 14 January 1797 to exchange pieces of property, Levi agreed to give Lenox 14 acres of *Mount Zion,* for 7 3/4 acres of his land called *Beall's Good Will.* This is a bargain and sale, giving metes and bounds on the two parcels. Signed by all three before Greenbury Howard, Wm Smith. Eleanor wife of Levi and Elizabeth wife of Lenox Martin released dower rights.

218-219. John Letton of Bourbon County, July 1800, from John H. Nicholls of Mason Co., Kentucky, his right to estate of John Wilcoxon Sr. John H. Nicholls having married a daughter of the aforesaid Willcoxon.

219-220. Adam Boon recorded 21 July 1800, from John Miller, bill of sale for one bay gelding, brown mare, cow and calf, eight sheep, shoat and 2 beds & furniture, table and all the rest of household and plantation utensils. Signed by mark before Wm Smith.

220-221. Eleanor Brook of Prince George's County recorded 22 July 1800, from Marsham Waring of Georgetown, deed made 7 May for 5 shillings and in consideration that he purchase for her with her money while she was sole, *Second Resurvey on William and John,* and part of *Rich Valley,* containing 105 ½ acres, conveyed by Isaac Waters 1 Oct 1796 recorded in G:322 & 323, also part conveyed by Samuel Harper, 1 Oct. 1796, containing 223 acres. Signed before Joseph Forrest, Tench Ringgold. Acknowledgment.

221-223. Joshua Sear recorded 24 July 1800 lease from William Sear, in consideration of the covenants herein, assigns lease of *The Slipe,* beginning at north side of William's Spring.

223. Samuel H. Wheeler recorded 26 July 1800, a list of slaves willed to him by his father, Clement Wheeler, 1 March 1788 in Prince George's County. Sam, a male 55 years old; Rit, a female 36 years old, brought from Loudon County, Virginia.

223-225. Robert Ferguson from Benjamin White Jones, Sheriff, deed. Whereas judgment was had by Glassford against Elias Hardy, Kinsey Hardy, Jesse Phillips and Mary his wife, Henry Wheeler and Rebecca his wife, Frederick Burns, and Barbara his wife, Lawrence Owen and Sarah his wife, Samuel Allison and Fielder his wife and Elizabeth Holland, coheirs of Samuel Hardy late of Montgomery County, land in Montgomery County called *Grandmother's Good Will,* which was sold at public sale.

225. Alexander Whitaker recorded 3 August 1800 from Aaron Rawlings, bill of sale for £28..2, sells beds and furniture, one grey horse, two cows. Provided always that if sum paid with interest, before 1 February next, then sale is void. Signed before Robert A. Whitaker, Thos B. Beall.

226-227. Orlando Griffith recorded 4 August 1800, from Samuel Thomas of Anne Arundel County, to Orlando Griffith, Charles Greenberry Griffith and John Howard Griffith, for part of *Gaither's Forest,* for 8 acres for $48. Deed made 21 June. Anne wife of Samuel Thomas released dower rights.

227-228. John Weems and William King Junr., recorded 5 August 1800, from Edward Gantt, of Georgetown, bill of sale to indemnify and save harmless Dr. Weems, security in a supersedeas obtained by Bordley Clark against me in General Court. Delivers and assigns a Negro man named Aaron about 38 years old, and Neptune about 45. Signed 21 July 1800 before Joseph Forrest, Thomas Ewell.

228-230. James Ray recorded 6 August 1800, from Hezekiah Ford deed for £200 lot of land #2 in town of Williamsburgh (or ½ thereof). Signed before John L. Summers, Elemelech Swearingen.

230-232. Ely Beall recorded 12 August 1800, from Rachel Beall, parcel *George's Delight,* for £45, in the low grounds of Little Monocacy, containing 20 acres, near a tract taken up by Thomas Willson, called *Subberbs.*

232-233. Elizabeth Forrest, wife of Joseph Forrest, recorded 19 August 1800, from Francis Deakins of Montgomery County, devisee of William Deakins, Jr., in pursuance of an exchange of lands.

233-234. Elizabeth Forrest (daughter of Benjamin Dulaney of Fairfax County) recorded from Benjamin Dulaney, for love and affection, tract of land called *Middle Plantation,* to be held by her and her heirs.

234-235. Solomon Holland and others, bond to state of Maryland recorded 13 August 1800, to be collector of the tax for the county levy court. Signed by Solomon Holland, Benjamin W. Jones and Honore Martin.

235. Jonathan Reed recorded 13 August 1800, from Benjamin Loveless, deed for £50, lot in Sugarland Hundred on *Twice Got,* 15 acres. Signed by mark. Chloe wife of Benjamin Lovelace released dower rights.
236. Samuel Robertson recorded 10 August 1800, from Isaac Russell, bill of sale for $30 sell one gray mare 9 or 10 years old. Signed by mark before Eleven Mobley.
236-237. Nicholas Travers recorded bill of sale 10 August 1800 from Thomas Lynch of St. Mar's County for $200, a Negro man slave named Joe or Joseph about 33 years old. Signed before Dan'l Reintzel.
237-238. George T. Winrode recorded 20 August 1800, from Benjamin W. Jones, deed. Whereas a judgment was obtained by William Duncan against Jonathan Rhodes for lot of ground in Clarksburgh, #4, sold at public sale for £11..15. Signed before John L. Summers, Patrick Magruder.
238-239. Susanna Holland recorded 20 August 1800, from Nathan Holland Senior, for 7 shillings, 6 pence paid by Susanna, daughter of Nathan, and also for love and affection, gives one Negro girl Henny, 15 years old. deed of gift. Signed before John L. Summers.
239. Thomas Nevitt delivers to Sheriff Benj. W. Jones, a schedule of goods and articles, August 18, 1800, including amount amounts due from William Lancton, Daniel Sly, James Harrison and Alexander Childs. Signed before Elemelech Swearingen, J.H. McPherson.
240-241. Hugh Riley recorded 21 August 1800, from William Murphey and Rebecca his wife, deed for part of tract called *Dann.* Indenture made 1 August for £200, sells tract, a part of 600 acres sold to William Penson by John Hide, beginning at end of 2nd course of said 600 acres, N 90 perches, N 13 W, 68 perches, then W 108 perches; then S 106 perches, then S 13 degrees E 36 perches, S 86 deg. east 129 perches to second line of parcel, then with said line to beginning, containing 100 acres more or less. Signed William Murphy, Rebeckah Murphy before Henry Brookes, J. H. McPherson.
241-242. Thomas Lyddane recorded lease 22 August 1800 from Ruth Trundle. For rents and consideration, leases the tenement whereon John Bowman formerly lived about 108 acres. Rent of $28/year. For term of 19 years, he is also to build a premises, and keep fence and orchard in repair. Signed in the presence of Ans Campbell, Laurence O'Neale.
243-244. Dorcas Harris recorded 26 August 1800 from George Busey Hays, executor of his father's will, William Hays, late of Montgomery County deceased; indenture made 25 August 1800. Dorcas Harris purchased two distinct parts of said land, for £23..10 sells tract called *Harris Loss,* contiguous to each other, beginning at end of first line of the *Resurvey on Jeremiah's Park,* containing 5 acres and ½0; Signed George B. Hayes before John Clarke, Greenbury Howard. Receipt. Acknowledgment.
244-245. Richard Gott recorded 29 August 1800, from Benjamin White & Becky Ogle White, his wife, for 5 shillings, deed for part of tract called *Second Resurvey on Wolfs Cow,* laid out for 7 ½ acres. Signed Benjamin White, Rebeckah Odel White. [sic]. Dower release.
246. Upton Beall and John Orme recorded 3 September 1800, bill of sale for their being security, in superseding a judgment obtained by Gilpins and Brown against me in the May term, I assign a Negro boy called Sam, about 18 years old. Nevertheless sale void if judgment paid. Signed Richard Orme.
246-247. Thomas Leech Jr., delivered schedule to Benjamin W. Jones, sheriff, recorded. Included accounts of Capt. Lloyd Beall, George Seyle and Richard Oden, signed before John L. Summers, J. H. McPherson.
247-248. William Hilton recorded 5 September 1800, from James Hilton and Priscilla, his wife, for 5 shillings, deed for part of *Mount Zion,* adjacent to *Prospect Hill,* given to them by the last will and testament of their father, Joseph Harris Sr. Priscilla released dower rights.
248-250. Francis Deakins recorded 5 September 1800 from Joseph Forrest & wife, for 5 shillings, deed for two parcels of land conveyed to Elizabeth Forrest by her father, Benjamin Dulaney.
250-251. Robert Peter recorded 10 September 1800 from Charles Hungerford, for £222..10, deed for *Resurvey on the Beginning.* Mary, wife of Charles Hungerford released dower.
251-253. James Perry recorded 18 September 1800, from Richard Wootton, deed. Whereas James Perry did purchase of Benjamin West, part of *Discontent,* adjoining his dwelling plantation, conveyed 13 November 1780, which Richard Wootton agreed to convey to James Perry.

253-254. Thomas Sparrow recorded 20 September 1800, for £18..15 one small mare from John Jennings. Signed by mark.

254. Commission issued to Thomas Plater and Thomas Davis, recorded 23 September 1800, appointed associate justices of Montgomery County.

254-258. Land commission to Elizabeth Harris recorded 24 September 1800. Granted 11 November 1799 by Montgomery County Court, appointing William Smith, Greenbury Howard, John Clarke and Lenox Martin, commissioners to examine evidence concerning the beginning boundary of land called *Basil's Lot,* notice published 24 February. Met June 9, 1800. George Hays aged about 48 or 49 years old, sworn and deposed regarding boundary of *Basils Lot,* by a certificate of resurvey made for Joseph Harris August 1786, called *Mount Zion,* on a line of *Basil's Lot,* and *Happy Choice.* Joseph Harris, age 38, deposed regarding his father, Joseph Harris' resurvey. The surveyor and the two chain carriers, Jesse Harris and Archibald Owen were sworn to the lines run by them.

258. Samuel Gue and Mary Gue recorded 27 September 1800, from Rebecca Gue, deed of gift for the love and good will I bear unto my grandson, Samuel Gue, a dark bay mare aged 9 or 10 years old, to be delivered out of my estate, likewise I grant to the said Samuel Gue, a red cow, 7 years old, and a red yearling ...

258-259. Lucy Scott recorded 29 September 1800, manumission from Joseph L. Belt before Daniel Reintzel.

259-260. Joshua Pigman recorded 29 September 1800, from James Beall of Samuel, deed for £150 for parcel called *Advise* in Montgomery and Anne Arundel County, containing 73 acres. Elizabeth wife of James Beall released dower.

260-261. Thomas Fletchall recorded 30 September 1800 from Thomas Plater, deed for part of *Brightwell's Hunting Quarter,* 45 acres. Martha Plater released dower rights.

261-263. Thomas Plater recorded 30 September 1800 from Thomas Fletchall, deed for 5 shillings, part of tract called *Sugar Bottom*, on Horse Pen Branch, for 39 ½ acres; 2nd part for 5 ½ acres. Signed and acknowledged.

263-264. Charles Catlet recorded 30 September 1800 from Alexander Catlet of Madison Co., Ky., power of attorney to sell tract of land called *New Holland,* and other land enumerated in Virginia.

264-265. Samuel Clagett recorded 1 October 1800 from Benjamin Ray Senr. For £51, 13 3/4 acres, part of *Leach's Lot,* originally granted Wm Leach for 25 acres, on second line of tract, *Mudhill,* signed before Elemelech Swearingen and J. H. McPherson.

265-266. Samuel Clagett recorded 1 October 1800, from Benjamin W. Jones, sheriff, deed made 26 July. Whereas a judgment for use of John Gwinn in general court was obtained against Benjamin Ray Sr and Samuel Clagett was the highest bidder at public sale, for £233..3..1, for tract called *Peace and Plenty,* for 403 acres. Signed before John L. Summers and Patrick Magruder.

266-269. John Burgess recorded 2 October 1800 from Philemon Griffith of Frederick County and Joshua Griffith, executor of Henry Griffith. Part of *Tusculum.* Whereas John Burgess did on 3 March 1793 agree with Henry Griffith for the purchase of the tract, containing 347 acres, which John Burgess did agree to pay the sum of £694, when Henry Griffith received a deed from Bordley. A decree in the Court of Chancery ordered Bordley to make a deed of conveyance to the executors. By virtue of the power of the will, they have actually sold unto John Burgess, tract known as *Barber's Lot* containing 53 acres by patent, and part of *Gaither's Forest,* adjacent to Zachariah Linthicum's part, containing 50 acres; and also one other piece being a part of three tracts, one called *Snowden's Purchase,* one called *Jones Chance,* and part of a tract called *Tusculum,* containing 55 acres. Signed before Daniel Reintzel and Edward Burgess Jr.

269-270. Gerrard Brooke paid £25 & Caleb Bentley for $20, recorded 3 October 1800, bill of sale from Ezekiel Jackson for all my crop of corn now growing, one spring colt, 10 fowls, 2 pair of horse gears, all my garden stuff and crop of turnips; signed by mark 2 October 1800 before Richard Green. Receipt.

270-271. Joseph Clagett recorded 10 October 1800 from Greenbury Gaither, deed made same date for £176, sells tracts *Friendship* and *Gravelly Hill.* Metes and bounds for 88 acres. Signed before John L. Summers, Elemelech Swearingen. Ann Gaither wife of Greenbury released dower rights.

271-273. John Buxton Jr. recorded 14 October 1800, from Richard Waters, deed made 23 August for $30. Sells one parcel in Clarksburg, lot #6, on the great road, ½ acre. Signed before Greenbury Howard, John Clarke. Margaret Waters released dower rights.

273. Charles Perry to the State of Maryland, bond as supervisor of the roads filed 15 October 1800. Signed Charles Perry, John Henderson, Wm Worthington.

273-275. John B. Dyson recorded 18 October 1800, from Edward Veirs, deed made 10 May for £60 sells part of *Resurvey on Non-Eaten* and part of *Mary,* containing 16 ½ acres. Signed before Laurence O'Neale, Aeneas Campbell. Receipt, acknowledgment.

275-276. Alexander Catlett, late of Montgomery County, now of Mason County, recorded 18 October 1800, deed made 26 July, between William Benson, Sarah Benson and Ninian Benson, infant heirs of William Benson deceased, and Nicholas Pegno. Whereas a decree of high court of chancery in favor of Alexander Catlett on his application for specific performance of a contract, allowed him to make a good deed with Pegno as guardian, now they, by their guardian, and for £29..15..4, sell part of *Pleasant Fields,* lying at the 5th line of *Lost Jacket,* to the 37th line of *Beautiful Meadow,* containing 35 acres. Signed by Nicholas Pegno, guardian of William, Sarah and Ninian Benson. Acknowledgment.

276-277. Benjamin White recorded 18 October 1800 from Richard Gott, deed for 7 ½ acres, a part of *Fertile Plains.* Signed Richard Gott before Aeneas Campbell, Thos B. Beall. Acknowledgment, wife of Richard Gott (not named) released dower rights.

277-279. Benjamin White from Townshend Dade, for £5, deed recorded 18 October 1800, tract *Liberty.* containing 2 9/10 acres. Mary Dade released dower rights.

279. Benjamin F. Daley qualified as deputy sheriff before John L. Summers, 20 October 1800.

279-280. Thomas Bartholow Junr. recorded lease 24 October 1800 from Edward Iglehart, for 50 acres of *Pembroke.* Bartholow to build a dwelling house, a tobacco house and plant an apple orchard. Signed by both parties before Jno Clarke.

280-281. John Dells recorded 24 October 1800, deed from Obed Leeke, for £45, part of *Gittings Hah Hah.* Receipt. Acknowledgment.

281-282. Leonard Marbury Deakins of Prince George's County recorded 27 October 1800, from Alexander Contee Hanson on behalf of the State of Maryland. Whereas a sale made by Commissioners of Confiscated British property, 25 October 1781, formerly the property of Daniel Dulaney son of Daniel for lot #1, for 120 1/4 acres, part of the tract *Concord,* gave bond. Metes & bounds given. Signed in the presence of Mary Jane Hanson.

282. Gustavus Easton recorded schedule of personal property 28 October 1800, to Benjamin W. Jones, sheriff. One bedstead and cord, one straw bed and cover, one pot and table, one pewter dish, six white plates, some old knives, forks, tea pot, cups and saucers, one looking glass, 5 pewter spoons, one pail, one piggen, 3 old barrels, some old bottles and 3 chairs. Signed by mark, before John L. Summers, J.H. McPherson.

283-284. Stacy Pancoast from Samuel Williams, bill of sale for £50..8, sells servitude of Negro man Neale for 7 years, 9 ½ months, then to be free. Signed before Wm Smith, 18 April 1794. Endorsements on back of indenture: I hereby make all right and title to this indenture unto James Higdon, 20 October 1797, signed Samuel Brayfield. Whereas the within Negro man, Neale, became the property of Samuel Brayfield by his marriage to Jane the widow of Stacy Pancost. James Higdon, remits the remainder of time of the said Negro man Neale to the said Negro after he served him for 3 years. Signed 5 October 1800 before William Smith.

284-285. Greenberry Howard recorded 1 November 1800 from Jonathan Browning, Jr., deed of trust. Whereas an application of the said Jonathan Browning for relief of insolvent debtors, and Greenberry Howard was appointed trustee, for 5 shillings Browning assigns his property.

285-286. Greenberry Howard recorded 1 November 1800 from John Kelly, deed of trust, Whereas an application of the said John Kelly for relief of insolvent debtors, and Greenberry Howard was appointed trustee, for 5 shillings Kelly assigns his property.

286-287. Samuel Leek recorded 3 November 1800, from Richard Thomas & Deborah Thomas his wife, for $20, assigns lot #44 in Brookeville.

287-288. Beall Gaither recorded 8 November 1800 deed from Samuel Thomas of Anne Arundel County. For $393, assigns tract of land conveyed by the Samuel Thomas to John Burgess. Anne wife of Samuel Thomas released dower.

288-289. James Hinton recorded 4 November 1800, from Benjamin W. Jones, sheriff. Whereas a judgment was obtained by James Gordon and others in Montgomery County Court against Rebecca Hinton, James Hinton, Thomas Hinton, Philip Hinton, Michael Hinton, Edward Ward and Mary his wife, Charles Anderson and Ann his wife, James Ball and Rachel his wife, heirs and legatees of Thomas Hinton, in pursuance of a writ of fieri facias, took parcel of land near Clarksburgh, called *Saplin Ridge,* for 100 acres. James Hinton was the highest bidder on property. Signed before John L. Summers, Elemelech Swearingen.

289-290. Joseph Williams recorded 4 November 1800 from James Hinton, deed made 25 Oct. For £172..12, sells part of *Sapling Ridge,* containing 92 acres. Catherine, wife of James Hinton, released dower rights.

291-292. Uriah Leaton from Francis Perry, recorded bill of sale 4 Nov. 1800 for £53, one Negro woman, Henn age 19, and child Amoria, 4 years of age. Sale void if sum paid by 21 Oct. 1801. Signed before Jno Clarke, William Wilson.

292-293. Deposition of Ally Hickman recorded 4 November 1800 by Zephaniah Plummer. On 9 Sept. 1800 at my own house, Alley Hickman was sworn and stated that last of August or first of September, George Ray, Robert Flemming and William Hall came to the house of Zephaniah Mockbee sometime after sundown. They came around to back door and met Mrs. Mockbee in the yard and inquired if she had seen old Mr. Mockbee. She said he had not been there for three years. He asked for water, and she invited them to sit and requested deponent to bring tumbler and bottle. Mr. Hall said he did not drink grog. By this time, Mr. Zephaniah Mockbee, her uncle came in, and asked for names and if they had any demand against him. They were asked to leave. They didn't. He struck hall with an auger and pushed him out of doors. Althea Hickman signed before Wm Smith.

293-295. Anacletus Dyer recorded 11 November 1800, from Solomon Veatch, mortgage for 3980 pounds crop tobacco, all that part of a tract formerly called *Progress* and one part of tract called *Narrow Lane,* and now resurveyed and called *Three Tracts Resurveyed,* metes and bounds given to a spring formerly made use of in common by John and Solomon Veatch, to a line of a deed for part of *Progress,* formerly conveyed to Ninian Veatch for 75 acres; and then to a tract conveyed by Solomon Veatch to Carlton Belt for 38 acres. Also for the second part of three tracts, formerly conveyed to John Veatch.' Signed before Laurence O'Neal, Ans Campbell. Ack.

295-297. Thomas Rhodes recorded 6 November 1800, from Jacob Howard of Prince George's County, deed for £210 for tract called *Friendship Enlarged.* For 140 acres, agreeable to patent granted William Hall in 1715, which was willed by Jacob Howard now deceased on 6th December 1792 to Cassandra Page for term of seven years from time of death, agreeable to commence, Thomas Rhodes agreed to take upon this condition. Signed Jacob Howard 14 June 1800, before Richard Cramphin, Richard L. Lowndes.

298. Lizza from Baldwin Dade, manumission recorded 6 November 1800 for £75. Mulatto woman aged 34 years.

298-299. Edward Jones recorded indenture of servitude, 6 Nov. 1800, Lizza a mulatto woman, formerly the slave of Baldwin Dade, for £75, she is to serve for the full term of 5 years. Signed by mark, Lizza, Edward Jones.

299-300. Thomas Linsted and Solomon Holland recorded 11 November 1800, bill of sale from William Pelly, for £31..5, for a bay horse with blaze, personal and farm property. Signed 6 November 1800 before John L. Summers.

300-301. William Stabler recorded 12 November 1800, from Richard Thomas and Deborah Thomas, deed made 31st day, 10th month, 1800, for $22. A lot in town of Brookeville. Signed before Richard Green, Thomas Davis.

301-303. James Barnes recorded 17 November 1800 from William Ballinger, tract *Meadowland.* Lydia Ballinger released dower.
303-304. Honore Martin recorded 17 November 1800, from Zachariah Prather & wife Ruth of Enfield District, South Carolina, assigns any right to real estate of John Allison, they may have under his last will. Signed by both before Wm Summers, James Summers. Receipt for £25.
305. Jonathan Monro of the City of Baltimore, merchant, recorded 18 November 1800, from James Barnes, deed of trust, for 5 shillings, assigns tract called *Meadow Land,* which was originally on 14 May 1796 granted William Ballinger for 20 acres conveyed by Barnes to Ballinger 4 June 1800. Signed before Owen Dorsey, John Moale.
306-307. Samuel Lazenby recorded 18 November 1800, from Zachariah Duly and wife for £97..10, tracts called *Addition to Girls Gift, Addition to Lazenby's Chance, Lazenby's Chance,* and *Samuel's Purchase,* late the property of Henry Lazenby, deceased, unto him the said Samuel Lazenby. Signed before Allen Bowie, J.F. Beall. Ann Duly released dower rights.
307. Michael McEntosh & wife recorded 21 November 1800. We the subscribers being appointed by William Hickman to settle a dispute between them, award that William Hickman pay £103..19 with interest before 1st day October next. Signed by Alexander Whitaker, Thos B. Beall,. Annexed to award was receipt for full sum, dated 29 October 1800, due them of all demands under the last will of John Fletchall of Montgomery County deceased, signed by Elizabeth Mackentush, Michael McTush by his mark.
307-309. Evan Jones recorded 21 November 1800, from Francis Deakins, devisee of William Deakins, deceased, deed. Whereas he is indebted to Evan Jones for $1,064, he assigns part of *Deakin's Range,* and two parts of *Middle Plantation,* to *Resurvey on Gravelly Range,* to the 10th line of *Overplus*. Eleanor wife of Francis Deakins released dower.
309-310. Frederick Scholl recorded 2 December 1800 from Ann Roberts for £65, parcel called *Hammer Hill,* beginning on SW side of main road from Frederick Town to Georgetown. Signed before Edward Burgess Jr., Greenberry Howard.
311. Lewis Beall and Thomas Perry recorded qualification as Deputy Clerks of Montgomery County Court 4 December 1800. Sworn before J. H. McPherson.
311. Negro Nancy recorded 9 December 1800, from Thomas Prater, manumission to be from the 9th December 1817, after the term above to be free. Signed before John L. Summers.
311-313. George Riley recorded 10 December 1800, from Hugh Riley and Amos Riley, deed made 20 October, for $882. Sells the following tracts: *Two Brothers,* beginning at a stake in an apple orchard, in two parts, laid out for110 acres. Signed before John L. Summers, J. H. McPherson.
313-315. Isaac Riley recorded 10 December 1800 from Hugh Riley, deed made 20 October for £100, part of *Howards Chance,* on south side of a spring branch by Ten Mile Creek, to part of *Conclusion,* adjacent to *Pork and Potatoes,* 32 3/4 acres and 50 acres. Signed & acknowledged.
315-316. George Riley recorded 10 December 1800, from Thomas King, blacksmith, for £200, deed made 24 October, for a lot of land in Williamsburgh, otherwise called Montgomery Courthouse. Signed Thomas King before John L. Summers, J. H. McPherson.
316-317. Solomon Holland recorded bond 12 December 1800, as Sheriff of Montgomery County. Signed by Solomon Holland, Honore Martin.
317. Robert W. Flemming, recorded 10 December 1800, qualification as deputy sheriff at the request of Solomon Holland.
317-319. Nathan Veirs recorded 10 December 1800 from John Veirs, deed. Whereas Daniel Veirs did in his lifetime, make a will, and bequeath to his son John Veirs 120 acres adjoining his dwelling, and the rest of his land to be divided to his two sons, Elisha and Nathan Veirs, these deeds are to clarify boundaries, and title to his brothers lands. Catherine Veirs, wife of John Veirs released dower rights.
319-321. Elisha Veirs recorded 10 December 1800, from John Veirs, deed Whereas Daniel Veirs did in his lifetime, make a will, and bequeath to his son John Veirs 120 acres adjoining his dwelling, and the rest of

his land to be divided to his two sons, Elisha and Nathan Veirs, these deeds are to clarify boundaries, and title to his brothers lands. Catherine Veirs, wife of John Veirs released dower rights.

321-322. William Jeffery recorded a schedule of goods and chattels and credits given to Benjamin W. Jones late Sheriff of Montgomery County, 13 December 1800. Included accounts due from Richard Studs, William Blandford, Jacob Shirock, Jacob Young, Lewis Lerminty, John Davis, Luke Thompson. Signed before John L. Summers, Elemelech Swearingen.

322. William Candler, recorded 16 December 1800, qualification as deputy sheriff at request of Solomon Holland.

322-323. Annistacia Dial recorded 18 December 1800, from Joseph Sprigg Belt, deed for $43, sells lot on east side of the road leading from Geo Town, opposite Tenly's and adjoining Theophilus Robey's lot. Signed before Dan'l Reintzel and Thos Corcoran. Receipt and acknowledgment.

323. Rev'd Plunkett from Henry Lansdale, letter recorded 17 December 1800. 27 August 1800: Rev. & Dear Sir: Whereas Frank, a free Negro, the bearer of this, and my Negro woman Judy wish to get married, I take the liberty of informing you that they have my free and full consent, not having objection thereto, as I conceive him to be an honest and orderly person. Henry Lansdale. On the back of the letter: Frank and Judy were married by me at Mr. Stephen Adams on the __ day of October 1800.

323-326. Peter Daniel Decandry of Baltimore County recorded 20 December 1800, made 16 December 1800, , mortgage of Peter Bouic, for £250 tract now known as *Normandie,* and formerly four tracts known by names of *Cyder and Ginger, Indulgence, Welfare* and *Farewell,* 151 acres, adjacent to *Edloe's Adventure.*

327-330. Peter Bouic recorded 20 December 1800 from Peter Daniel Decandry. Deed made for £1440 tracts as above. Signed before Justices of the Peace of Baltimore County.

331. Henry Lansdale recorded 23 December 1800 qualification for deputy sheriff, at the request of Solomon Holland.

331. Leonard P. Higdon recorded 23 December 1800 power of attorney from Thomas Higdon, who appoints his son and friend, his attorney to recover any debts due, and to sell and real estate or personal property. Signed by mark before Laurence O'Neale and Thos B. Beall.

332. Basil Leatch, schedule recorded 29 December 1800, credits on account, Nicholas Baley, £4..19, Erasmus Hart, 1..17..9; Josiah Leatch. Note in hands of constable of Prince George's County. Signed before John L. Summers, J.H. McPherson.

332-333. Kesiah Beckwith and George Beckwith record deed from Lamach Beckwith of Shendandoah County, Virginia, for £100, his part of the estate of Charles Beckwith, to indemnify them a security in a replevin bond to John Belt. Witness: John Beckwith, Walter Daniel.

333-334. John L. Trundle, recorded 31 December 1800 bill of sale from Charles Hungerford and John Fyffe, for £102..10 Negro boy, Coolman. Signed before William Higgins, Wm Wilcoxon.

334-335. Schedule received for Joseph Beck 1 January 1801, for relief from debts and for 5 shillings turns over all belongings to Richard Beck, trustee on behalf of creditors of Joseph Beck.

335-336. Terrance Nowlan recorded 5 January 1801, bill of sale from John Lynch of St. Mary's County, for Negro woman Rachel about 37 and boy Lewis about 4 years old. Signed by mark before Thos Corcoran, Wm Cary.

336. Edward Janes recorded 7 Jan. 1801, goods delivered to the Sheriff of Montgomery County, Solomon Holland. Consisted of two iron pots, one iron oven, two bar share ploughs, two shovels. Signed by mark before John L. Summers, Elemelech Swearingen.

336-337. Samuel Wright recorded 7 Jan. 1801, from Richard Thomas Jr., & Deborah his wife, deed for $12. For lot #18 in Brookeville.

337-341. David Newlin recorded 7 January 1801, from Thomas Moore and Mary his wife, deed made 31st 10th mo., 1800 for £80, part of tract called *Addition to Brooke Grove,* beginning at a maple sapling, standing below David Newlan's mill dam, containing 4 acres. Also access to the two streams, the condition that he not erect a mill for the purpose of grinding the following kinds of grain: wheat, rye, Indian corn or buckwheat, unless it shall happen that Richard Thomas Junr. At any future time neglect to keep a mill for grinding grains where his place now stands or within half a mile thereof. Witnesses, Richard D. Green, Thomas Davis.

341. John D. Travers qualified as deputy sheriff, 8 January 1801.

341. Commission to Justices of Levy Court: Thomas Davis, Allen Bowie, John L. Summers, John Clarke, and James Lackland, Thomas B. Beall and Adam King. By the honorable Alexander C. Hanson, Chancellor.

341-343. Richard Wootton recorded 17 January 1801, from Richard Keene, of the County of Bath in Virginia, for £50, deed for part of *Exchange and New Exchange.*

343-344. George Riley recorded 20 January 1801, from Henry Hardy of Baptist, Mary West, and Frances Hardy wife of Henry, part of *Two Brothers,* and *Hobson's Choice,* formerly the property of William West. Frances Hardy released dower rights.

345-346. Benjamin Gittings recorded 22 January 1801, from Samuel Brooke Beall of Allegany County, deed for tract of land called *Benjamin,* between the road that leads from Walter Beall's mill to Georgetown, and Henry Clark's land which Clark purchased of Samuel Beall, containing 21 3/4 acres. Signed before Joseph Forrest and Thomas Corcoran.

346 Elias Earvin, recorded 22 January 1801, from Francis Perry for $100, bill of sale for one Negro woman called Bett, formerly the property of Thomas Aldridge, now of Kentucky. Signed before Edward Burgess Junr.

346-348. Charles Carroll of Carrollton recorded 23 January 1801, from Charles Courts Jones, mortgage made 15 January. Whereas Charles C. Jones is indebted in sum of £750 to be paid in two yeas with interest annually, he mortgages, parcel on east side of Rock Creek, on road leading to Jones Bridge, to mouth of Conquelain Run, and the tract on which the grist and saw mill belonging to Jones stands, 22 acres plus improvements. Signed Charles Courts Jones before Joseph Forrest, Uriah Forrest.

348-349. Israel French recorded 23 January 1801, from Richard Thomas and Deborah Thomas, his wife, deed for $12 for lot in town of Brookeville, #46. Signed before Richard Green, Thomas Davis.

349-350. Deborah Phillips recorded 23 January 1801, from Richard Thomas & Deborah, his wife, for $12. deed, lot in Brookeville #41. Signed before Richard Green, Thomas Davis.

350-351. David Clagett recorded 24 January 1801, from Thomas O. Offutt, deed. For £87..13.. Sells parcel, part of *Three Brothers Industry*, signed before John L. Summers, J.H. McPherson.

351-352. Sarah Collyar (relict of William Collyar) recorded 2 February 1801, from Charles Greenfield, deed for £1200 sells part of parcel *Pleasant Hill.* Adjacent to tract *Brother's Industry.* And also *Tryall.* containing 315 acres. Elizabeth wife of Charles Greenfield released dower.

352-354. Charles Greenfield recorded 2 February 1801 from Sarah Collyer, deed for £1200 tract as above.

355-356. John Clarke recorded 3 February 1801 from John D. Coffee of Mason County, Ky, and Ann Roberts for £350, sells parcel called *Moneysworth,* part of *Hammer Hill,* part of *Woodport,* and part of *Resurvey on What You Will,* beginning at Timber Creek, formerly conveyed by John Belt to James Coffee for 158 13/4 acres, and part formerly conveyed to Michael Dowden for 93 ½ acres. At second division made between John Clary and Esther his wife. Basil Roberts and Ann his wife, Solomon Sympson and Dorcas his wife.

356-358. John D. Coffee and Ann Roberts recorded 3 February 1801. from John Belt for £102..5, four distinct parcels called *Wood Port,* and part of *Moneysworth,* for 158 3/4 acres, as formerly conveyed from John Belt to John Coffee, adjacent to *Timber Creek,* and *What you Will,* another part containing 7 3/8 acres; Signed before Edward Burgess, Greenberry Howard.

358-359. George Campbell recorded lease 5 February 1801 from Edward Crow, made 22 January 1801, land he purchased of Ignatius Pigman called *Goshen Mills,* part of *Resurvey on Benjamin Square* and *Fertile Meadows,*

360. Joseph Nourse, certificate of slave, Moses, 21 years old, his slave in Washington, D.C., being moved to Maryland to work.

360. John Beall recorded 10 February 1801, bill of sale from Levin C. Beall for slave girl, Sall, 12 years old.
360-361. Erasmus Perry recorded February 1801, from Zachariah Duley, bill of sale for £25, two beds, other personal property remaining in my household and plantation, void if sums paid. Signed before J. F. Beall, Benjm Perry.
361-363. William Vinson recorded 11 February 1801 from Richard Thomas Senior, lease. Memorandum of an agreement on tract called *Thomas Discovery,* containing 200 acres for 22 years. He agrees to pay rents and to build a dwelling house and two framed tobacco houses, also a peach orchard and a cherry orchard. Signed before Wm Thomas, Wm Smith.
363. Negroes Janny aged 25 years old, and Nancy aged 20 years old, , manumission recorded 18 February 1801, from Henrietta Thomas. Signed before Wm Smith.
363-364. John Rawlings recorded 14 February 1801, deed from Samuel Offutt for 463 ½ acres of tract *Final Conclusion.* Signed Samuel Offutt before John Tomlinson.
364-365. Samuel Nicholls records list of Negroes brought in from Virginia, from his marriage with Ann Finch of Virginia. Negro woman Flora about 30 years old. 21 Feb. 1801.
365. Henry Lodge recorded certificate of qualification as a deputy sheriff 21 Feb. 1801. Oath before John L. Summers.
365. Nathan Holland Junior recorded certificate of qualification as a deputy sheriff 21 Feb. 1801. Oath before John L. Summers
365-366. Richard Johns recorded 27 February 1801, made 26 Feb. from Archibald Orme, for $19.83 deed for parcel about ½ mile below Seneca Falls, beginning at a bounded sycamore on Potomac River, containing 4 ½ acres. Signed and acknowledged before Thomas Prather.
366-368. Elizabeth and Otho Luckett of Frederick County, Maryland; recorded deed 27 February 1801 from William Hough of the County of Loudon, Virginia. For carrying into effect a contract from Thomas Hussey Luckett the late husband of Elizabeth and father to the above named Otho, and also for £1186..10 part of a *Resurvey on Discord.* Containing 171 acres. Wit: Aeneas Campbell, Laurence O'Neale.
368. Thomas Rigdon and Robert Peters recorded bond unto Richard Fenwick, 2 March 1801. Whereas the said Richard Fenwick is confined in the public Jaol of Montgomery County, and the said Thomas Rigdon and Richard Fenwick hath disposed of his property in such manner as his creditors object to the discharge of the said Richard Fenwick, the above bound Thomas Rigdon is to satisfy all damages and costs the said Richard Fenwick shall sustain. Signed in presence of John Weems.
368-369. Leonard Mackall and Aquilla Beall to State of Maryland, bond. For £1000, obligation is such that Leonard Mackall is appointed tobacco inspector. Signed before Henry Harding and Edward Harding, by Leonard Mackall, George Beall, Aquilla Beall.
369-370. John Leeke recorded 3 March 1801 from Richard Thomas Junr and Deborah Thomas his wife, sell lot in Town of Brookeville, Lots no 10 & 11.
370. John Pool Junr. Recorded 3 March 1801, from Jonathan Reed, for £45, deed for tract of land conveyed by John Nobbs to Henry McGlocklin and from McGlochlen to John Yates and from John Yates to Benjamin Loveless and from Benjamin Loveless to Jonathan Reed. Signed before Aeneas Campbell, Thos B. Beall. Susannah Reed, wife of Jonathan released dower.
370-372. Charles C. Jones recorded 3 March 1801 from John Carroll of Baltimore, a bishop of the Catholic Church, Notley Young and Robert Brent Esq. Of the City of Washington. Under the last will of Daniel Carroll deceased. Whereas Daniel Carroll by his will made 9 April 1796, did give all his estate to his brother John Carroll, and his friends Notley Young and Robert Brent, in trust for his grandchildren, to dispose of as they might think proper. Now for £990 they assign parcel, part of *Joseph's Park,* beginning at east side of Rock Creek, a dividing line of the lands between Daniel Carroll and Daniel Carroll Jr., to the east side of road leading to a bridge over Rock Creek called Jones Bridge, metes and bounds continue to contain 88 acres. Signed before Joseph Forrest.

373. William Marbury of Georgetown recorded 9 May 1801 from Benjamin Stoddert of Georgetown, mortgage made 13 February. Whereas Benjamin Stoddert by deed of 13 March 1797 assigned parcels in Allegany County, recorded in record books of the General Court of the Western Shore, now to more fully secure payment of sums he mortgages part of tract *Friendship,* the same being farmed about 5 miles from Georgetown on road leading to Frederick town, about 283 acres; also a tract of 15 acres adjoining land belonging to William Diggs, Joseph Sprigg Belt, Frances Valdenare and William Thornton, together with all improvements. Rebecca Stoddert wife of Benjamin Stoddert released dower rights.

375. Stephen Shaw recorded 3 March 1801 from Sylvester Sullivan, bill of sale for $199.39 personal property. Horse, bridle, household goods and implements. Signed before Allen Bowie

375-377. Hezekiah Thomas recorded 4 March 1801, from Edward Crow, deed for £741..15, tract called *Abels Levels,* containing 126 acres, part of *Resurvey on Shady Grove* and *Addition to Abel's Levels,* adjacent to *Samuels Chance,* 27 acres; part of *Samuel's Chance,* 61 1/4 acres, and 16 acres, also *Jacobs Mistake,* 14 acres. Signed before Greenberry Howard, John Clark. Acknowledgment.

377-378. Caleb Bentley recorded March 1801, bill of sale from Cornelius Sullivan for £4..3 sells five pigs, one black horse, 2 shots, one Dutch oven, hoes, common shares, plough, weeding hoes, common chairs, putting Caleb Bentley in full possession by the delivery of one spoon in the name of the whole property. Signed before Thomas Davis, Remus Riggs.

378-379. John Henderson and Samuel Bealmar from John Hartlove, bill of sale for £20, sells personal furniture, other farming and cooking utensils. Signed before John L. Summers.

379. Greenberry Howard recorded 9 March 1801 from Evan Belt, deed of trust. For benefit of insolvent debtors, for 5 shillings he assigns all of his property excepting wearing apparel to be sold to pay debts. Witness: John L. Summers, Elemelech Swearingen.

379-380. Uriah Leaton recorded 10 March 1801 from Hugh Coupland and Michael Heffner of Frederick County, sells a lot on east side of road #9. Signed before Greenberry Howard, John Clarke, acknowledgment.

381. Walter Magruder recorded 10 March 1801, and others to State of Maryland, Inspector's bond for tobacco. George B. Magruder, L. Mackall.

381. Solomon Green recorded discharge 14 March 1801. The bearer hereof, Solomon Green having fulfilled his engagement with me as a servant for the term of 18 months, this is to certify to all whom it may concern that he is free from me and at liberty to pass and repass and enter into whatsoever employment he may think proper for his own benefit. January 20, 1801, Washington Bowie.

381-383. Robert Peter of Georgetown, recorded 14 March 1801, from Mary Smith, bill of sale for £2000 sells Negroes, Ben Senr., Sam, Bob, Charles, Cate and her two youngest children Ben Junr., Charles, Grandison, Horatio, Massey, Ally, Fil, Duke, Cassey and her two children, Charity and Liz; Liz, Mary, Sharlotte, Violett, Jane, Maria, Rose, Matilda, Munday, Rose Letty, Jerry, Jim, and Ajay mother to the last mentioned six Negroes; also all the other Negroes now in the possession of the said Mary Smith or any other person which she may have any right or title to, with the increase thereof at present on the plantation in Montgomery County aforesaid, being part of a tract of land called *Course Basket*, now in the possession of the said Robert Peter, together with their increase. That Negroes Mary, Jane, Maria, Rose Violet and Grandison shall remain in the possession of the said Mary Smith aforesaid to her separate benefit, and disposal. Signed 28 February 1801, by Mary Smith and Robert Peter before James S Morsel, Daniel Reintzel.

383-385. Thomas Clagett recorded 19 March 1801, from Benjamin W. Jones, late Sheriff. Whereas a judgment obtained by Ignatious Davis, administrator with the will annexed of Sarah Perry in the general court for the Western Shore of Maryland, against a certain John B. Magruder, and in pursuance thereof, a judgment on 8 November 1799 directed the sheriff to sell tracts called *Ruturs Purchase,* and *Oversight,* property of the aforesaid John B. Magruder, in obedience to her will, they were exposed to public sale, and in consideration of the sum of £133..15 sells tracts called *Rulers Purchase,* beginning at a tract called *Rum Punch* and *Resurvey on Dublin*, *Samuel's Lot*, to *Resurvey on Dickerson's Lot*, to first line of John Beall

Magruders tract, *Resurvey on Rum Punch,* to beginning as now measured off by Thomas Orme, surveyor for 92 ½ acres. And beginning at a tract called *Oversight,* adjacent to *Samuel's Lot,* containing 6 3/4 acres. Signed by Benjamin W. Jones before John L. Summers, J. H. McPherson.

385. Negro Andrew age 4, Negro Isaac aged 1 year, Jerricam 2 months; Girl Mary age 2 years to be free at ages 21 and 18 years respectively. Signed 2 January 1801, Henrietta Thomas before William Smith.

385-386. Gerrard Brooke recorded 24 March 1801, between Richard Thomas and Deborah his wife for $40. Lot in town of Brookeville. Wit. Richard Green, Thomas Davis.

386-387. John L. Summers from Caleb Letton, power of attorney recorded 26 March 1801. I John Letton of the County of Bourbon, commonwealth of Kentucky. Whereas John Wilcoxon late of Montgomery County, departed this life intestate leaving an estate both real and personal, and whereas I the said John Letton having intermarried with one of the daughters of John Wilcoxon, I am entitled under the laws to an equal part of portion of the estate; and whereas John H. Nicholls in Kentucky, having also married one of the daughters, has transferred his interest to me in a bill of sale 11 July 1800, which stands of record in the Clerks office of said County, I appoint my brother Caleb Letton of the County of Bourbon and Commonwealth of Kentucky my true and lawful attorney to make a division of said real and personal estate. Signed John Letton, in Bourbon County before John Metcalfe, Thos Jones.

387-388. Caleb Letton recorded 26 March 1801, an award. Whereas John Willcoxon, Senr., died interstate, and Caleb Letton married a daughter of his, and was employed by him as an overseer for four years of his business, and during that time Caleb received from the said John a certain tract of land, the quantity of 20 bushels of wheat, 5000 pounds of tobacco and $40 which said Caleb contents were given him by the said John Wilcoxon Senr. For his securing the business of the said John and certain other persons hereafter named. We Caleb Letton, Erasmus Riggs, Jesse & Wilcoxon Jr. and parties interested do hereby appoint Edward Harding, Benjamin W. Jones, Solomon Holland and Daniel Beall as four referees and have appointed a fifth to proceed to value and make an award. Commissioners came to the opinion that he was entitled to the lands aforesaid, as well as wheat, and money for his services and not chargeable to the estate. That the balance will be equally divided by the number of persons entitled.

389. John L. Summers recorded power of attorney March 1801. I Caleb Letton of Bourbon County, Commonwealth of Kentucky send greeting. Whereas John Wilcoxon late of Montgomery County, departed this life with an estate both real and personal, and Caleb Letton, John Letton and John H. Nicholls (of Mason County) all of Kentucky and all married daughters of John Wilcoxon, appoint Caleb Letton as their attorney to divide estate.

390. Deed between Lewis Bealmar and Samuel Bealmar recorded 26 March 1801, for £12..18, part of tract called *Valentines Garden.* Signed before John L. Summers, J. H. McPherson.

390-391. Christopher Miller recorded 1 April 1801 from John Belt, for £85 deed. Assigns tract called *Resurvey on What You Will*, to second line of *Grandmother's Good Will.* 28 ½ acres. Signed, acknowledged.

391-392. Marsham Waring recorded 2 April 1801 from Bernard O'Neal, for 5 shillings assigns deed of trust for all he owns, as he has applied for benefit of insolvent debts. Wit: Uriah Forrest, Daniel Reintzel.

392-393. Thomas Waring recorded 3 April 1801, from Basil Waring, Eleanor Waring, Jane Beall, Walter Brooke Beall, Anne Waring, Mary Waring, Sarah Waring, Priscilla Waring, and Edward Gantt Waring, for 5 shillings, sells tract called *Younger Brother,* containing 203 acres. Signed before Richard Cramphin, T. Lawrence.

393-394. John Self from Rebecca Self, agreement. They have mutually agreed to live separate and apart, 2 April 1801. Wit. Hezekiah Veatch, Thomas Veatch.

394-395. William Redman, schedule of personal property recorded 4 April 1801.

395. Hanbury Jones recorded 4 April 1801, bill of sale from Leven S. Beall for 55 Spanish Milled dollars, Negro girl Tabitha. Signed before Lawrence O'Neale.

395-397. William Scott recorded 6 April 1801, from Thomas O. Offutt, deed for part of *Brother's Industry.* Charity Offutt released dower.
397. William Fisher recorded 9 April 1801. from Elizabeth Magruder and Elizabeth Lynn, bill of sale for £100, sells Negro man Watt, about 25 years of age.
397. Benjamin Howse recorded 13 April 1801, to Solomon Holland, Sheriff, schedule of personal property, including 3 cyder casks, frying pan, old knives and forks.
398. Archibald Browning recorded 14 April 1801, from Jonathan Browning for 5 shillings. *Resurvey on Long Looked for,* containing 44 acres. Witness Edward Burgess, John Clark.
399-400. Laurence O'Neal recorded 14 April 8101, from Honore Martin, for £40 deed for lots #40 and 41, in town of Williamsburgh, alias Montgomery Courthouse, acknowledgment. Sarah Martin released dower rights.
400. Basil Soper recorded 14 April 1801 from John Belt, deed for £3..1..1, part of *Resurvey on Maple Branch,* containing 13 acres. Signed before John Clarke, Greenberry Howard.
401-402. Erasmus Perry & Sam'l Wheeler recorded 17 April 1801, from Ann H. Harding, bill of sale for £175 sells Negroes Daniel, Fanny and child called Tilghman. However, if I pay before 19 January 1808, then this bill of sale is void. Signed before Eneas Campbell by Ann H. Harding.
402-403. Samuel Riggs recorded 25 April 1801, from Philemon and Joshua Griffith, as executors of Henry Griffith, part of *Tusculum,* and part of *Resurvey on Griffith's Chance,* adjacent to *Linthicum's Chance,* for £425. Signed before Edward Burges, John Clark.
404. Richard Kirk recorded in April 1801 deed from William Kirk for £22 for part of *Lockall,* adjacent to *Willson's Inheritance.* Suzanne, wife of William Kirk released dower.
405-406. Richard Kirk recorded 29 April 1801 from John Cecil, for £22..10 , sells 7 ½ acres of *Locks All*, adjacent to *Willson's Inheritance*, containing 7 ½ acres. Mary wife of John Cecil released dower.
406-407. Nicholas L. Dawson recorded 2 May 1801, from John James, for £750 deed for part of *Mother's Delight* and *Second Resurvey on William and John,* signed by mark. Sarah wife of John James released dower.
407-408. Elizabeth Matthews, aged about 35 years, recorded 1 May 1801, from Nathan Musgrove, manumission. Signed before Thomas Davis, Samuel Brooke.
408-409. Henry Poole recorded 4 May 1801 from William Inman, for £17..10 deed made 4 April, sells part of *Inman's Adventures.* Signed before Greenberry Howard, John Clarke.
409-410. Joseph Nourse recorded 5 May 1801, from Francis Deakins, both of Washington, D.C., part of a tract called *Chevy Chase,* containing 28 acres in two parts. Mentions tracts *Friendship,* and *Fletchall's Purchase,* on 5 ½ acre part. Signed before Joseph Forrest, Patrick Magruder.
410-411. James Anderson recorded 5May 1801 from Allen Bowie and Thomas Cramphin, for £300, one half acre lot no. 5, in town of Williamsburgh, commonly called Montgomery Court House, on south side of West St. & east of 1st St. Ruth Bowie released dower.
411. Jeremiah Watkins recorded 5 May 1801 from Henry Lashare, for £9..1..9 bill of sale for one feather bed and furniture, six pewter plates, one iron pot, Dutch oven, table, one plow, all the wheat now growing on his plantation, and five hogs. Signed before John Clark.
412-413. Leonard Hayes recorded 5 May 1801 from Christopher Miller, for $114 deed for tract of land called *Westport,* for 28 ½ acres. Anne Miller released dower rights.
414-415. Joshua Owen recorded 5 May 1801 from Nathan Pelly and Solomon Pelly for £128..11..5 all of their interest in tract of land called *Wickham's Choice,* which fell to the said Nathan Pelly and Solomon Pelly by the death of their father Calvert Pelly. Signed before J. H. McPherson, John L. Summers. Acknowledgment and Massy wife of Solomon released dower.
415. Brice Letton recorded qualification as deputy sheriff. On 14 May 1801, taking oath before John L. Summers.

415-416. Benjamin Berry, recorded 16 May 1801 from Solomon Holland, Sheriff. Whereas judgment obtained by Aza Beall against Robert B. Beall, tract *Charles and Benjamin,* conveyed by Charles Perry now property of Henry Clark. Signed Solomon Holland before John L. Summers, J.H. McPherson.
417-418. George Riley recorded 18 May 1801 from Nathaniel Beall & Daniel Lee, mortgage. in consideration that the aforesaid George Riley hath this day given his bond with Nathaniel Beall and Daniel Lee to Charles Carroll of Carrollton for £211..17..7 sterling with interest thereon from 17 October 1798, and £13..14..7 ½ Maryland for further consideration of 5 shillings, releases unto the aforesaid George Riley the following tracts, and also the following Negro slaves, to wit, one tract of 80 acres called *Snowden's Manor;* one tract called *Lay Hill,* 250 acres; one tract called *Labyrinth,* 71 acres and one tract called *Clean Shaving,* 97 acres; one tract called *Joseph's Park,* 100 acres, all in Montgomery County. The following Negro slaves: Rachel, Ben and Tom, now the property of Nathaniel Beall and Sarah, Sook, George and Nell, now the property of Daniel Lee, to hold the said land and Negroes. The condition nevertheless, and it is the true intent and meaning of these presents that if the said Nathaniel Beall and Daniel Lee, do well and truly pay the aforesaid Charles Carroll of Carrollton, then this is void. Signed before Thomas Davis, J. H. McPherson. Acknowledgment.
418-420. John Magruder recorded 22 May 1801, made 18th April, from Edward Magruder, deed for 5 shillings, tract called *Addition to Brooke Grove,* on 18th line of tract sold Edward Magruder from John Dorsey, laid out for 300 acres.
420. Basil Soper recorded 22 May 1801, from John Breese, bill of sale for £8..15 two iron grey mares, both about 5 years old. Signed John Brice by mark in the presence of John Clark, Samuel Soper.
421. Upton Beall, certificate and bond as Clerk of Court. Recorded 23 May 1801. Bondsmen, Upton Beall, Leonard Mackall and Charles Perry. Witnesses Lewis Beall, Joseph Mountz, Thomas Perry, Zedekiah Moore.
422-423. Lenox Martin, Thomas Moreton, Levi Hayes, Jesse Hayes, Vachel Hall, William Hilton and George Norris recorded deed 26 May 1801 from Barton Harris and Sarah Harris, in consideration of the rent money of 5 shillings, deed in trust for the meeting house already built, called Bethel Chapel of Methodist Episcopal Church. A part of tract called *Mount Zion.* On the north side of the main road, containing 8/10 of an acre. Signed before Aeneas Campbell, Laurence O'Neale.
423-425. Honore Martin recorded 26 May 1801, from Simon Nicholls & wife, deed. Whereas Charles Beckwith late of Montgomery County, died intestate seized of property, including *Hills and Dales,* on or about the month of April 1799, and the property descended to his children. Whereas Barbara, one of the children was married to a certain Simon Nicholls of Monongahela County, Virginia, and the said Simon and Barbara his wife, sell their interest for $500 unto Honore Martin. Signed before John Simpkins, Jesse Tomlinson. John Simpson and Jesse Tomlinson are justices of the peace in Allegany County.
425-426. Caleb Darby recorded 28 May 1801 from William Veirs, Senior, John Balmear, and John Veirs of Daniel, all of Montgomery County, for £33, deed for tract called *Resurvey on Noneaten,* adjacent to tract *Grandmother's Delight,* and tract conveyed to John Bealmear called *String About,* signed by three parties. Mary wife of John Bealmear, and Catharine wife of John Veirs released dower rights.
426-428. William Veirs recorded 28 May 1801 from John Viers of Dan'l & John Bealmear, deed for part of *Resurvey on Noneaten,* adjacent to *String About,* signed before Laurence O'Neale, Thos B. Beall. Dower releases same as above deed.
428-429. Elijah Veirs record ed 28 May 1801 from William Veirs and John Balmear, and John Veirs of Daniel, for £30 deed for part of *Resurvey on Non Eaten,* 17 1/4 acres. Same dower as above, plus Mary wife of William Veirs released dower.
429-431. Henry Hardy, turner, recorded 2 June 1801, made 3 March from Thomas O. Offutt of Montgomery County, shoemaker sells part of *Brothers Industry,* to the 7th line of David Clagetts part, adjacent to *Offutt's Pasture,* now laid out for 151 3/4 acres.

431-433. Thomas Buxton recorded 6 June 1801 from John Buxton and William Buxton, deed for 5 shillings, *Resurvey on Harrison's Delight,* for 16 acres. Sarah wife of William Buxton relinquished dower rights.
433. Elizabeth Williams from Martha Clagett, deed of gift recorded 8 June 1801, for affection she bears to her daughter Elizabeth Clagett who married Edward O. Williams, gives Negro man, James about 32 years old. Signed Martha Clagett, 10 May 1801 before Honore Martin, Sally Martin.
434-435. Joseph N. Chiswell recorded 1801 from Henry Culver Pierce, deed for all his right to tract, *Fortune.* Elizabeth Pierce released dower.
435-437. Thomas Drane Sr. recorded deposition 12 June 1801. To Mr. Kinsey Gittings son of Kinsey Gittings and administrator of Kinsey Gettings. Notice to take deposition in Georgetown at Robert Peter Sr., in May touching his knowledge of the transaction on which suit was brought in Montgomery County but now removed to the general court. Washington Drane swore before Patrick Magruder that the notice to appear was delivered.
The deposition of Robert Peter aged 75 years, deposeth that the said Kinsey Gittings in the year 1768 during his life time had considerable dealings with this deponent then agent of John Glassford at his Rock Creek Store, and at the time of the death of the said Gittings he was considerable indebted to the said store, and after the death of said Gittings; Rachel the widow of said Gittings gave her bond for what she and William Douglass (?) The administrator said was the amount of the personal estate of said Gittings, or perhaps something over, and this deponent being the more confined in this deposition from the circumstance of having been applied to afterwards by Rachael the widow of William Douglas aforesaid or both to make a discount from the bond aforesaid for the amount of a judgment which a certain Beall had obtained for a sum to the best of this deponents knowledge of about £9 against the said Gittings or the estate aforesaid. Further, Rachel Gittings widow of Kinsey Gittings, on the 26 April 1768 did pass her bond to the af'said John Glassford for 2000 lbs. Heavy crop tobacco at Rock Creek ware house, and £175 was for so much of the debt so due and owing as aforesaid from Kinsey Gittings Senior to the said John Glassford.. William Douglas the administrator of Kinsey Gittings signed the bond as witness Said Rachel Gittings in about four or five years afterward paid the whole of the tobacco and money for which the bond was given and the interest thereon and the bond was delivered up to her as paid off and discharged. Taken before Daniel Reintzel
437-438. Richard Shekels recorded 17 June 1801, from Samuel Williams, bill of sale for $100. Sells bay gelding about 8 years old. Signed before Wm Smith.
438. Kenelm Gray qualification as Deputy Clerk 18 June 1801. Before J. H. McPherson.
438-439. Hugh Riley recorded 20 June 1801 from Edward Owen & Rachel, his wife, deed for receipt of a certain claim Hugh Riley had on account of being an heir of Archibald Beall, deceased, assigns all that parcel called *Trial,* containing 63 acres.
440-441. James Redman recorded 2 July 1801, from Solomon Holland, for $327.50 deed for tract, *Beautiful Meadow.* Signed before John L. Summers, Benjamin Gaither. Margaret wife of Solomon Holland released dower rights.
441-442. Solomon Holland recorded 3 July 1801, from Benjamin White Jones, sheriff, deed made 1 July 1801. Whereas a judgment was obtained by Hardage Lane exec. of Ninian Beall against Alexander Catlett, for tract called *Pleasant Fields.* 32 3/4 acres was taken for payment and exposed to public sale for $327.50. Signed before John L. Summers, Benjamin Gaither.
442-444. Solomon Holland recorded 3 July 1801 from James Redman, mortgage made 1 July for £273..1..10, assigns 32 3/4 acres of *Pleasant Fields.* Nevertheless if James Redman pays the above sum by 30 November next, sale is void. Jane Redman releases dower rights.
444-445. Patrick Lyddane recorded bill of sale 4 July 1801. I James Langton Junr., for £10 bed and furniture belonging thereto. Provided always that if paid with interest from 29 June 1799, sale is void, and the further sum of 5 shillings 4 pence at suit for which Samuel Busey obtained a judgement against me, the said Patrick Lyddane superseded forms. Signed before J. H. McPherson.

445-446. James Page recorded 15 July 1801, from Francis Page, bill of sale for £75 sells dark bay mare, one bright bay mare, one cow and calf, one feather bed, 15 head of hogs, also crop on the ground. Signed before John L. Summers.

446-447. Armstead Long recorded list of Negro slaves 15 July 1801, a citizen of Virginia being possessed of an estate in inheritance, as follows, males Billy 30 years of age; Billy 23 years; Perremus 16, Paris 1 year 6 months, Daniel 34; Prince 36, Henry 9 and George 6 and females Rose 45, Milly 6, Esther 4, Hetty 26, Jenny 26, Nancy 5, Esther 3, Alice 1 month and Lucy 1 year 6 months. Signed 31 May 1801.

447-448. Benjamin White recorded 21 July 1801 from Samuel Hepburn of Prince George's County, for £375 deed made 28 April, part of *Resurvey on Hanover,* 100 acres. Signed before Thomas Bowie, Francis Magruder. Receipt, acknowledgment. Jane Hepburn released dower.

449-450. Abednego Baker recorded 21 July 1801 made 23 March from William Ballenger of Frederick County, for £379..18, of which William Ballenger acknowledged but £50 for the land, the said Abednego Baker allowed to Samuel Poole for his improvement, on tract *Henry and Elizabeth Enlarged,* the greater part in Montgomery County, beginning at end of 4th line of Peter Burges part of said land. Containing 167 acres. Signed William Ballenger before Belt Brashears, Sam'l Thomas. Acknowledgment. Lydia Ballinger released dower rights.

450-451. John Fleming recorded 23 July 1801 from Rebecca Russell of the City of Baltimore, relict of Thomas Russell, for $110, released her rights of dower, which she may have to several tracts in Montgomery County, known by names of *Beals Addition, Resurvey on Content.* Signed by Rebecca Russell, acknowledged before Wm Russell, Rd H. Moale, justices of the peace of Baltimore County.

451-453. Stephen Basford recorded 23 July 1801 from Martha Howard, surviving executor of Joseph Howard, who in 1782 sold to Francis White of Anne Arundel County, part of *Henry and Elizabeth Enlarged,* and empowered Benjamin Howard, executor to convey same. For a valuable consideration. Signed Martha Howard, before Edward Hall, and Bruce Worthington of Anne Arundel County.

453-454. Robert Peter recorded 24 July 1801 from Francis Deakins, deed recorded 24 July 1801. Whereas William Deakins Jr. Deceased, did in his lifetime on14 August 1782, pass his bond to Charles Hungerford to convey 181 3/4 acres of a tract called *Friendship,* for payment of £232, which he did pay, and Charles Hungerford did on 8 April 1795 assigns to Robert Peter for value received the bond and assignment; therefore this indenture made between Francis Deakins, executor and devisee of the aforesaid William Deakins, deceased, conveys to Robert Peter, tract called *Friendship.* Signed before John L. Summers, J. H. McPherson. Acknowledgment.

455-456. William Bennett recorded 27 July 1801, between Vachel Hall for £7..10, part of tract called *Resurvey on Jeremiah's Park,* lot #1, on north side of main road containing 2 acres of land. Signed and acknowledged before Greenberry Howard, John Clark. Margaret wife of Vachel Hall released dower rights.

456. Negro Henny recorded receipt 1st August 1801. Received of Mr. Edward Owen £3 , 6 pence. it being the amount of sold woman by the name of Henny formerly the property of Robert Beall of James, taken and sold for officers fees on the 18th July, at which time she said Henny became the highest bidder for the above sum. Benjamin W. Jones, late sheriff.

456. Basil Dyson recorded 3 August 1801, from Hezekiah Veirs, bill of sale for a Negro boy named Bill Chiclum, in consideration of security in a bond. If the said Hezekiah Veirs satisfy the judgment then this bill of sale is void.

457-458. Samuel Browning recorded 3 August 1801 from Jonathan Browning Sr for $1. Tract called *Resurvey on Maple Branch,* containing 40 ½ acres. Signed before Edward Burgess Jr., John Clark. Elizabeth Browning wife of Jonathan Browning released dower rights.

458-459. William Willcoxon recorded 3 August 1801, from Richard Purdy, bill of sale for 2000 pounds merchantable crop tobacco, sells 2 cows and calves, one bay mare, one black gelding, bed and sheet and blanket, 2 iron pots, 10 bushels of wheat, 10 bushels of rye, 400 pounds tobacco in bulk, a crop of corn Signed Richard Purdy by mark before Wm Smith.

459-461. Thomas Nicholls of Simon recorded 4 August 1801 from Benj. W. Jones, late sheriff. Whereas a judgment obtained against John Hayman Nicholls, and in pursuance of a writ of fieri fascias by Thomas Nicholls against him took title to his claim and interest in tract called *Prevention,* 331 acres, and part of *Hermitage,* 274 ½ acres, and *Exeter,* 220 acres, he was best bidder for $20.

461-462. Charles Miles recorded 6 August 1801, from Philemon Griffith and Joshua Griffith, executor of will of Henry Griffith, deed for part of *Cow Pasture,* for £187..7, adjacent to Amon Rigg's part. Signed before Thomas Davis, Edward Burgess.

462-463. Charles W. Davis of Fauquier County recorded 11 August 1801 from Basil Brooke, for £50 tract called *Fair Hill,* standing on east side of road leading from Mouth of Monocacy to Baltimore, containing 10 acres. Mary Brooke released dower. Signed before Richard Green, Thomas Davis.

463-466. William Inman of Frederick County, recorded 11 August 1801, from Edward Inman of Berkeley County, Virginia, for £25, deed made 27 March for tract called *Inmans Adventure,* beginning at 5th line of a tract called *Solomon's Roguery,* originally granted 2 March 1774 to George Cook for 495 acres, adjacent to tract *Henry and Elizabeth Enlarged,* to 15th line of *Resolution.* Signed by mark Edward Inman before Wm Van Lear and James Davis, two Justices of the Peace of Washington County, Maryland. Elizabeth wife of Edward Inman released dower rights. O. H. Williams, clerk of Washington County attested to signatures.

466-467. William Wood recorded 11 August 1801 from William Inman, deed made 9 April 1801, for £50, sells part of *Inman's Adventure,* surveyed 10 May 1788, for William Inman, his father, for 72 acres, and lately granted to him by same William Inman. Signed before John Schley, Jno Baltzell, Justices of the Peace of Frederick County. Attested to by William Ritchie clerk of Frederick County Court.

467. Robert Ferguson of Charles County, recorded 12 August 1801 from Benjamin Jones, late sheriff of Montgomery County. Whereas a judgment obtained by James Gordon, surviving partner of John Glassford & Company, against Elias Hardy and others, the heirs of Samuel Hardy, deceased, by writ of fieri fascias, a parcel of land in 1799, and exposed to public sale for 100 pounds of crop tobacco. Tract called *Grandmother's Good Will,* for 67 acres. Receipt, acknowledgment.

469. Aquilla Wathen recorded 14 August 1801, from Ignatius Wathen, bill of sale for the good will, love and affection which I do bear unto my son, and for $2. Grant Negro slaves, namely Ruth 30 years, Esther about 20; Anthony about 3, Matilda about 3, and Jesse about14 years of age. Signed by mark before Laurence O'Neale, Leonard Combs by mark, Gabriel Wathen.

469-470. Joseph Wathan recorded 14 August 1801, from Ignatius Wathen, bill of sale in consideration of the good will, love and affection which I do bear unto my son, and for $2, grant and sell the following Negro slaves, Dick about 20, Dark about 20, Terry about 22, Nell about 25, Charles about 10 years of age. Signed by mark before Laurence O'Neale, Leonard Combs by mark, Gabriel Wathen.

470-472. Honore Martin, merchant, recorded 15 August 1801, from James Hodges, of Prince George's County, deed made 8 June 1801 for £300, sells tract called *Wickham's Good Will,* for 247 acres. James Hodges did heretofore convey a part to Benjamin Hodges, which he hath since sold to Honore Martin. Signed before Robert Bowie, Thomas Bowie of Prince George's County, Justices of the Peace. Martha wife of James Hodges, released dower rights.

472-473. Richard Beall recorded 17 August 1801, made 11 April, from Barton Harris for £10..17, tract adjacent to *Beall's Good Will,* called *Mount Zion.* Containing 3 5/8 acres. Sarah Harris released dower rights. Signed before Aeneas Campbell, Laurence O'Neale.

473-474. Solomon Holland recorded 17 August 1801 to State of Maryland, collectors bond for £5990. Signed Solomon Holland, Benjamin W. Jones, Edward Owen.

474-475. Barton Harris recorded 17th August 1801, from Richard Beall, deed for £21..5 sells tract *Bealls Good Will,* containing 4 1/4 acres. Signed before Aneas Campbell, Greenbury Howard. Anne wife of Richard Beall, examined apart released dower rights.

476-476 ½ John O'Neale recorded 17 August 1801 from Benjamin W. Jones, sheriff. Whereas a judgment obtained by Isaiah Boone against John Ball, and a writ of fieri fascias for use of William Lodge was issued for tract *I Will Not, Yet I will,* for 118 acres, and *Scrub Hill,* for 15 acres, the property of John Ball and his wife, for £120. Signed before John L. Summers, J. H. McPherson.

476 ½ -478. Joseph N. Chiswell recorded 21 August 1801, from Samuel Hepburn of Prince George's County, deed made 28 April, for £521..5 sells *Resurvey on Hanover,* adjacent to land formerly conveyed to Christian Hempstone, 174 7/8 acres. Signed before Thomas Bowie, Frances Magruder, Jane Hepburn released dower before J.P.'s Prince George's County..

478-480. The President and Directors of the Bank of Columbia recorded mortgage 18 August 1801, made 6 May from William Thornton of the city of Washington, for $7,550, the repayment with interest by William Thornton and Samuel Blodget, mortgages property herein. Parcel now in his tenure in Montgomery County, on east and west sides of road leading from Georgetown to Frederick Town, formerly occupied by Bernard O'Neale, which William Thornton purchased from John Hoskenstone, of about 500 acres. It is agreed that $7550 therein mentioned due is an accommodation granted Thornton by the bank on sundry notes, viz; $600, 9 May in favor of Mrs. Ann Brodraw, and endorsed by her and Leonard Harbough, and also on the 16 May, for $1950 to the same parties; and another for $5000 drawn in favor of John Weems on 16 May and endorsed by John Weems and Nicholas Voss, all of which will become due within 60 days. Signed William Thornton.

480. Benjamin Cracroft recorded 24 August 1801, from Washington Owen, bond of conveyance for £1000, to convey tract which said Washington Owens has from his father Robert Owens and part thereof from his late brother, which came to him at his death. 150 acres. Signed before Kenelm Gray, Joseph Mounts.

481. Joseph Mountz and Nathan Suter, qualification as Deputy Clerks recorded 24 August 1801.

481-483. John Veirs recorded 26 August, 1801, from Nathan Veirs, deed for £432..5, sells tract called *Susannah,* adjacent to *John's Delight,* to *Mother's Delight,* to *Grandmother's Delight,* containing 108 1/16 acres. Signed Nathan Viers before Ans Campbell, Lawrence O'Neale. Dorcas wife of Nathan Viers released dower rights.

483-485. Gerard Brooke recorded 27 August 1801, made 4 August between James Brooke for £645, part of *Brooke Grove,* adjacent to *Charles and Benjamin,* running on the line of division between James Brooke and William H. Dorsey. 107 acres. Signed James Brooke before Richard Green, Thomas Davis, Hester Brooke, released dower rights.

485-486. David Clagett from Henry Hardy, deed recorded 27 August 1801, for £254, for *Brother's Industry,* adjacent to *Outlett,* to *Offut's Pasture,* containing 153 ½ acres. Signed Henry Hardy before John L. Summers, J.H. McPherson. Anne Hardy released dower rights.

486-488. John Laird, recorded 29 August 1801, deed from the Sheriff, made the same date. Whereas William Digges, in suit against Robert Beall of James obtained a fieri fascias, the Sheriff Benjamin White Jones sells the parcel *Robert's Choice,* containing 9 acres and 96 perches. Signed before J. H. McPherson, Elemelech Swearingen.

488. Mesheck Browning recorded 1 September 1801, a bill of sale for a 7 year old gray mare and other property, but if Nathan Bennett pay the sum of £27..10..6, then sale is to be void. Signed by Nathan Bennett before Greenberry Howard.

489. Kenelm Gray recorded articles of agreement, which were made between John Day with William T. Beall. Said Day to occupy house and pay ground rents.

489-492. Caleb Bentley recorded 2 September 1801 between David Newlon for 5 shillings and to better secure payment of a note of $1173, made 10 August 1800, mortgages tract, a part of *Addition to Brooke Grove,* below the mill dam. Signed before Richard Green, Thomas Davis.

492-494. Zachariah Offutt recorded 6 September 1801, made 7 August from Thomas Plater, for £2962, sells two tracts, parts of *Zoar,* and *Resurvey on Younger Brother,* beginning at tract called *The Lost Hatchett,* also the beginning of *Belt's Desire,* metes and bounds given, containing 287 acres, as in a deed from Edward Burgess to Thomas Plater, and adjoining 71 1/4 acres of tract. Signed before Wm Smith, Henry Bowles. Acknowledgment, and Martha Plater wife of Thomas Plater released dower.

494. Thomas B. Evans recorded list of Negroes, late of Berkeley County, Virginia now of Washington, D.C., seized in his own right by inheritance, to work on an estate of Montgomery County, slaves were acquired to marriage with Eliza Cooke of Berkeley County. Lydia 38, Lear 21, Daniel 17, Bill 10, London 8, Nancy 4, Amy 4, Joseph 2, Ben 3 and Richard 1; and Negroes George 24 and Davy 22, acquired by deed of gift from Walter Evans. Signed 7 September 1801.

495-497. Thomas Beall of George recorded September 1801, deed from James Lackland following a chancery court degree, that trustee should sell all the interest and claims of a certain William Smith, Samuel William Sr., Lenox Martin, Hardage Lane and Thomas Martin, reference to decree in case of 11 April 1801. After said James Lackland followed the decree in chancery, Thomas Beall of George purchased the land, a part of tract called *Seneca Ford, Addition to Seneca Ford,* and *Resurvey on part of Thomas's Discovery, Middle Plantation,* which were conveyed to the aforesaid William Smith and Samuel Williams and Thomas Beall son of George as tenants in common by Bernard O'Neale and William Deakins Junr., 17 June 1796, and also the interests of the aforementioned William Smith, Samuel Williams, Lenox Martin, Hardage Lane and Thomas Moreton and all of them.. James Lackland signed and acknowledged deed. Octavia Smith wife of William Smith released dower rights. Entered along side of margin: Elizabeth Williams wife of Samuel Williams released her dower rights to the tracts known as *Seneca Mills.*

497. Edward Iglehart recorded 7 September 1801 from Thomas Barthelow for $40. sells crop of corn and tobacco. Signed before Edward Burgess, Junr.

498. Joseph Forest recorded 7 September 1801, bill of sale from Samuel Etchison, for rent due said Joseph Forrest, sells gray mare, etc. Signed by mark before John Aldridge, Wm Smith.

498-499. Joseph Forrest recorded list of Negroes, 7 September 1801. Negro Selena 20 and her female child of 15 months; Nanny 40 years old and Peter 12 years old, who were property of Joseph Forrest while he resided in Georgetown, except for Peter, who is the property of Dulaney Forrest the son of Joseph Forrest. Negro Milly about 16 years acquired by gift from Mrs. Penelope French and Benjamin Dulaney to Eliza Forrest wife to Joseph Forrest. Signed Joseph Forrest.

499-500. Garrah Davis of Columbia Co., Georgia, records bill of sale from William Ogle of Montgomery County for £280, sells one Negro man, George, 20 years of age, one bay horse and one brown horse, feather bed and furniture. Signed 31 August 1801 before John L. Summers.

500-501. Cyrus Bowen recorded 11 September 1801, from John Beale Magruder, for £45, deed for part of tract *Good Spring,* adjacent to *Charles and Benjamin,* and *Batchelor's Forest,* for 45 ½ acres. Signed before Elemelech Swearingen, J.H. McPherson.

501-502. James M. Lingan of Washington, District of Columbia, recorded 17 September 1801, from Thomas Plater for 10 shillings, a 23 acre tract. Signed before Henry Brookes, Wm Smith. Martha Plater released dower.

502-504. Jacob Kinley and William Kinley recorded 21 September 1801, from William Ballenger, of Frederick County, deed. made 23 March, for £131..10, for part of *Henry and Elizabeth,* adjacent to *Quaker's Bite, None Such,* and *Hall's Resurvey,* for 121 acres. Lydia Ballinger released dower rights.

504. Wm & Joseph Burns from Adam Ramsour, for £45, bill of sale. for a Negro woman, Chane with a child at her breast of about 10 months, to serve for the term of 4 years, 3 months, then she is to become the property of Isaac Gardner, but if she has any children during the term of service, they are to belong to the said William and Joseph Burns, as well as the child at her breast. Signed before Greenberry Howard.

THE END of LIBER I

Montgomery County Liber K, Land Record Abstracts

1-2. Thomas Morton recorded 23 September 1801, from Barton Harris, deed made 11 April 1801, for £61..13 sells tract, formerly called *White Oak Swamp Enlarged,* and *The Dutchman's Disappointment,* now called *Mount Zion,* metes and bounds given, to Thomas Morton's mill dam, crossing the cabin branch, containing 24 1/4 acres. Signed Barton Harris before Laurence O'neale, Ans. Campbell. Receipt. Acknowledgment, and Sarah wife of Barton Harris released dower rights.
2-3. Thomas Plater recorded 25 September 1801, from Charles Gassaway, deed made 19 September 1801 for £271..5 specie, 54 ½ acres *Pleasant Hills.* Signed before Wm Smith, Jas Lackland. Receipt. Ruth Gassaway released dower rights.
4-5. Richard Lowe Hall recorded 28 September 1801, from Robert Ferguson of Charles County, deed for tract he sold to Kinsey Hardy, called *Grandmothers Good Will,* conveyed to Benjamin W. Jones, sheriff. Signed by Robert Ferguson before James Freeman, Sam Chapman.
5-6. Rezin Spates and Thomas Hickman recorded 28 September 1801, from John Scrivener, bill of sale for one Negro girl, Letha, purchased by Scrivener from Martin Fisher. Sale is nevertheless void if mortgage paid.
6-8. Solomon Pelly recorded 1 October 1801 from William Pelly, deed as directed by Chancellor, from Chancery Court June Term 1801. Tract, *Wickham's Choice.* Indenture made 15 August 1801 for £100 for 150 acres.
8-9. Jane Russell recorded 3 October 1801, from James Croke, bill of sale for £35 for one sorrel mare, one colt, 2 beds and furniture. Signed by mark, before Wm Smith.
9-11. Caleb Dorsey recorded 5 October 1801, from Charles Gassaway & Ruth, his wife, for 5 shillings, deed for tract which was heretofore conveyed by Charles & Ruth Gassaway, Alexander and Susanna Catlett, Hardage and Rachel Lane, Zachariah and Eleanor Offutt, John and Mary Watkins Jr., Benjamin and Margaret Edwards and Charles and Tabitha Beall on 5 August 1777, recorded in Liber A:31-34, 253 acres part of *Vienna,* conveyed to Gassaway by Hezekiah Beall.
11-12. Joseph Waters recorded 6 October 1801 from William Shanks, deed. Whereas Shanks applied for relief as an insolvent debtor for 5 shillings assigns to Joseph Waters as trustee all of his property.
12-13. William Magrath and Joseph West recorded 6 October 1801 from Alice Casey, they having become securities for me in a replevin bond, assigns a Negro woman Chloe and her child, provided nevertheless that if sum is repaid, this bill of sale is void. Signed by mark before J. H. McPherson.
13-14. Zadock Browning recorded 7 October 1801 from Jonathan Browning, Senr., deed for part of *Resurvey on Maple Branch,* 55 acres. Signed by mark. Elizabeth Browning released dower rights.
14-15. Jesse Browning recorded 7 October 1801, from George Harris, deed made 25 May for $100 sells one lot of land in Clarksburg. Signed by mark before Greenberry Howard and John Clarke.
15-17. Jonathan Browning Junr., recorded 7 October 1801 from Jonathan Browning, Senr., deed made 14 April or £1..2..6 confirms tract, a part of *Resurvey on Maple Grove.* Signed by mark before Edward Burgess Jr., John Clarke. Elizabeth Browning released dower rights.
17-18. Nathan Browning, Jesse, Zadock & Meshach Browning recorded 7 October 1801 from Jonathan Browning, Senior, deed for £50 sells and assigns on lot of land in Clarksburgh, a part of lot #1. Signed by mark before same witnesses. Elizabeth Browning released dower rights.
18-19. Leonard Hayes recorded 7 October 1801, from Vachel Hall, deed made 18 July for £4..10 for part of *Resurvey on Jeremiah's Park,* formerly conveyed to William Barnes, for 2 acres. Signed before Greenberry Howard and John Clark. Acknowledgment. Margaret Hall, wife of Vachel Hall, released dower rights.
20-21. John B. Dyson recorded 9 October 1801 from Nathan Veirs and Dorcas his wife, deed for £58..10, for part of *Resurvey on NonEaten,* also *Thomas Discovery,* which land formerly descended from Samuel

Dyson, late of Montgomery County to his daughter Dorcas, now wife of Nathan Veirs. Signed before Aeneas Campbell, Laurence O'Neale. Dorcas Veirs released dower rights.

21-22. John B Dyson recorded 9 October 1801 from Samuel Dyson, deed for part of *Thomas Discovery,* which he inherited from his father Samuel Dyson, which he assigns to John Baptist Dyson. Signed before Eneas Campbell and Laurence O'Neale.

22-24. Zadock Summers from Elemelech Swearingen, deed for parcel willed to William D. Swearingen by the will of Thomas Swearingen deceased, and conveyed to Elemelech 4 April 1796, part of *Trouble Enough,* containing 78 ½ acres. Signed before John L. Summers, J. H. McPherson. Susannah Swearingen, wife of Elemelech released dower rights.

24-27 Talbott Allnutt recorded deed 12 October 1801, from George Coonce & Sarah Coonce, his wife. In Chancery June term 1801, Deed ordered to be made by the authority of the court, to sell their undivided one fifth part of tract containing 171 acres, or about 35 acres, devised by will of James Allnutt deceased, to Sarah aforesaid, his daughter. Deed made by George Coonce and Sarah his wife of Hampstead County, Virginia, for £20 assigns parcel to Talbott Allnutt.

27-28. Henry Ayton, Thomas Rawlings, & John Rawlings recorded 16 October 1801, as tenants in common, from Benjamin Ray Senior, bill of sale for Negroes Harry, Peter, Nace, Sam, Nelson (called Norman), Jerry, Jude wife of Harry, Kate wife of Peter, Darby, Cassandra, Rose and Beck; wagon and team of five horses and all furniture, mortgaged. Sale is void if paid by date. Signed before Jeremiah Townley Chase.

28-30. John Benson recorded deed 17 Oct. 1801 from Samuel Hepburn, for *Resurvey on Hanover,* whereon Samuel Plummer now lives, adjacent to tract in possession of said John Benson, containing 100 acres. Signed before Gabriel Peterson VanHorn, and Francis Magruder, Justices for Prince George's County. Jane Hepburn, wife of Samuel released dower rights.

30-31. Henry Cowley recorded 19 October 1801, from Archibald Cecil and John Cecil, for £18..5, tract *Squirrel Trap,* Priscilla wife of Archibald Cecil and Mary wife of John Cecil released dower rights.

31-32. John Poole Junr. from Thomas Higdon & Rachel Higdon, his wife, of Nelson County, Kentucky, signed power of attorney 4 Sept. 1801, and attested to on 10 Oct. 1801, by Leonard P. Higdon witnessing that he saw Thomas and Rachel Higdon sign the power of attorney.

33-34. Joseph Newton Chiswell recorded 22 October 1801 from Thomas Higdon and Rachel, his wife, of Nelson County, Kentucky, deed made by John Poole Jr., for one undivided fourth part of tract *Fortune,* descended to them from Rachel's brother, John Baptist Pierce, and also dower right of Elizabeth Pierce.

34-35. John Hoyle recorded mortgage 29 October 1801, from Leonard Hoyle, for £350, several tracts, *Rock and Timber,* 10 3/4 acres; *Luck's All,* 23 acres; *Tryal,* 12 1/4 acres, and tract *Three Angles,* provided nevertheless that if sum paid, sale is void.

36. Enoch Beall recorded 30 October 1801, from Samuel Beall, bill of sale for 7 shillings, for one Negro girl, 5 years old called Milly. Signed before Elemelech Swearingen.

36-37. Anna Beall recorded 30 October 1801, from Samuel Beall, bill of sale for 7 shillings for one Negro women, for term of 12 years hereof, Ellen, age 22 years, she and her increase, they are to be manumitted when they reach the age of 25 years. Signed before Elemelech Swearingen.

37-38. Elijah Beall recorded 30 October 1801, from Samuel Beall, bill of sale for 7 shillings, for one Negro girl, 5 years old called Airy. Signed before Elemelech Swearingen.

39-40. John Fletchall from Jacob Stires, deed for £35..15, on *Resurvey on Brandy,* conveyed to Rezin Spates by John and Elizabeth Scrivener, said Spates conveyed to Basil Beckwith, for 1 6/10 acres. Margaret wife of Jacob Stires released dower rights.

40-42. John Baker Sr., recorded 31 October 1801, from John Snowden, of Anne Arundel County, lease on land now in his possession for 19 years, to pay yearly rent of 3000 pounds of tobacco.

42-44. Stephen Adams recorded 2 November 1801, from George Riley, deed for £150. Lot #28 in town of Williamsburgh, adjoining lot #27 the property of William J. Beall. Signed before John L. Summers, J.H. McPherson. Sarah Riley released dower rights.

44. Anthony Baston and William Stabler, to State of Maryland, recognizance for £30, for support of a male bastard child of which Dinah Williams was delivered the middle of May last, of which she accused Anthony Baston of being the father. 16 March 1801.
44-46. Nathan Musgrove recorded 3 November 1801, from Thomas Blackwood of Shenandoah Co., Va., and Mary his wife, daughter of the late William Selby, deceased, deed made 27 October, for £188..10, tract known as *Snowden's Mill Seat,* part of the land which William Selby died possessed. Signed before Thomas Davis, Edward Burgess, Junr.
46-48. Jesse Willcoxon recorded deed 3 Nov. 1801, from Thomas Clagett Willcoxon of Prince George's County, for 100 acres, part of *Drane's Purchase*. Verlinda Wilcoxon released dower.
49. Elizabeth Luckett recorded 3 November 1800, from Eleanor Hough, release of dower. Whereas William Hough acknowledged sale to Elizabeth and Otho Luckett, on *Resurvey on Discord,* she appears 8 October 1801 before Lawrence O'Neale and Thos B. Beall.
49-50. Entry begun on page 49, for Negro Sam, and then lined through. Negro Sam recorded 3 November 1801, from William Norris, of George, manumission for boy aged about 5 or 6 years, to be free at age 30, if he is faithful. Witnesses: Greenberry Howard, James Lackland.
50-51. Henry Lashear recorded 4 November 1801, from John Mauxley, of Anne Arundel County, lease for 130 acres of *Ambush.*
51-52. John Sheets recorded 4 November 1801, from John Mauxley, lease for tract called *Pembroke.*
52. Singleton Ricketts recorded 5 November 1801, from Drusilla Ricketts, bill of sale for Negro woman Luce, boy Charles, boy Abram, six chairs, etc.
53-55. Joshua Owen recorded 5 November 1801, from Solomon Pelly, deed. Whereas Calvert Pelly died seized of 50 acres, and William Pelly one of the sons conveyed to Solomon Pelly his interest in tract, sells same for £60. Mercy wife of Solomon released dower right.
55-57. Joshua Owen recorded 5 November 1801 deed from James Pelly of Brooke County, Virginia. He sells for £60, his claim on real estate of Calvert Pelly, his father. Receipt and acknowledgment.
57-59. John Cecil and Benjamin Cecil recorded 6 November 1801 from Joshua Cecil of Frederick County for £199..13, part of *Resurvey on Wild Cat Spring,* 45 1/8 acres. Mary wife of Joshua Cecil released dower.
59-60. Obed Swearingen recorded 8 November 1801, from Leonard P. Higdon of Nelson Co., Ky., for £102..10 bill of sale for one Negro boy named Daniel and one girl named Henny. Signed before J. F. Beall, Thos H. Wilcoxon.
60-62. John Gardner, joiner, recorded deed 14 November 1801, from William Duncan, of the city of Baltimore, shoemaker, for £55, lot #7 in Clarksburgh. Martha Duncan released dower rights.
62-63. John L. Summers recorded 14 November 1801, from Hezekiah Veirs, bill of sale for Negroes Hannah aged 30 years, and Grace aged 7 years. Signed before J. H. McPherson.
63-65. Thomas Beall of George of the Territory of District of Columbia recorded 16 November 1801, from Robert Dorsey of Baltimore, for £1241..12 deed for part of *Addition to Brooke Grove,* and part of *Fair Hill,* from Ann Dorsey's allotment of her part of her deceased grandfather's land, the land of James Brooke, as filed in Chancery Court. M&B for 359 acres.
65. Benjamin Talbutt recorded 26 November 1801, from John L. Summers, release of all his interest in Negro "Sal," sold by Hezekiah Veirs.
65-66. Robert W. Fleming recorded 27 November 1801, from Francis Jarboe, bill of sale for $60 for one bay mare 3 years old. Signed before John L. Summers
66. Thomas B. Evans, late of Virginia, now of the District of Columbia, recorded 30 November 1801, a list of Negroes brought into the state: Negro boy James, one year old son of Negro Leithy, and property of the subscriber.
66-68. George Frances Winrod recorded 1 December 1801, from John Gardner, deed for lot #7 in Clarksburgh. Part of tract called *Moneysworth.* Cassandra Gardner released dower rights.

68-69. Richard Gott recorded 3 December 1801 from Robert Peter, for £816 release of interest in mortgage of Negroes: Will, Jerry, Sarah, Eve, Hagar, Peter, and Harry mortgage recorded previously.
69-71. John Duvall recorded 2 December 1801, from Thomas Orme for £196.. 17, tracts called *Hickory Ridge,* and *Richardson's Range.* 175 acres. Ack. Before John L. Summers, J. H. McPherson
71-72. Nathan Cooke recorded 5 December 1801, from Richard Waters for £50, deed for land on Luke Cabin Branch, containing 14 acres. Margaret wife of Richard Waters released dower right.
72-74. Basil Darby recorded 5 December 1801, from Richard Thomas, lease for 184 acres, part of *Thomas Discovery Fortified.* Tract begins near an Ivy Bank of Seneca Creek. To fence the tract, and maintain for term of 18 years. Signed by both before Rich'd Green, J. F. Beall.
74-75. Negro Clarissa, aged 18 years, and Richard aged 1 year 24 Feb. next, from Israel Leeke, manumission recorded, Clarissa to be free in 1 January 1803, and Richard to be free at age 21 years.
75-77. Thomas Rhodes of Prince George's County, recorded 9 December 1801, from Basil Lucas of Harrison Co., Virginia, for $1187. Tract called *Hard Struggle,* at end of 3d line of *Friendship Enlarged,* containing 111 3/4 acres. Signed before Wm Smith, Lawrence O'Neale.
77-79. Thomas West recorded deed 9 December 1801 from Lawrence O'Neale, for £80 tract called the *Race Ground,* beginning at tract, *Two Brothers.* 32 acres. Ack before John L. Summers, J.H. McPherson.
79-81. John Benson recorded deed 9 Dec. 1801, from Nathan Harding of Brooke Co, Va., for £364..10 tract called *Forest,* adjacent to *Two Brothers,* and part formerly conveyed to Elias Harding for 158 acres and another part of 96 acres. This deed is for 121 ½ acres.
81. Patrick Magruder and Benjamin White Jones, Commission, Associate Justices recorded 10 December 1801.
81. John Dells recorded 14 December 1801, from Basil Mullikin, bill of sale for Negro man Tom, aged 25 years for £150. Signed before Richard Green and Archibald A. Beall.
82-83. William O'Neale Senr., recorded 14 December 1801 from William Prather Williams, deed for £75 for lots #69, 70, 71, 72 & 73 in town of Williamsburgh agreeable to survey by Archibald Orme.
83. William Ray of Benjamin, qualification as deputy sheriff recorded 17 December 1801.
83-85. Daniel Beall, Nathan Holland, Stephen Shaw, Ely Beall, trustees, recorded 15 November 1801, from Samuel Beall & Edward Owen, deed for 5 shillings, grant lot of ground on *Batchelor's Forest,* to build a house of worship for the Methodist Episcopal Church of the United States of America. Witnessed by William Smith, Jno Clark. Rachel wife of Edward Owen released dower rights.
86-87. Laurence Snyder recorded deed 18 December 1801, from John Clarke, for 5 shillings, tract beginning at 8th line of *Moneysworth,* formerly conveyed to James Coffee, and adjacent to *Benton's Lott,* for 11 1/4 acres. Signed before Greenbury Howard, Edward Burgess Jr.
87. Cephas Lazenby recorded 19 December 1801, to Negro Rachel, manumission. Rachel to be free at expiration of the year 1815. Signed 19 December 1801 before John L. Summers.
87-88. Solomon Holland recorded bond as Sheriff with Henry Brookes and Erasmus Perry, 22 December 1801.
88-89. Nathan Macklefresh recorded power of attorney 22 Dec. 1801 from Richard Macklefresh and Susanna Macklefresh his wife, of Fayette County, Pennsylvania, to make good conveyance of property to James Brown. Signed before John P. Allen, Peggy Allen.
89. James Brown recorded from Richard Mackelfresh & wife, bond of conveyance dated 29 July 1799 for tract called *Benjamin Heskith's Choice,* on hill on west side of Snowden's River, containing 50 acres. Signed Richard Mackelfresh by mark, Susannah Mackelfresh, before John P. Allen, Ephraim Douglas Pro.Ntry.
90-91. Deed for same property by Nathan Mackelfresh, witnessed by Archibald Beall, Richard Green.
91. Negro George recorded 23 December 1801, from William Duley, manumission. Slave to be free after 20 January 1805. Signed before J. F. Beall, James A. Beall.
92. Gerard Brooke recorded 24 December 1801, from Samuel Wright, deed for lot #18 in Brookeville. Signed before John Clarke, Jas Lackland. Phebe Wright released dower.

93-95. George Chandlee recorded deed 24 December 1801 from George Hardy, of Anne Arundel County, for £194..1, part of *Hammond and Geist,* for 28 3/4 acres, on east bank of Snowden's River. Signed before Richard Green, Thomas Davis. Priscilla Hardy released dower.

95-96. James Norwood recorded deed 26 December 1801 from Henry Poole, for £500, part of *Henry and Elizabeth Enlarged,* for 83 acres, plus 18 acres. Signed before John Clarke, Edward Burgess, Jr. Amelia Poole released dower.

96-97. Enoch King recorded deed 29 December 1801 from Francis Deakins, of Washington, D.C., for £40, tract called *Fruitful Plains*, adjacent to *Resurvey on Happy Choice.* 20 acres.

97-98. Daniel McCarthey recorded 31 December 1801 to the Sheriff of Montgomery County, schedule of property including one feather bed and bedstead, one table, two chairs, one cupboard, one breeding sow, one amount on account, due from Mordecai B. Offutt, £7..6.

98-99. George Riley recorded deed 31 December 1801 from Amos Williams, of Albemarle County, Virginia, for $548 land devised to him by his father, William Williams. Signed before Henry Brooke, John L. Summers. deed

99-100. Thomas Orme recorded deed 2 January 1802, from Thomas Beall of George, of Washington, D.C. for £400 several tracts of land. *Discovery,* 89 acres; *Portland,* 13 ½ acres; *Red Oak Bottom,* 11 acres; *Then or Now,* 43 acres; *Sporting Ground,* 96 acres; *Denmark,* 19 acres; *Sapling Ridge,* 21 acres; *Hyspaniola,* 10 1/4 acres; *Hold Fast, Enough,* 12 acres; *Mount Airy,* 21 ½ acres; *Glasgow,* 4 3/4 acres; and tract at the Great Falls of the Potomac called *Mount Vernon,* 135 acres. Nancy, wife of Thomas Beall released dower rights.

101-102. Isaac Riley recorded 5 January 1802, made same date, from Martin Honore & wife, for £350, deed for lot in Rockville. Signed Honore Martin before J. H. McPherson, John S. Summers. Sarah Martin released dower rights.

102-103. Henry Pool recorded 6 January 1802, from Jesse Hyatt, deed made 16 December 1801, for £205, part of *Ivy Reach,* beginning at 5th line, 20 ½ acres. Signed before Greenbury Howard and John Clarke. Ann Hyatt released dower.

103. John Clarke recorded 6 January 1802. from Edward Burgess, Senr., for $350. bill of sale for one Negro man, James. If sum paid before 25 December next, then sale is void. Acknowledged before Edward Burgess Junr., J.P.

104-105. Edward Crow recorded 6 January 1802, from William Willson, for $500. bill of sale for Negro Kate and her two children, Harry and Frederick. Acknowledged before John Clarke.

105-106. Samuel Soper recorded deed 8 January 1802 from John D. Coffee, for $8. Part of *Hazard.* 5 acres. Signed before Greenbury Howard, Jno Clark.

106. John Bealmear recorded 13 January 1802 from John L. Summers, release & bill of sale. John Bealmar did convey in trust a Negro by name of Eve as security of his own and also for Archibald Mullikin which he was security for, now releases all rights. Signed John L. Summers.

106. Tyson Beall recorded 14 January 1802 from Robert L. Beall, for £35 bill of sale for one Negro boy, Bob, 17 years of age, and three feather beds. Signed before John L. Summers.

106-107. Robert Beall and Walter Greenfield Junr., Henry Baggerly and Tyson Beall recorded 14 January 1802, to the State of Maryland, bond to keep bridge in repair

107-108. Thomas Riggs of Samuel recorded 16 January 1802, from Joshua Griffith, bill of sale for £120, sells one Negro man called Benjamin or Ben. Signed Joshua Griffith of Hy, before Archibald A. Beall.

108-109. William Brewer Jr. recorded deed 16 January 1802 from Joseph Newton Chiswell, for $1, part of first resurvey on tract, *Wolf's Cow,* 60 acres. Signed before Ens Campbell, Laurence O'Neale. Eleanor Chiswell released dower.

109-110. Thomas West recorded deed 19 January 1802 from Joseph D. West, for £575..10 all his right and title to parcel, *The Two Brothers.*

110-112. George Culp recorded 19 January 1802 from Laurence O'Holt & Jno B. Allison. Whereas Elisha Allison by his will 28 June 1796 devised ½ of his estate to some of Richard Allison's family, conformably to will aforesaid, James B. Crafford, who married widow of said Elisha Allison, and Ann Crafford his wife, did on 28 Dec. 1799 convey to John B. Allison, son of Richard Allison, ½ of the property aforesaid and Laurence O. Holt, trustee of James B. Crafford and Ann his wife. Elisabeth Allison wife of John B. Allison released dower.

112-113. Ruth Constable, Nancy Constable and Eleanor Constable recorded deed 2 January 1802 from Richard Kirk, for $200. Tract *Lucks All,* beginning at 4th line of *Wilson's Inheritance,* surveyed for Jonathan Wilson, 14 Sept. 1785, containing 15 acres more or less. Mary Kirk released dower.

114-115. Ninian M. Clagett recorded deed 23 January 1802 from Joshua Owen, for £300, part of *Owen's Conclusion.* 166 1/4 acres. Mary wife of Joshua Owen released dower.

115-116. Robert Peter recorded deed 27 January 1802 form John McDonald, of Frederick County, Virginia, eldest son and heir at law of Angus McDonald, for £408..13 tract called *Fork of Grubby Hills,* containing 305 acres.

116-117. William O'Neale recorded deed. 27 January 1802, from David O'Neale. Whereas William O'Neale, John O'Neale, Henry O'Neale and David O'Neale, did on 6 December 1785, survey jointly a tract called *Resurvey on Wheel of Fortune,* into the name of *Partnership,* with 10 acres of vacancy, which appear to be part of a tract called *Pleasant Mountain*, by mistake included, and now deducted, leaving only 71 acres. For 5 shillings, agreements reached.

117-118. Eneas Campbell & others: William Smith, Lawrence O'Neale, Richard Dyson, Henry Brookes, Thomas Davis, Allen Bowie, John L. Summers, Greenbury Howard, Edward Burgess Junr., Josias Fendall Beall, Elemelech Swearingen, Benjamin Gaither, John Clark, Josias H. McPherson, James Lackland, Archibald A. Beall, John Turnbull, Walter Magruder, Lewis Duvall of Hyatts Town, Ozias Offutt, John Thomas, John Burgess, Howard Griffith, William Culver, Richard Turner, Thomas Simpson and Lennox Martin, commissioned as Justices of the peace

118. Burgess Willett recorded 1 February 1802 qualification as Deputy Sheriff

118-119. John Purdom recorded deed from Thomas Orme for £24..17. Part of *This or None,* at beginning of *Cow Pasture,* also the beginning of *Benjamin's Second Beginning,* adjacent to a *Resurvey on Locust Bottom,* containing 17 acres.

119-120. Zachariah Gatton Senr recorded 4 February 1802 from Abraham Stallings, bill of sale for 2000 lbs. Tobacco, one bay mare 6 years old, one black mare 10 years old, one iron grey mare

120-121. Aquila Magruder recorded deed 4 Feb. 1802, from Walter Magruder. Whereas Nathaniel Magruder of Alexander did execute a will on 28 November 1793. And devised to his son Walter Magruder 41 acres, and real estate by will to be equally divided between his two sons Walter and Aquila Magruder. Margaret, wife of Walter Magruder released dower.

121-123. Walter Magruder recorded 5 February 1802 from Aquila Magruder, deed in division of *Grubby Thicket,* above real estate, left them by their father, Nathaniel Magruder. Mary Ann wife of Aquila released dower.

123. Richard Kirk Sr. to Solomon Holland, Sheriff of Montgomery County, recorded schedule 8 February 1802.

123-125. Nicholas Pegno, administrator of William Benson, recorded deed 8 February 1802, from Lancelot Warfield, deed. Whereas William Benson, did in his lifetime, contract to buy parcel called *Peckerton,* containing 210 acres of land, but deed not made before his death. Rachel, wife of Lancelot Warfield released dower. Signed before Allen Quynn, Jno Brice.

125. Commission for the Justices of the Levy Court for Montgomery County recorded 8 February 1802. To Thomas Davis, Allen Bowie, John L. Summers, John Clarke, Henry Brooke, Eneas Campbell and Edward Burgess Junr.

125-126. Edward Crow recorded deed, 9 February 1802 from Nicholas Pegno, as administrator of William Benson. Whereas William Benson, did in his lifetime, contract to buy parcel called *Peckerton,* containing

210 acres of land, but deed not made before his death, and did further contract to sell 112 ½ acres, this makes good deed for sum of £333.10 .
126-128. John Fletchall recorded 9 February 1802 from Thomas Fletchall, deed for £1350 parts of *Cyder and Ginger,* and part of *Three Springs.* Adjacent to part conveyed to William Hickman, containing 225 acres. Sarah, wife of Thomas released dower.
128-130. Thomas Fletchall recorded deed 9 February 1802, from John Fletchall, for £1350 parts of *Blantrye, Cors Basket,* and *Preston's March.* Adjacent to part of *Brightwell's Hunting Quarters,* 151 acres. Dorcas, wife of John released dower.
130-131. Stephen N. Chiswell recorded deed 9 February 1802, from Joseph N. Chiswell, for $500 part of *Resurvey on Hanover,* Eleanor wife of Joseph N. Chiswell released dower.
131-133. Thomas Hickman, Ann Hickman, Elizabeth Hickman, Mary Hickman and William Hickman, children of William Hickman deceased recorded 9 February 1802 from Elizabeth Hickman, widow of William Hickman, for 5 shillings, deed for *Preston March*, *Cyder and Ginger*, *Three Springs*, and *Resurvey on Three Springs.*
133-134. John Poole Junr. recorded deed 9 February 1802 from Vachel Hall, for £115, part of *Resurvey on Jeremiah's Park*, adjacent to line of deed conveyed by Vachel Hall to Robert Sollers, for 1plus acres; containing 38 5/8 acres. Margaret, wife of Vachel Hall released dower.
134. Lewis Duvall, recorded 9 February 1802, qualification as a Justice of the peace
135-136. Benjamin S. Dailey, recorded 10 February 1802, Qualification as deputy sheriff
136. Joseph Compton recorded 11 February 1802 from Charles Carroll, release. In consequence of Mr. Wm M. Beall paying me £80, relinquish all title to Negro Rachel and her son Robert unto Mr. Zedekiah Swann. My right is under a bill of sale from Joseph Compton Jr. and Joseph Compton Sr. Made 16 April 1799, redeemed before 16 April 1801. Signed Charles Carroll.
136-137. Samuel Leeke and Caleb Bently recorded 11 February 1802 from Israel Leeke, bill of sale for £15 for one feather bed, and other household items and livestock.
137-138. William Mullican recorded 12 February 1802, from Mrs. Elizabeth Crabb, deed made 16 Jan. 1801. Whereas the late Charles Greenbury Griffith died possessed of a tract called *Friday,* 3 acres, Elizabeth Crabb is sole heiress, beginning at 5th line of *Chestnut Ridge.*
138. Patrick Magruder, qualification as Associate Justice of Montgomery County Court recorded 19 February 1802.
138. Elizabeth Allison, Thomas Allison and William Fields recorded 16 February 1802, from Nicholas Umpstatd, for £50, bill of sale for one Negro boy called Harry, age 14 years. Signed before John Summers.
138. John L. Summers recorded qualification as Justice of the Peace 19 February 1802.
138-140. Richard Clagett recorded 20 February 1802, from Honore Martin & Sarah his wife; Edward O. Williams and Elizabeth his wife of Berkeley Co., Va., sells two parts, containing 150 acres of *Dann,* one conveyed by Pharoh Riley to Richard Clagett Jr. And the other by Thomas Conn, to Richard Clagett Jr., of which Richard K. Clagett, died seized. This indenture fulfills a prior agreement with him.
140. Lenox Martin recorded 22 February 1802, qualification as Associate Justice of Montgomery County Court, oath made before Aeneas Campbell.
140-141. Zachariah Hayes recorded 22 February 1802, from Vachel Hall for £4..10, part of *Resurvey on Jeremiah's Park,* 3/4 acre lot, adjacent to lot conveyed to Leonard Hays. Signed before John Clark, G. Howard. Margaret Hall released dower rights.
141-144. Thomas Cramphin recorded 22 February 1802, from James Dunlap, indenture made 3 February, whereas John Heugh's by indenture dated 9 November 1796, recorded in G:348-351, conveyed to said Dunlap, several tracts in trust, after death of Sarah to sell and divide lands among the named sisters of John Heugh, to wit: Elizabeth, Sarah, Ann, Jane, Mary, Harriott and Christina, one of the sisters is now married to Walter C. Williams, and the land is sold to Cramphin for £4,506..5, called *Leek Forest*, resurvey 28 November 1785, at end of 3d line of part of *Dan,* conveyed to Thomas Clagett, to second line of *Forest*, to

a tract called *Labyrinth,* containing 456 3/4 acres. Signed before Elizabeth Heugh, Sarah Heugh, John L. Summers, J. H. McPherson.

144-146. Thomas Cramphin recorded 22 February 1802, deed made 3 February from John Heugh, Elizabeth Heugh, Sarah Heugh, Ann Heugh, Jane Heugh, Mary Heugh, Harriot Heugh, Walter C. Williams and Christina his wife. Whereas John Heugh by his deed recorded 4 November 1796 conveyed to James Dunlap, the tract mentioned in trust after the death of Sarah Heugh his mother, and divide the purchase money among his sisters the said Elizabeth, Sarah, Ann, Jane, Mary and Harriot Heugh and Christina Williams, and as the said Sarah Heugh the mother is dead and the tract has been sold to the said Thomas Cramphin for £4,506..5 paid on account to the said grantees, and granted with previous knowledge and consent of the aforesaid parties, this deed of conveyance and deed of confirmation is made. All parties signed deed in the presence of John L. Summers.

146-147. Thomas Cramphin recorded covenant, 22 February 1802,. Whereas Thomas Cramphin of Montgomery County has purchased of James Dunlap a tract called *Leek Forrest,* as will more fully appear by reference to deed of conveyance bearing even date with John Heugh, Elizabeth Heugh, Sarah Heugh, Ann Heugh, Jane Heugh, Mary Heugh, Harriot Heugh, Walter C. Williams and Christina Williams his wife, have by their deed of confirmation confirmed and released to said Cramphin, part of the said lands, formerly the estate of Andrew Heugh deceased, of which he died seized in fee, that their may be some liens and encumbrances upon the said lands by means of judgments or otherwise, whereby the said Cramphin may hereafter incur some loss of injury, now we do covenant and agree, that we and each of us, shall and will at all times hereafter fully indemnify and save harmless the said Cramphin by reason of any incumbrance affecting the lands sold. Signed by same parties as above.

147-148. Joseph Clagett recorded 23 February 1802, made 15 February, from Greenberry Gaither, deed for £100..7 sells tract called *Gravelly Hill,* part of a tract called *Mitchell's Range,* metes and bounds given. Ann, wife of Greenberry released dower.

148-150. Arnold Warfield recorded deed 1 March 1802 from Thomas Kirk Junior, for £27 lot #11 in Clarksburg. Mary Kirk released dower. Signed before Edward Burgess, John Clark.

150-151. Basil Mullican recorded 2 March 1802, from John Dells for $800. Part of *Gittings Hah Hah* Sarah wife of John Dells released dower rights.

151-153. Edward Lancaster recorded 2 March 1802, from Benjamin Berry from the city of Baltimore, for £209..1, deed for part of tracts, *Resurvey on the Grove,* and *Resurvey on James and Mary,* for 159 acres. Elizabeth Berry released dower.

153-155. William Abbington Needham recorded 2 March 1802, from Uriah Forrest, tract patented to Thomas Whitten by name of *Hope Improved,* and whereas 109 acres was conveyed to George Cullum in 1762, with two other tracts, *Maple Spring,* 28 acres and one other tract conveyed by Cullum to Charles G. Griffith in 1779, and then to Daniel Jenifer Adams in 1779, then to Hugh Young, and land conveyed by Hugh Young to a certain Richard Ridgely in 1791 conveyed to William Deakins Jr. and Uriah Forrest as joint tenants. William Deakins has since died, leaving title with Uriah Forrest by his survivorship. Several tracts containing 149 acres. *William and Mary*, 42 acres; *Maple Spring* 11 1/4 acres, sold for £252..16..3. Signed before John L. Summers, J. H. McPherson. Rebecca, wife of Uriah Forrest released dower.

155. Eleanor Harper and Francis Harper filed 2 March 1802, to Montgomery County, recognizance bond for £30. Whereas Eleanor Harper was lately delivered of an illegitimate male child, this bond is to indemnify county from all charges relative to maintenance of child. Signed by both parties before William Smith.

156. Negro Richard, age 33, recorded 2 March 1802, from Amy Nixon, for good cause sets free Negro. Signed 20 February 1802, before J. F. Beall, James A. Beall.

156-159. Hezekiah Harris, Charles Hays Harris, Nancy Harris and Rebecca Harris recorded 2 March 1802, from Nathan Harris for 5 shillings, deed made 19 July 1795 from Joseph Harris Sr., recorded in Liber G:296-198, for *White Oak Swamp Enlarged,* but now resurveyed and called *Mount Zion,* beginning on south side of Little Monocacy containing 153 acres. Also tract called *That's It,* conveyed to Charles Beatty, heretofore

in 1789 passed his bond to Nathan Harris, tract adjacent to *Hopewell,* and *Father's Gift,* at end of the line of William Norris's (son of William) part of *That's It Resurveyed.,* also personal property including coopers and joiners tools. Dorcas Harris wife of Nathan Harris released dower.
159-161. Samuel Sprigg recorded 2 March 1802 from Thomas Drane & Mary his wife, deed. Whereas Walter Harding, deceased, by his will[2], gave to his wife, Mary, as long as she remain widow, 1/3 of estate, and then to his five children: Anna, Elias, Mary, alias Polly, Elizabeth and Philip. Mary, widow of Walter Harding, has since intermarried with Samuel Sprigg, and Mary, alias Polly is intermarried with Thomas Drane.
161-162. Zachariah Musgrove recorded 2 March 1802 from Richard Morgan, for £30 sells two feather beds, and furniture, one dark horse, one grey mare. Signed before John L. Summers.
162-163. Jesse Phillips recorded 3 March 1802, from Joseph Hall, for bill of sale for $140, Negro girl Cilla, 6 years old, Negro boy John, 3 years old. Signed before Aeneas Campbell, Adam Robb.
163-164. James Hawkins recorded deed 4 March 1802, from William Dison, for £9..7, lot in Clarksburgh, being the lot conveyed from Jonathan Browning to William Dison. Signed William Dyson before Greenbury Howard, John Clark. Acknowledgment.
164-166. Laurence O'Neale recorded deed 11 March 1802, from Samuel Hepburn, for £129 part of *Hanover*, adjacent to 2nd line of The *Turnip Patch.*
166-168. Charles Mackelfresh of Frederick County, recorded deed 5 March 1802 from Joseph Newton Chiswell, for $250. Part of *Resurvey on Hanover.* Eleanor Chiswell released dower.
168. Charles Rogers recorded 5 March 1802 from Benjamin Ricketts, bill of sale for valuable consideration, 2 year old bay colt, roan horse, 3 sheep. Signed by mark before John L Summers.
169-170. John Laird recorded 6 March 1802 from Thomas Dick of Bladensburg, deed for tract called *Bells Hunting Quarter,* conveyed to Dick by John Heugh. Margaret, wife of Thomas Dick released dower rights.
170-171. Thomas Cramphin recorded 9 March 1802 from Eleanor Magruder, bill of sale for $290 one mulatto slave man named Abraham, 34 years old the 23 October last. Signed before John L. Summers.
171-172. William Jones recorded deed 9 March 1802 from John L. Summers. Whereas John L. Summers, purchased of David O'Neale 10 acres, for which he was to pay in settlement of a debt for which he became special bail for Rebecca Lane, at Philip Jenkins suit. Now for £30 he assigns to William Jones. Anne M. Summers released dower.
172-173. William Jones recorded deed 9 March 1802 from David O'Neale, for £3..2..6, 5 acres granted him in partition by William O'Neale, John O'Neale, William Lodge, assignee of Henry O'Neale and David O'Neale on 3 Sept. 1794, recorded in Liber E:532-538, part of *Wheel of Fortune,* and other tracts.
173-175. William Jones recorded 9 March 1802 from Solomon Holland, sheriff, deed. Whereas a judgment was obtained against David O'Neale by Thomas Cramphin, John Bowie, Thomas Perry Willson and Laurence O Holt. Tract as sold above for £3..2..6, parts of *Wheel of Fortune,* and *Come by Chance.*
175. Francis Clements recorded 9 March 1802 from Oswald Clements, bill of sale for £16, one sorrel horse, 7 years old.
175-176. John H. Cushman recorded 11 March 1802, from Patrick Dempsey for £25, two feather beds, furniture and 200 weight of bacon.
176-178. John Worthington Warfield recorded deed 9 March 1802 from Greenberry Gaither for £439..4, part of *Mitchell's Range,* and part of *Gravelly Hill,* adjacent to *Martha and Mary,* for the other part of *Mitchell's Range,* said Gaither purchased of John Worland for 4 ½ acres, but tract found to contain 5 acres, beginning at given line of tract sold by Edward Gaither to Thomas Prather and by said Prather to said Worland, at given line of 45 acre part heretofore sold by Thomas Prather to John W. Warfield. Signed by Greenberry Gaither before Wm Smith, Benjamin Gaither. Ann Gaither released dower.

[2]Will dated 6 May 1782, probated 16 August 1782, recorded in Montgomery County.

178-179. Solomon Viers recorded 11 March 1802, from Hezekiah Viers, bill of sale for £100 one Negro girl, Suk, two horses, one dark bay 8 years old called Buck, and one 4 years old called Dauphin; and a bay colt, six head of cattle, 15 hogs, 3 feather beds, 8 windsor chairs, 3 tables, one Beaufat, the furniture thereon, and 3 bedsteads. Signed before Wm Smith, Patrick Dempsey.
179-180. George Willson recorded 11 March 1802, from Zedekiah Willson, release on bill of sale for one Negro named Jack, one called Charity and her child Poll, one other called Phillis and her child Bob, Eleanor, Bill and Ben. Whereas George Willson has satisfied me, release them back to him. Signed by mark.
181-182. Mordecai Burgess Offutt recorded 11 March 1802, from Nathaniel Offutt (of Edward), for £75 deed for all part of *Outlet,* beginning at a stone planted by a white oak stump on south side of a spring commonly called Meeting House Spring, to dividing line between Nathaniel Offutt and Henry Townsend. Signed. Deborah wife of Nathaniel released dower rights.
182-183. Mordecai B. Offutt recorded 11 March 1802 from George Washington Offutt, for £45 deed for tract called *Barren Hill* containing 6 3/4 acres. Cassandra, wife of George W. Offutt released dower rights.
183-184. George W. Offutt recorded 11 March 1802 from Mordecai B. Offutt, for £45 deed for part of *Smithfield.* On main road leading from Georgetown to the mouth of Watts Branch, 6 3/4 acres. Jane, wife of Mordecai Burgess Offutt released dower.
184. Solomon Holland, sheriff recorded schedule 12 March 1802 from Philip Daugherty, schedule.
184. State of Maryland, commission Jurors Levy Court dated 11 March 1802, to Allen Bowie, John L. Summers, John Clarke, Aeneas Campbell, Henry Brookes, Edward Burgess Junr., and Richard West, appointments.
185. State of Maryland commission Justices of the Peace, dated 11 March 1802 to Eneas Campbell, William Smith, Laurence O'Neale, Richard Green, Hy Ren, Henry Brookes, Allen Bowie, John L. Summers, Greenberry Howard, Edward Burgess Jr., Josias Fendall Beall, Elemelech Swearingen, Benjamin Gaither, John Clark, Josias H. McPherson, James Lackland, Archibald A. Beall, John Turnball, Walter Magruder, Lewis Duvall of Hyattstown, Ozias Offutt, John Thomas, John Burgess, Howard Griffith, William Culver, Richard Turner, Thomas Simpson, Lenox Martin, Richard West.
185-187. Henry Pool recorded 13 March 1802 from Elizabeth Fleming and John Fleming, executrix and executor of James Fleming deceased. For £165 tract *Bealls Addition,* adjacent to *Moneysworth,* 132 acres.
186a-186b. Sheet inserted, Road Act of General Assembly, Session, 1801, to open a road leading from John Orme's plantation to main road leading from William Darne's to Montgomery Court house. Plat signed by Charles Gassaway and William Darne Jr. Reverse side plat shows "Beall and Lackland's merchant mill"
187-188. John Moxley recorded deed 16 March 1802 from George Chandler, for £389..5, tract *Pembrooke,* 259 ½ acres. Signed before Richard Green and Thomas Davis. "The wife" came and released dower rights.
188-190. Nehemiah Moxley recorded 16 March 1802 from Henry Ridgely of Henry, of Ann Arundel County, executor of Henry Ridgely deceased. deed for part of *Friendship,* Henry Ridgely sold him in 1786, but now called *Prospect Hill.* On main road leading to Gaither's Store, known as Bucy's Road, adjacent to Shadrach Penn's part of *Friendship,* containing 200 acres.
190-191. Nehemiah Moxley of Anne Arundel County, recorded deed 16 March 1802 from George Chandler, for £171..7..6, part of *Resurvey on Mount Radner,* for 114 acres. The wife of George Chandler released dower rights.
191-192. Honore Martin recorded 17 March 1802, from Zachariah Allison, deed for all his rights to the real estate of his father, John Allison, deceased.
193-194. Thomas Peter recorded deed 18 March 1802 from Francis Deakins, executor & devisee of Wm Deakins, deed for 200 acres of *Conclusion.* Signed before John L. Summers, JGH McPherson.
194. William Fields recorded 18 March 1802, from John Ball, bill of sale for Fields becoming security unto William O'Neale of John, grants bay horse, 5 years old and one sorrel horse. Signed before J. H. McPherson.

194-195. Leonard A. Johns brought into this state a Negro man, Clem, 22 years old, acquired by purchase from Washington Bowie, of Washington, District of Columbia to work on his farm in Montgomery County.
195-196. William Abbington Needham recorded 19 March 1802, from Francis Deakins Exec. & devisee of Wm. Deakins, deed for *William and Mary, the Maple Spring,* and *Small Hopes,* conveyed to William Deakins and Uriah Forrest jointly.
196. Jesse Phillips recorded 20 May 1802, from Walter Mitchell, for $60, bill of sale for one small black mare, one black & white cow, specified furniture, joyners tools: chisels, auger, handsaws. Signed before Ens Campbell, George Hoskinson.
197-198. Jesse Hyatt and others, recorded plat and certificate of Hyattstown 22 March 1802. Signed by Jesse Hyatt, Henry Poole, Lewis Duvall, John Clarke, Charles Busey, Francis Pastuer, Michael Rians, James Herston, Charles Macklefish, William Burgess, Joshua Dorsey, Jacob Smith, John Barnes.
199-201. William Magrath recorded 23 March 1802 from Richard Allison, John B. Allison, David Allison, Enoch Allison, Barbary Allison, John Day and Lily Day his wife, Edward Archy and Elizabeth Archy his wife, for £180 46 acres, part of *Resurvey on Martha's Delight,* conveyed to Richard Allison by Samuel Beall Jr. In 1771. Signed by parties. Sarah Allison, wife of Richard Allison examined apart released dower rights.
201. Hezekiah Viers recorded 27 March 1802 from John L. Summers, release on bill of sale for Negro woman Jane, having sold her to James Higdon.
It should be noted here that page numbers are not visible on microfilm version, and they appear to have been filmed loosely, removed from binding. A page or two may be missing or out of order. The edges on many of the pages are torn, so there is some speculation in the following deed regarding amount paid, and ------burgh as Clarksburgh.
201-202. Rebecca Clay of Frederick County recorded 27 March 1802, deed from Laurence Snyder of Montgomery County for 5 shillings, lot in Addition to Clarksburgh containing one acre. Eve Snyder released dower rights before Greenberry Howard, John Clarke.
202-203. Harriet Beall recorded 28 March 1802 from Sarah West, bill of sale for the natural love and affection which I have for my daughter, Harriet, I give her Negro woman named Hester. Signed by mark before Charles Philpot. Attested to in Frederick County.
203-203a, 205. Evan Thomas recorded deed 29 March 1802 from Henry Culver of Prince George's County for £20 tract, a part of *Addition to Culver's Chance,* adjacent to Samuel Luken's part and tract *Two Farms,* also outlines agreement regarding use of and access to the Northwest Branch. [numbering from the on-line deeds, MDSA]
204. Agreement regarding location of streets, alleys and lots in Hyattstown, to make and return plat. Signed by Jesse Hyatt, Henry Poole, Lewis Duvall and witnessed by Meschach Hyatt and [—torn page] Hyatt.
205-206. John Poole Junior recorded 30 March 1802 from John Poole Senr. Tracts *Happy Choice, and Happy Choice Fortified.*
206-207. John Poole Senr., recorded 30 March 1802, from John Poole Junr and Prissa, his wife, for £250 part of *Happy Choice,* the aforesaid land having descended to the heirs of Frederick Sprigg of Montgomery County, his three daughters, Peggy, Mary Belt and Prissa Woodward, the said Prissa W. Having intermarried with John Poole Jr.
207-208. Thomas B. Beall of George of Washington, D.C., recorded mortgage 1 April 1802 from Armistead Long, on 134 acres on *Black Walnut Island,* signed before Ens Campbell, Laurence O'Neale.
208-210. Mary Harrison recorded deed 5 April 1802 and others from Josias Harrison, for natural love and affection for Mary, widow of my son Nathan Harrison, and Laney, Ann, Rebecca, and Sarah Hawkins Harrison, children of my son Nathan Harrison, deceased, in consideration of above and for their better support assigns 50 acres of *Locust Bottom.*
210-211. Thomas Knott recorded deed 7 April 1802 from Zachariah Knott, for £100, part of *Conclusion,* 100 acres. Jane wife of Zachariah Knott released dower.

212-213. John L. Summers recorded power of attorney April 1802 from John Letton of Bourbon County, Kentucky. Whereas John Wilcoxon, late of Montgomery County, deceased, died intestate, leaving considerable real and personal property, and John Letton married one of his daughters, and one John H. Nicholls of Mason County, Kentucky, married another of his daughters and transferred his share by bill of sale, John Letton authorized John L. Summers to act on his behalf.

213-215. Robert Plummer recorded 26 April 1802 from Nacy Waters, executor of the will of Richard Waters, deceased, deed for £114 assigns part of *Water's Conclusion,* adjacent to *Gattrel's Good Will,* and *Water's Forrest,* 178 ½ acres. "Signed, sealed and delivered."

215-216. Robert Plummer recorded deed 26 April 1802 from Nacy Waters, deed for £50 tract called *Gartrell's Good Will,* 50 acres. Signed before Henry Brookes, Benjamin Gaither. Ann, wife of Nacy Waters released dower.

216-217. Marsham Waring & Notley Young recorded deed 16 April 1802, from Thomas Sim Lee, of Washington, D.C. Whereas Waring and Young at the request of Lee have devised to Bank of Columbia £10,000 of which Lee is the drawer, to indemnify them assigns a parcel of land adjoining the District of Columbia, purchased of a certain John Murdock deceased, conveyed to him in by Murdock's trustees in 1798.

218-219. James W. Perry of Prince George's County, recorded deed 24 April 1802 from Tyson Beall, for £5, part of *Fair Prospect,* adjacent to *Bear Garden Enlarged,* conveyed by Archibald Beall to Joseph Perry, containing 72 perches (one and 9/10 acre).

219-220. Tyson Beall recorded deed 24 April 1802 from James W. Perry, for £5, part of *Bear Garden Enlarged,* and part of *Second Mistake,* part of *Perry's and Beddow's Covenant,* adjacent to tract called *Deer Park,* contiguous containing 2 9/10 acres.

220-221. Clement Green, schedule delivered to the Sheriff of Montgomery County recorded 23 April 1802 includes a hoe, 6 pewter spoons, one table, one bar shear plough, accounts due from Col. John Thomas £16..17..6, Thomas Hall £7..16..3, Francis Green £1..10 and Joseph Sharp, £..3..7,

221. Erasmus Earp to the Sheriff of Montgomery County, schedule recorded 23 April 1802, included amount due from Mrs. Hill on account , linen wheel, various tools. Signed by mark.

221-223. William Hempstone recorded deed 21 April 1802, from Samuel Hepburn of Prince George's County, for £787..15..7 part of *Resurvey on Hanover,* Jane Hepburn released dower. Witnessed Thomas Bowie, James A. Magruder, Justices of Prince George's County.

223-224. John B. Dyson recorded 19 April 1802, from Barton O'Neale & wife Mary O'Neale, heirs of Samuel Dyson, Senior, for £10, tract called *Non Eaten,* and a tract called *Thomas's Discovery,* Both signed by mark before Wm Smith, Lawrence O'Neale.

224-225. Zachariah Knott recorded deed 17 April 1802 from Greenberry Gaither, for £8..5, tract, a part of *Gaither's Bastion,* adjacent to 3rd line of *Gaither's Range,* laid out for 8 1/4 acres. Ann Gaither released dower.

226. Negro Daniel from Isaac Lansdale, certificate recorded 17 April 1802. "I hereby certify that the bearer, Daniel Blackman, is free. Signed Isaac Lansdale.

226-227. Benjamin W. Jones and Henry Jones recorded deed 17 April 1802 from Greenberry Gaither, for £8..5 part of *Gaither's Bastion,* below *Mitchell's Range,* containing 25 ½ acres. Ann Gaither released dower rights.

227-228. Thomas Clagett recorded deed 14 April 1802 from John Orme, for $150 part of tract called *Wet Beginning,* Sarah Orme released dower.

228-229. Basil Magruder recorded deed 12 April 1802 from Archibald Orme, for £4 part of tract called *Resurvey on Rich Bottom,* adjacent to *Brooke Range,* and *Resurvey on Gravelly Ridge,* conveyed by Archibald Orme to Basil Magruder, containing 10 ½ acres. Signed before Wm Smith, Jas Lackland.

229-231. Warring Magruder recorded deed 8 April 1802 from Honore Martin, for £75 parcel called *Cleland,* it being originally called *Black Oak Thickett Enlarged,* escheated by Thomas Cleland, 24 November 1774, for 30 acres. Signed before Patrick Magruder, Associate Judge, Richard Turner. Sarah Martin released dower.

231-233. Zachariah Knott recorded deed 7 April 1802 from Samuel Hepburn of Prince George's County, for £550..2..6, part of *Resurvey on Hanover,* adjacent to parts where James Plummer now lives, and land sold to Ignatius Wathen and Samuel Sprigg, and the tract *Turnip Patch,* 180 ½ acres. Jane Hepburn released dower right.

233-234. Zachariah Linthicum, recorded deed 1 May 1802, from the executors of the will of Johnsey Gaither: Mary Gaither, Charles Gassaway and Greenberry Gaither, for 5 shillings, deed for part of tract *Good Luck,* adjacent to land of Zachariah Linthicum called *Resurvey on Wolf Pit*, and *Pig Pen*, for 9 ½ acres. Said tract was conveyed by bond to Greenberry Gaither, but not paid in full, and he had assigned to Zachariah Linthicum for payment.

235-236. Zachariah Linthicum recorded deed 1 May 1802, from Greenberry Gaither, for £15, part of *Mitchell's Range,* adjacent to *Resurvey on Wolf Pit,* and *Pig Pen,* 4 ½ acres. Ann Gaither wife of Greenberry Gaither released dower.

236-237. Zachariah Linthicum recorded deed 1 May 1802, from Greenberry Gaither, for £25, parts of several tracts, *Wolf Pit,* and *Pig Pen,* by another survey name called *Vienna,* and tract *Mount Airy,* called by name of *Mitchell's Range,* lands up Seneca Creek, for 18 3/4 acres. Ann Gaither released dower right.

237-239. Thomas Edmonston recorded 8 May 1802 from James Beall of James for £5, part of *Bear Garden,* adjacent to part formerly conveyed by Archibald Beall to Joseph Perry for 8 acres. Elizabeth Beall, wife of James released dower right.

K: 239-241. Basil M. Perry recorded 8 May 1802 from Thomas Edmonston. Whereas James Beall of James, did heretofore 28 February 1765 by deed sell to Joseph Perry, father of Basil Perry 240 acres, deed for a tract called *James and Mary,* recorded in Liber I:1065 of Frederick County. In Joseph Perry's will be devised the land to Basil Magruder Perry who has discovered the quantity of 14 acres lies within the lines of an older tract called *Deer Park.* The property of Thomas Edmonston, whereas the said James Beall has conveyed to Thomas other lands in lieu of the 14 acres, Thomas Edmonston will convey the land for 5 shillings, part of *Deer Park,* beginning at end of 40 perches on 5th line of *Bear Garden,* also the 5th line of *James and Mary,* S 50E 8r pc. To last line of *Deer Park,* S 55 W 50 pc., N 20 3/4 W, 84 pc., then to beginning. Signed by Thomas Edmonston. No dower released.

242. Carlton Belt, Junr., recorded 8 May 1802 from John Belt, deed for £30 part of *Woodport,* formerly called *Moneysworth,* Witnesses Greenberry Howard, John Clark.

243-244. Samuel Welsh Senr. of Anne Arundel County, recorded 10 May 1802 from Isaac Webster, Junr. of Baltimore City, formerly of Harford County. Whereas Isaac Webster, his father, did on 9 Oct. 1770 by his bond, assign to Lewis Duvall tract called *Richardson's Range,* then to Richard Morgan, about 380 acres, and tract called *Bristol,* 50 acres, lying in Montgomery County. Isaac Webster in his lifetime received purchase money from Lewis Duvall, who assigned his interest in bond of conveyance to Samuel Welsh. Signed before Lewis Duvall, Ephraim Shipley.

244-245 Jesse Phillips & Hezekiah Willson recorded constables bond, 10 May 1802.

245-246. Tyson Beall recorded deed 13 May 1802 from James Willson Perry, of Prince George's County, for £44..10, for part of *Deer Park,* 6/10 of an acre.

246-248. Peter Kemp recorded deed 13 May 1802, from James Willson Perry, for £16..10, part of *Deer Park,* containing 2 acres and 2/10.

248-249. William Price Junr. Recorded 14 May 1802 from Richard T. Chesaldine. Whereas Chesaldine has filed for relief under states insolvency laws to the Chancellor, he assigns all his property.

249-250. Honore Martin recorded deed 15 May 1802 from Thomas Allison, for £27, sells all his right to real estate of his father, John Allison, late of Montgomery County, deceased.

250-251. Thomas Cramphin recorded 19 May 1802, deed from John Heugh, for £78..5, part of *Dan,* beginning at Rock Creek, to given line of Hugh Riley's part, 7 7/8 acres. Ann wife of John Heugh released dower right.
251-253. Honore Martin recorded deed 24 May 1802 from George Beckwith for £300. Whereas Charles Beckwith, late of Montgomery County, died intestate in April 1790, seized of *Hills and Dales,* leaving five children, assigns his undivided fifth part. Anna Beckwith wife of George released dower right.
253-254. Marsham Waring, Robert Brent, Benjamin Young and Nicholas Young recorded 25 May 1802, from Thomas Sim Lee of Washington County, District of Columbia, bill of sale to indemnify parties for note drawn on bank, assigns Negroes on tract *Friendship:* to wit: Carpenter Charles, Tom, Tally, George, Kate, Bet, Sall, Rachel, boy Bernard, also old Sukey, Peg daughter of Sukey, boy Will, Jenny and all her other children. Signed before John L. Summers.
254-255. William Lee recorded 25 May 1802, from Thomas Sim Lee bill of sale for natural love and affection, assigns Negro slaves: old Charles and his wife, Jenny, Jack and his brother Bob, the sons of Robin and Rachel, and Sukey, and four children, plus Henny, sister of Sukey, both daughters of Robin and Rachel, also Will, son of old Sukey. Signed before John L. Summers.
255. Josias F. Beall, qualification as magistrate recorded 27 May 1802.
255-256. Honore Martin, Edward Owen Williams and Richard Clagett recorded deed 2 June 1802, from Martha Clagett, for 5 shillings, the property that Richard Keene Clagett, the late husband of Martha Clagett died seized.
256-257. William Lee recorded assignment of lease 4 June 1802, from Thomas Sim Lee, for 5 shillings and natural love and affection for his son, assigns tract near Montgomery Courthouse, the plantation farm estate of Ignatius Digges of Prince George's County, lately deceased, patented under the name of *Burgundy,* during the natural life of said Thomas Sim Lee.
257-259. Thomas Waters Senior recorded deed 14 June 1802, from Thomas Snowden of Prince George's County, and Charles Alexander Warfield, of Anne Arundel County, for £119, *Water's Lot,* and *Water's Purchase,* at second line of tract called *Mother's Gift,* and running to the Patuxent River, containing 52 acres. Second parcel containing 30 acres. Elizabeth Warfield and Ann Snowden released dower rights.
259-261. Arnold Warfield recorded 9 June 1802, from Benjamin W. Jones, late sheriff, deed. Whereas judgment obtained by John Clark, against the property of Jonathan Rhodes, an absconding debtor for lot in Clarksburg, sold to Joshua Purdum as the highest bidder for £9..15 who paid the sum, and assigned the lot to the said Arnold Warfield.
261-262. John Rousby Plater recorded deed 10 June 1802 from Uriah Forrest, of Washington, D.C., for $3000, lot #9, 100 acres; lot #13, 126 acres and lot #7, only 9 ½ acres and lot #4, containing 158 acres and lot #3, containing 3 1/4 acres, all being part of *Bradford's Rest,* in Montgomery County, Rebecca Forrest released dower rights. Signed before Patrick Magruder, Associate Justice.
262-263. John Rousby Plater recorded deed 10 June 1802 from Uriah Forrest, for $1900. Assigns part of *Bradford's Rest,* lot #18, adjacent to Mrs. William's Lot, containing 199 ½ acres. Rebecca, wife of Uriah Forrest released dower rights.
264. John Rousby Plater recorded 10 June 1802, from Uriah Forrest of territory of Columbia, bill of sale for $1,300. Negroes: James, Stephen and Jacob, also black cattle, hogs, horses. Signed before Patrick Magruder.
265. Robert Peter recorded 11 June 1802, instrument of writing, involving debts due from Richard Henderson, Doctor Ross and Mr. Robert Duck. Others involved: William Douglas Sr., Nin. Edmonston and William Clagett. (Signed April 30, 1766). Mortgage released to Robert Peter on tract *Sugar Bottom,* May 22, 1776.
266. Clement Jarboe to State of Maryland, bond as constable recorded 19 June 1802 Signed Clement Jarboe, Henry Bellwood, in presence of Lawrence O'Neale.

266-267. Basil Darby recorded deed 15 June 1802 from Talbott Allnutt, deed for £50, one undivided fifth part of tract called *Thomas's Discovery* conveyed to the said Talbut Allnutt by Basil Darby, the lawful attorney of Richard Pack and Mary Pack his wife on 21 March 1798.

267-268. Gerrard Brookes recorded 18 June 1802, from Ezekiel Jackson, deed for £70 one hogshead of tobacco, now packing by Caesar Williams and one by horse, ten years old. Sale void if sums paid. Signed by mark before Jno Thomas 3d.

269-270. John H. Summers recorded 21 June 1802, made 10 April, from Vachel Hall, deed for £7..7 part of *Resurvey on Jeremiah's Park,* lot formerly conveyed to James Barnes for 2 acres. Signed before Greenberry Howard, Lenox Martin, Margaret Hall released dower rights.

270-271. Henry Culver of Vansville in Prince George's County, recorded deed 22 June 1802, from Evan Thomas, for £30 part of tract called *Two Farms,* to the beginning of a tract called *Drumeldry,* containing 4 acres of land.

272. Greenbury Murphy recorded 22 June 1802 from John Keath, for £10 bill of sale for all personal property. Signed by mark before John Burgess

272-273. Negro David recorded 22 June 1802, from Mrs. Margaret Beall widow of Brooke Beall, manumission for faithful service and 5 shillings. Signed before J. H. McPherson.

273-274. John Laird of Georgetown, recorded deed 24 June 1802, from Thomas Hewitt of Prince George's County, for $1 assigns tracts, *Thomas and Mary,* lying in Prince George's County on the Beaver Dam Branch of the Eastern Branch of the Potomac, and *Wilson's Enlargement,* where said Hewitt recently resided, and tract called *Jackson's Improvement,* in Montgomery County on the Northwest Branch of the aforesaid Eastern Branch, and *Hard Struggle,* adjoining thereto; and two lots in the town of Bladensburg inherited from his deceased father, Thomas Hewitt. Ann Hewitt released dower.

274-276. John Laird of Georgetown, recorded deed 24 June 1802, from Catherine Hewitt of Bladensburg, Prince George's County, widow of the late Thomas Hewitt Sr. Deceased, for $400, assigns her rights to above tracts.

276-277. Richard Wootton recorded deed 24 June 1802 from Thomas West, for £20 tract called *the Two Brothers,* 3 1/10 acres. Signed before Thos P. Willson, Charles Willson.

277-279. Thomas Magruder Clagett recorded deed 25 June 1802 from Joshua Owen, for £375, tract called *Pleasant Plains of Damascus,* 167 acres. Mary, wife of Joshua released dower.

279-280. Meshack Tucker recorded deed 29 June 1802 from Matthew Reed, for £150 part of lot #7 sold by William Duncan to Meshack Tucker, laid out for 1/4 of an acre.

280. Edward Crow recorded receipt 8 July 1802 John Clarke, for release of mortgage for $700.

280-281. John Candler recorded bill of sale 10 July 1802, from Joseph Tippet, bill of sale for £15 for one sorrel mare and one young colt.

281-282. John Larken of Frederick County, recorded 10 July 1802 from Lawrence Snyder, deed for £30 lot of ground, a part of *Moneysworth,* lot on west side of road for one acre, two roods and 16 perches, Eve, wife of Laurence Snyder released dower.

283-284. Robert Dent recorded deed 15 July 1802 from Vachel Hall, for £7..10, for part of *Jeremiah's Park,* adjacent to part conveyed to William Bennett, containing 3/4 of an acre. Margaret, wife of Vachel Hall released dower.

284-285. Basil Poole Junr., recorded 17 July 1802, from Philemon and Joshua Griffith, executors of Henry Griffith, deceased, deed for part of *Cow Pasture,* and part of *Hope Improved,* adjacent to Charles Mill's part. Signed before Archibald A. Beall, John Burgess.

285-287. Charles Rogers recorded lease 17 July 1802, from Charles Gassaway. In 1797, he laid off a number of lots on tract called *White Oak Springs,* in town called Charlesburg, for rents of 20 shillings, he assigns for 99 years lots #27 and 28.

287-289. Nathaniel E. Magruder recorded deed 20 July 1802 from William Law, for £75 tract called *Law's Purchase,* adjacent to *Mud Hill,* 51 3/4 acres.

289-290. Abednego Baker recorded deed 27 July 1802 from William Inman of Berkeley County, Virginia, for £24..15, part of tract called *Inman's Adventure,* adjacent to *Henry and Elizabeth,* containing 16 ½ acres.
290. Joseph Slater brought into Maryland a Negro man named Cirus, 22 years old a blacksmith by trade from the District of Columbia. Recorded 27 July 1802.
290-291. Philemon Plummer recorded 30 July 1802 from John Thompson of John, bill of sale for $150, for crop of corn, crop of tobacco in the ground, one bay horse, one grey horse, housewares.
291-292. Thomas West recorded deed 31 July 1802 from Richard Wootton, for £20, *Rocky Point Fortified,* 3 and 6/10 acres. Signed before Thos P. Willson, Charles Willson.
292-293. Jesse Phillips with Hezekiah Willson recorded 2 August 1802 to the State of Maryland, bond as constable.
293. Zachariah Musgrove to the State of Maryland, recorded bond as constable 2 August 1802, with Nathan Musgrove.
293-294. Isaiah Nicholls, Thomas Nicholls Sr. and Hendry Allison recorded bond 2 Aug. 1802, to State of Maryland to build a bridge over Seneca Creek, near Smith and William's Mill.
294-295. John R. Campbell to the state of Maryland, recorded constable's bond, 2 August 1802 with Josiah McPherson and Kinsey Gittings of Kinsey.
295. Solomon Holland, Erasmus Perry, and Henry Brookes recorded bond to state of Maryland for £10,000, to State of Maryland, for Solomon Holland to serve as Sheriff.
296. Leonard Hayes, recorded constables bond to state of Maryland, 4 Aug. 1802 with Meshack Browning and William Willson.
296. John Darby, recorded constable's bond 4 Aug. 1802, to state of Maryland with Samuel Darby, and Aden Darby.
296-297. George Missicope recorded bill of sale 4 Aug. 1802, from Christopher Missicope, for £30 sells one bay horse, a cart and gears, two beds, bedsteads, two iron pots.
297-298. Solomon Holland with Benjamin Jones and Henry Brookes, bond for £6148..7..6 to State of Maryland, to faithfully pay to the Justices of the Levy Court.
298-299. Jesse Willcoxon recorded deed 17 Aug. 1802 from Lewis Willcoxon, for £40, part of *Dann,* on main road leading from William Glaze's schoolhouse to Newport Mills, for 11 to 12 acres.
299. Plat and certificate of a road laid out by John Orme (Lackland's Mill) beginning at a road opposite Archibald Orme's plantation, to corner of fence by Thomas Nicholls of Simon's plantation; page torn. No plat.
300-301. Levi Hays recorded 7 August 1802, made 8 July 1802, from Jesse Harris, for £71..5, deed for tract formerly called *White Oak Survey Enlarged,* resurveyed 24 August 1786, and now called by the name of *Mount Zion,* in Montgomery County adjacent to Little Monocacy. Containing 9 ½ acres. Signed Jesse Harris before Wm Smith, Lenox Martin. Dorcas wife of Jesse Harris released dower.
301-302. Thomas Morton recorded 10 August 1802, made 15 May, from Samuel Hunter of the State of North Carolina, and County of Rowan, attorney for Susanna Griffith, the wife of Zadock Griffith. Whereas a certain Henry Hunter of Maryland, but now deceased, did by his last will named Susannah his executrix, who is the Susannah Griffith above mentioned, took out letters on her late husband Henry Hunter. And whereas Thomas Morton has now paid the purchase price, this deed is maid with her power of attorney, to sell tract called *Beall's Good Will,* adjacent to *Rays Venture,* containing 251 acres. Also another part of *Beall's Good Will,* beginning at the 4th line of Peter Klem's land called *Rays Adventure,* to the fourth line of William Norris's land called *Pretty Spring,* to the given line of John Tannihill's land. Containing 10 ½ acres, together with all the dwelling houses, out houses, mills and all other improvements. Signed Samuel Hunter, attorney in fact for Susannah Griffith. Receipt dated 15 May 1802. Acknowledgment. Recorded: I, Susannah Griffith, wife of Zadock Griffith of Rowan Co., N.C., signed power of attorney.
304-305. Henry Poole recorded 12 August 1802, from William Burgess of Hyattstown, for $206 bill of sale for all goods and stock. Signed before John Lee Bell.

305-307. Solomon Holland and Benja. Jones recorded mortgage 12 Aug. 1802, from Samuel B. White, for their serving as sureties in a special bond, to secure them from loss and for 5 shillings, assigns tract purchased of Henry Ridgely called *Prospect Hill,* 142 ½ acres; Negro girl, Nan; one bay gelding, one black gelding, one sorrel gelding, five milch cows, five yearlings, 18 hogs, 3 feather beds and furniture, household and kitchen furniture and plantation utensils, crops of wheat and tobacco. Samuel B. White. Witnesses Henry Brookes, Richard West.

307. Commission for justices of the levy court 18 Aug. 1802: Allen Bowie, John Clarke, Henry Brookes, Eneas Campbell, Edward Burgess Junr., Richard West and Thomas B. Evans.

307-310. John Laird of Georgetown, and Thomas Dick of Bladensburg, Prince George's County, recorded deed of trust 18 August 1802, from James Miller of Glasgow in Great Britain, but formerly of Bladensburg, for $1 tract called *Conclusion,* 560 acres on Seneca Creek, appoints William Hammond Dorsey and John Murdoch his attorneys for sale. Witness Robert Miller. Margaret Miller, wife of James Miller released dower.

310. Commission for Justices of the peace for Montgomery County recorded 18 August 1802, to Eneas Campbell, William Smith, Lawrence O'Neale, Richard Green, Henry Brookes, Allen Bowie, Greenberry Howard, Edward Burgess Junr., Josias Fendall Beall, Elemelech Swearingen, Benjamin Gaither, John Clarke, Josias H. McPherson, James Lackland, Archibald A. Beall, John Turnbull, Walter Magruder, Lewis Duvall of Hyattstown, Ozias Offutt, John Thomas, John Burgess, Howard Griffith, William Culver, Richard Turner, Thomas Simpson, Lennox Martin, Richard West and Thomas Bevans.

311. Aquila Johns recorded 31 August 1802 from Archibald Orme, for £140 bill of sale for Negro man Stephen, son of Moll. Signed before J. H. McPherson.

311-312. Sheriff of Montgomery County recorded 11 September 1802, from Basil Beall, deed for personal property, one small looking glass, one pail. Signed before Elemelech Swearingen, J. H. McPherson

312-313. Joshua Cecill recorded deed 14 September 1802 from Philip Witten, for 5 shillings, all his interest in tract called *Resurvey on Wildcat Spring.* Deed made 5 Sept. 1802, in territory northwest of Ohio River.

313-314. John Laird of Georgetown, recorded deed 15 September 1802, from Richard Cramphin of Prince George's County, the trustee appointed by the Chancery Court, in the case of John Livingston and Martha his wife, William Hewett, Mary Hewett, John Hewett, James Hewett against John Laird, Thomas Dick and Henry Hewett, as directed by court deed made for sum of $3291 to John Laird for tracts called *Jackson's Improvement,* 194 acres and adjoining *Hard Struggle,* for 50 acres in Montgomery County, and also tract *Willson's Enlargement*, 102 acres, in Prince Georges County and two lots, #31 and #32 in Bladensburg.

314. William Willson recorded 18 September 1802 from William Higgins, for £34..10..3 bill of sale for one Negro woman, Mill.

314-315. Matthew Stone recorded 20 September 1802 from John Thomas the 3d, for $590 bill of sale for one mulatto man, Joe, 36, a blacksmith by trade; boy Isaac, 15 years old, mulatto boy David, 7 years old, 29 head of sheep, 2 cows and one calf, one set of blacksmith's tools, one carriage and cart. Signed before J. H. McPherson.

315-317. Armistead Long of Leesburg, Loudoun County, Virginia, recorded deed 25 September 1802 from George Beall, of Georgetown, for £7000, tract called *Lubberland,* granted 16 May 1734 to George Beall and James Edmonston, 54 acres, and *Resurvey on Lubberland,* granted George Beall 29 Sept. 1761 for 134 acres, tracts are part of Black Walnut Island in the Potomac. George Rose acted with power of attorney for George Beall in transaction. Elizabeth Beall wife of George released dower right.

317-318. Richard Beall recorded deed 27 September 1802 from William Willcoxon, for £174..11, part of *Prospect Hill,* adjacent to *It May be Good in Time,* and south line of *Woodstock,* 66 ½ acres. Ann, wife of William Willcoxon released dower.

318-319. Edward Berry recorded deed 29 Sept. 1802 from Jeremiah Berry, for natural love and affection and $1 assigns *Berry's Chance,* a part of tract called *Two Farms,* 2 plus acres.

319-321. John Benson recorded deed 29 Sept. 1802, from Richard Beall, for £174..11 part of *Prospect Hill,* adjacent to *It May be Good in Time,* and south line of *Woodstock,* 66 ½ acres. Anna, wife of Richard Beall released dower.

321-323. Thomas Cramphin recorded deed 29 Sept. 1802, from Richard Clagett, Honore Martin and Sarah Martin his wife for £1800. Whereas Richard Keen Clagett father of the aforesaid Richard and Sarah, died seized of a large tract called *Dann,* part being conveyed to Richard Clagett, father of Richard Keen Clagett, 13 Feb. 1749 by Pharoah Riley, recorded in Liber B:137; the other part conveyed to him by Thomas Conn, 149 ½ acres. Signed by Richard Clagett, Honore Martin and Sally Martin.

323-324. Basil Darby recorded deed 2 Oct. 1802 from John and Susanna Forster, of Frederick County, Virginia. Whereas James Allnut, late of Montgomery County, deceased, in his will bequeath to his wife her thirds in tract *Thomas Discovery,* directing that it was to be divided among his five daughters, after her death, viz: Ann Coats, wife of Charles, Sarah wife of Thomas Price deceased; Mary Pack wife of Richard Pack, Susanna Alnut and Rebecca Alnut. Susanna is entitled to an undivided fifth part of a third part of tract. She has since married to John Forster. For £50, sells their interest in tract to Basil Darby.

324. William Orr recorded order 2 Oct. 1802, to give up his bond, that he gave in common form, to us for building the new jail. Signed Allen Bowie & Saml Turner, order.

324-327. Beal Gaither recorded deed 4 Oct. 1802, from Samuel Thomas of Anne Arundel County, for $349.50 part of *Richard's Levels,* and part of *Gaither's Forest,* adjacent to John Burgess's part and tract deeded to Orlando Griffith, containing 58 1/4 acres. Anne, wife of Samuel Thomas released dower.

327. Thomas Offutt Junr., brought into this state from Virginia, a slave girl, Minie, aged 16 years, a gift from his mother, Ann Minor. 4 October 1802.

327. Negro Cate recorded 6 October 1802, from John Clarke, manumission for good causes she to be free after 1 March 1812, and all her issue to be free at age 25 years. Signed 3 May 1802, before Greenberry Howard, William Wilson.

327. Negro Sall & others from James Day, manumission recorded 6 October 1802, Negro freedom dates: Sall after 1806, Polly after 1809, Pris after 1812, Rier after 1820, Charlotte after 1822, and their male issue. Signed before John Clarke, Samuel Bennett.

328-330. Bernard Gilpin recorded deed 6 October 1802 from Samuel Brooke, selling property by decree of the court of chancery in the case of the creditors of Peter Casanave, deceased and Nicholas Young. Bernard Gilpin was the high bidder for sum of £937..10, for part of *Addition to Brooke Grove,* beginning at 8th line of James Brook's part of his deceased father's land, on main road leading to Frederick Town, and adjacent to *Turkey Thickett,* to head of a glade that falls into Rock Creek, containing 200 acres.

330-332. Samuel Bealmar recorded deed 6 October 1802 from George Riley, for £287..5, tract *Hobson's Choice,* 47 acres, 3 roods and 20 perches. Sarah wife of George released dower rights.

332-334. William Magrath recorded deed 11 Oct. 1802 from Laurence O. Holt, trustees of James B. Crafford and Ann Crafford and John B. Allison. Whereas Elisha Allison by his will dated 4 June 1796 devised ½ of his land to Richard Allison's family, and conformable to the will, James B. Crafford who married the widow of Elisha Allison, and his wife Ann Crafford, conveyed to John B. Allison, son of Richard Allison, one half of tract *Rock Spring,* and they conveyed property in trust to Lawrence O. Holt, and William Magrath became purchaser of the tract, adjacent to *Martha's Delight,* and the part of *Burgundy,* conveyed by Richard Allison to his son Elisha Allison, containing 85 acres more or less. Signed Lawrence O. Holt, trustee, and John B. Allison. Elizabeth Allison, wife of John B. Allison released dower.

334-336. Lawrence O. Holt, trustee of James B. Crafford and Ann Crafford his wife, recorded deed 11 Oct. 1802 from John B. Allison. Same conditions as above deed, for ½ of tract *Rock Spring.*

336-338. Richard L. Hall recorded deed 16 Oct. 1802 from Josiah Harding of Frederick County, Virginia, part of *Pleasant Plains,* 42 1/4 acres..

338-340. Nathaniel E. Magruder recorded deed 22 October 1802 from John Orme, for £38..6..10, *The Two Republics,* metes and bounds to Samuel Clagett's division line, on *Resurvey on Rich Meadow,* as purchased from John Golden, Benjamin and Richard Ricketts, from the part remaining for Drusilla Ricketts, Singleton Ricketts, Joshua Tippett and John Chambers, to beginning of *Hamilton's Lot,* 14 1/4 acres. Sarah, wife of John Orme released dower.

340-341. Benjamin Becraft recorded deed 25 Oct. 1802, from the Rt. Rev. John Carroll of Baltimore, and Robert Brent, as trustees of Daniel Carroll, deceased, for £918..2..3, part of *Joseph's Park,*

342. Negro Aquilla, aged 14 years, recorded 27 October 1802, from Ann Chambers, manumission. Signed before James Lackland and John Chambers of Wm.

342-343. Kenelm Selby Gray recorded deed 28 Oct. 1802 from Edward O. Williams, of Jefferson County, Virginia, for £75, lots #31, 50 & 84 in town of Williamsburg. Elizabeth, wife of Edward O. Williams, released dower.

344-345. Basil Magruder Perry recorded deed 1 Nov. 1802 from John Wells, for £122..10, tract called *The Honest Man,* beginning at 11th line of tract *Greenland,* resurveyed for James Beall, 137 ½ acres. Sarah Wells released dower.

345-346. Daniel Garrett recorded deed 1 November 1802 from Francis Deakins, part of *Fruitful Plains,* for 5 acres. Signed before Benjamin W. Jones, Associate Justice.

346-348. Lewis Bealmear recorded deed 2 November 1802 from Samuel Bealmear for $258, part of *Valentine's Garden Enlarged,* containing 5 acres.

348. William Ellson Willson, bond to State of Maryland recorded 2 Nov 1802, to well and truly serve as constable. Co signed by Nathaniel Willson, and Benjamin Gittings.

348-349. William Trail recorded deed 3 November 1802 from Daniel Jarrott for £7..10 part of tract called *Fruitful Plains,* beginning at end of 6th line of tract called *Hobson's Choice.* Acknowledged before Greenbury Howard, John Clark.

349-350. William Trail recorded deed 3 November 1802 from Daniel Jarrott and Margaret his wife, for £600 sells part of *Resurvey on Happy Choice,* resurveyed for Frederick Sprigg on or about 1st September 1781, as *Happy Choice Fortified,* containing 207 acres. Signed before Greenbury Howard, Lenox Martin.

351-352. Alexander McDonald & Nicholas G. Ridgely, of Baltimore, merchants, recorded mortgage 3 November 1802 from Robert Brooke Beall, for £195..16..8 have delivered to said Mackdonald and Ridgely the Negro slaves following: Davy, Airy, Arch, Mint, Abraham and Kate, together with all my right and title thereto; provided always that this writing be of no effect, on the said Beall's paying to the said McDonald and Ridgely the said sum on six months from the date. Signed before Richard Ridgely.

352. Christopher Scype recorded 4 November 1802 from Joshua Talbert, bill of sale for silver watch and other items.

353. Negro Viney aged 22 years and her son, Evan, aged 17 months, from Philemon Plummer, Senr., manumission recorded December 1802, before Richard Green, Margaret Raney by mark.

353-354. Hezekiah Magruder recorded 5 November 1802, slave Negro boy Charles from Frederick Co., Virginia. Said slave fell to him by decease of Eleanor Talbot of Virginia.

354. George B. Magruder, brought into this state a Negro boy named William, from Virginia, Said slave fell to him by deceased of Eleanor Talbot of Virginia.

355. Warren Magruder from George Magruder, bill of sale recorded 9 November 1802 for 5 shillings, for the purpose of securing debts and indemnifying Thomas Turner, sells three Negro men: Will, Rezin and Truman and Negro women, Charity and Lethy and their children, and a Negro boy, Charles. Signed George Magruder, before Patrick Magruder.

355-357. William O'Neale recorded 13 November 1802 from Thomas Garrett, Elizabeth his wife and George Washington Haymond for £227, tract called *Adamson's Choice,* 102 acres.

357-358. Nathan Cooke recorded 20 November 1802, from Zachariah Selby in consideration of a bond passed, from his father Thomas Selby Senr. To Thomas Selby Junr. To convey certain lands, which bond has since been assigned to Nathan Cooke by said Thomas Selby Junr., and also for having his father's contracts fulfilled, with 2nd and 3rd vacancies, *Fair Rosamond's Bower,* containing together 11 1/4 acres. Signed by mark before Henry Brookes, Benjamin Gaither.

359-360. Nathan Cooke recorded 20 November 1802 from Thomas Selby Senr., assignment of bond. Thomas Selby Senr. Bound to Thomas Selby Junr., 6 Jan 1787, did heretofore in May 1786, at request of Thomas Selby Junr., obtained from the land office a special warrant of resurvey on *Fellowship* and part of *Charles And John,* which he is now seized, and an additional amount of vacant land, Signed Thos Selby Senr. Before Wm Smith, Richard Selby. Now for a valuable consideration in hand paid by Nathan Cooke, on 19 December 1797, assign bond. Thos Selby signed before Brice Selby.

360-361. Dennis Costigan recorded deed 20 November 1802 from Zachariah Selby, for £200 sells tract, part of *Resurvey on Charles and John*, and also part of *Fellowship,* lately resurveyed, and now called and known by the name of *Fair Rosamond's Bower.* Containing 120 acres willed by the last will and testament of Thomas Selby, deceased. Signed by mark before Henry Brookes, Benjamin Gaither. Mary Selby, wife of Zachariah Selby relinquished dower.

361-363. Walter Dorsey of Baltimore County, recorded deed 20 November 1802 from William H. Dorsey & Ann Dorsey, his wife, of Washington, District of Columbia, for 5 shillings, tract of land called *George Third,* containing 47 acres. Also all that farm or plantation called *Fair Hill,* on which William Dorsey heretofore resided, being a part of *Charley Forrest,* and part of tract called *Brother's Content,* containing 397 acres.

363-364. William O'Neale Senior recorded deed 23 November 1802 from Robert Peter trustee defendants, adjudged in a suit between James Suiter complaint and Thomas Willson by Robert Peter, that he should convey to the said James certain land, *Resurvey on part of Exchange and New Exchange Enlarged*, adjacent to part sold by James Dick to Barton Harris, containing 100 acres.

364-365. John Stanton recorded bond 23 November 1802 from James Suter, in penal sum of £50 that James Suter shall make over tract called *Pyramid,* containing only 2 acres by certificate. Signed before Richard Morgan, John Suter.

365-367. Benjamin Hues recorded 2 December 1802 from John Alexander Brown, for £60 deed for part of *Brooke Grove.* Sarah Brown released dower.

367. Joseph Mahor, William Mahor and Elizabeth Mahor recorded 3 December 1802. I Jane Mahor in consideration of love and affection for my children, gives inventory of personal property and livestock. Signed by mark before Joseph Howell, John Hawood, Hezekiah Willson, Joshua Saers.

367-368. Thomas W. Crow recorded 9 Dec. 1802, qualification as deputy sheriff

368-369. Charles Jones recorded deed 9 Dec. 1802, from Aquilla Johns of Prince George's County, for $10. Assigns Lots #9 & #10 containing 429 acres more or less. Whereas the said Aquilla Johns stands indebted to George Hawkins for $3000 for which he is willing to give day of payment until 1st January next, securing to him, Mrs. Mary P. Johns, wife of Aquilla, released dower.

369-370. Solomon Holland, Sheriff of Montgomery County recorded 11 December 1802, schedule of property from Thomas Beck. One pair shears, one taylors goose, two press boards, one notch board, four bodkins, one razor and case, one small bowl, one small wigg, one inkstand, one thimble one pen knife, 11 needles, Accounts of Clement McDermott 18..9; Edward Viers 18..6; Elie Standage 1..3; John Bowman 1:3; Edward Biggs, 11..4; Richard Parr 2..6. Signed before Greenbury Howard, J.H. McPherson.

370-371. Richard Hoggins Junr. recorded 15 December 1802, from Richard Hoggins, Senr., bill of sale in consideration that Richard Hoggins Sr. Became security for payment of 300 lbs. Tobacco to Edmund Jennings, he assigns one Negro girl Katy 6 years old and one Negro boy Henson, 3 yrs. Old, six chairs, 2 feather beds and furniture, 2 cows, 6 years old, all of which is now in his possession; but if he pays the above sum, then this sale is void. Signed before John Clarke.

371. Henry O'Neale recorded 15 December 1802 from Anthony Reintzel of Georgetown, for £150, deed for all his right to land mortgaged by Benjamin Ward of Joseph to James Smith and Anthony Reintzel on or

about 19 August 1783, and conveyed to them 6 July 1790, and afterwards James Smith conveyed his right to tract to Anthony Reintzel. Signed before Patrick Magruder.

372-374. Thomas Beall of George of Washington, D.C., recorded deed 15 December 1802 from Henry O. Neal, for £1025 part of tracts called *Crumford,* beginning at road commonly called the Sugarland Road, 101 acres; parts of *Bealls Design*, 29 2/3 acres, and 6 acres; Margaret, wife of Henry O'Neale released dower.

374-375. Clement Thompson recorded deed 19 December 1802 from Elijah Williams, Harriett his wife, Rezin Davis and Eleanor Palmer, heirs of Ludwick Davis, deed. Harriett and Rezin are his children, and Eleanor Palmer his widow who intermarried with a certain Jonathan Palmer and has become a widow again. Two of her sons Ludwick Davis and Rezin Davis, consented to division. Part of *Resurvey on Benjamin's Square*, and part of *Davis Content.*

376. Negro Dick, alias Richard Swearingen, from Richard Wootton and Robert P. Magruder, manumission. before J. H. McPherson and Lewis Beall.

376. Joseph White to clerk of Montgomery County, recorded his mark 20 December 1802 for his cattle, sheep and hogs. A crop & slit under bit in right ear and a crop and slit in left ear.

376-378. William Brewer recorded 24 December 1802 from Robert Peter, deed for one part of *Fortune,* which William Gale Pierce one of the heirs of John Baptist Pierce, deceased conveyed, except for the right of dower of Elizabeth Pierce, widow of John Baptist Pierce. Elizabeth, wife of Robert Peter released dower.

379-380. William Brewer recorded 24 December 1802 from Joseph N. Chiswell, deed for undivided two of four parts of *Fortune,* the parts of Thomas Higdon and Rachel his wife and Henry C. Pierce, heirs of John Baptist Pierce conveyed. Eleanor wife of Joseph N. Chiswell released dower rights.

380-381. Henry Poole recorded 27 December 1802 from Francis Pasters, for $226 lots #5 and #59 in Hyattstown. Anastacia Pasters released dower rights.

382. Negro Harry and others recorded January 1803, from George Fee, manumission for Harry, William, Sukey from 1 January 1820, Cate and Jacob, Mary from 1 January 1823, and Sarah from 1 January 1821. Signed before Richard West, Alex. Adams.

382-384. Hezekiah Thomas recorded 4 January 1803 from Aquila Johns of Prince George's County for £850, tract called *Samuel's Chance,* 350 acres. Mary Pierce, wife of said Aquila Johns released dower rights.

384-385. John Purdum recorded 6 January 1803 from Thomas Orme, deed for £26..10, part of tract, *This or None,* beginning at tract called *Pleasant Spring,* granted Hugh Green, to a line of *Benjamin's Second Beginning,* for 25 acres.

385. Thomas Dunn to the Sheriff of Montgomery County, schedule recorded 7 January 1803. Sundry balances per book of accounts, credit to the sheriff, £5..12..7; amt of claim of Charles Gassaway note obtained, witness Henry Brookes, J. H. McPherson.

386-387. William Veirs Sr. Recorded deed 4 January 1803, from Elisha Veirs for £10 part of tract called *Mary,* beginning at part formerly conveyed to Daniel Veirs for 220 acres, containing 1 3/4 acres. Sarah his wife released dower.

387. Negro Richard and Ann, recorded 11 Jan.1803, from Edward Crow, manumission for Richard after 21 February 1804, Ann to be free after 29 December 1827. Signed before William Smith, Edward Crow Jr.

387-389. Harry W. Dorsey recorded deed 11 Jan. 1803, from Thomas Pleasants, of Goochland County, Commonwealth of Virginia, for $1566. tract called *Conclusion,* beginning at 12th line of Thomas Pleasant's part of *Addition to Brook's Grove,* containing 174 + acres. Signed before Wm Pledge [J.P. for Goochland County], Harriett Pleasants, Wm Pleasants. Recorded before John Thomas 3d, Wm Culver.

389-390. John Rawlings recorded release 13 January 1803, from Thomas Perry Willson, redemption and release of bill of sale of Negro girl Milly, heretofore mortgaged in August 1799.

390. Commission for Justices of the Levy Court, for 1803 recorded 15 January 1803, to Allen Bowie, John Clarke, Henry Brooke, Edward Burgess, Jr., Richard West. Thomas B. Evans, and Ozias Offutt, Justices of Levy Court.

390-391. Commission for Justices of the Peace for Montgomery County for 1803 recorded 15 January 1803, to William Smith, Laurence O'Neal, Richard Green, Henry Brooke, Allen Bowie, Greenberry Howard, Edward Burgess Jr., Elemelech Swearingen, Benjamin Gaither, John Clarke, Josias H. McPherson, James Lackland, Archibald A. Beall, Lewis Duvall of Hyattstown, Ozias Offutt, John Thomas, John Burgess, William Culver, Richard Turner, Thomas Simpson, Lenox Martin, Richard West, Thomas B. Evans, Nehemiah Stone, Alexander Whitaker, John Adamson, Amon Riggs, Samuel Williams, Camden Riley, Warren Magruder, Walter Fitzgerald, Richard Beall, all of Montgomery County, gentleman.
391-393. Thomas Fletchall recorded deed 20 January 1803 from Joseph Newton Chiswell, for $296, part of *First and Second Resurvey on Wolf's Cow,* beginning at a corner of the Roman Catholic Church lot, to tract called *Resurvey on Hanover,* Eleanor Chiswell released dower.
393-394. Peter Kemp recorded deed 24 Jan. 1803 from John Sutton Crawford, for £180, *Snowden's Mill Land,* Elizabeth, wife of John released dower.
394-395. Vachel Hall recorded deed 28 Jan. 1803 from William Bennett, for £20, part of *Resurvey on Jeremiah's Park,* on north side of the main road leading from Monocacy to Green's Bridge, ½ acre. Aletha, wife of Wm Bennett released dower.
395-396. John Simmons of Frederick County recorded deed 28 January 1803, made 24 January 1803, from Vachel Hall, for £9, part of *Resurvey on Jeremiah's Park,* beginning at end of 3d line of lot whereon John Glissan is now building, one acre. Margaret, wife of Vachel released dower.
396-398. Vachel Hall recorded deed 28 Jan. 1803, from Joseph Harris, son of John Harris, for 5 shillings, tract *Mount Zion,* beginning at 1st line of *Resurvey on Jeremiah's Park,* 35 1/4 acres. Wife of Joseph Harris (not named) released dower.
398. James Glisan recorded deed 28 Jan. 1803 from Vachel Hall, part of *Resurvey on Jeremiah's Park,* at 3rd line of lot laid out for Henry Camden, on north side of road leading to Green's Bridge. One acre. Signed before Greenberry Howard, Lenox Martin. Margaret Hall released dower.
399-401. Leonard Hayes recorded deed 28 Jan. 1803 from Ann Sollers, for £104.. 7 ½ pence, tract *Friendship,* 30 acres. Signed by mark.
401-402. James Holland recorded 31 January 1803, from John Burgess, for £4000 deed for part of tract originally called *Hartley's Lot,* but now called *Hold Fast What You Have Got,* beginning at bound oak on *Abel's Levels,* containing 125 acres. Signed John Burgess, before Edward Burgess Junr.
402-403. John Thompson Veatch recorded bill of sale 5 Feb. 1803 from Leonard Watkins for $61.25, bill of sale made 28 January for a black mare and colt. Signed Leo Watkins. Witness: Lenox Martin.
403-405. William O'Neale Senr recorded deed 2 February 1803 from Archibald Orme, for £61, *Piney Grove,* beg. At 3rd line of *Eleanor's Green,* 28 acres. Elizabeth Orme released dower.
405-407. Leonard H. Johns recorded deed 5 Feb. 1803 from John Carroll of Baltimore, and Robert Brent, of Washington, D.C. for £972, part of *Joseph's Park,* to 1st line of Thomas Cramphin's part. 162 acres.
407-409. Nathan Musgrove recorded deed 8 Feb. 1803 from Thomas Pleasants, of Goochland Co., Va., for $710, part of tract taken up by James Brooke, beginning at *Treed Land,* to line of *Plummer's Content,* to *Hygham,* to line of *Addition to Brook's Grove,* to 3rd line of *Hygham,* 29 1/4 acres, to 10 line of *John and Sarah*. Signed before William Pledge and others.
409-411. Thomas Davis recorded deed 8 Feb. 1803 from Nathan Musgrove, for $164.12 ½ for two pieces of *Addition to Brooke Grove,* for 1st piece, beginning at line of *Plummer's Content,* to *Hygham,* to the bank of the River, the 2nd tract called *Treed Land,* with 6th line of *Mill Seat,* 13 acres, 42 perches. Ann Musgrove released dower.
411-412. Ann Sollers recorded deed 9 Feb. 1803 from Leonard Hays, for £30, part of *Resurvey on Jeremiah's Park,* 1/4 acre. Elenor Hays released dower.
412-413. Robert Moore delivered schedule to the Sheriff of Montgomery County, 9 Feb. 1803. Sundry balances of book accounts due from John M. Guien, Dennis Griffith, Richard Scott, John Quarterman, and indenture for 1 year, from 1 Jan. 1803 for mulatto Nat, property of Joseph Jones.

413-414. Lewis Beall recorded 9 February 1803 from Eleazar Standage for valuable consideration, bill of sale for Negro man Peter, 30 years old, notwithstanding that if sum of £37..6 is paid, then this sale is void and redeemable. Signed before Ozias Offutt.
414. Zadock Dickerson recorded 9 February 1803, form James Suter & Ruth Suter, bill of sale for 5 shillings, Negro man, Aleck 22 years and Negro girl Rachel, 9 years old. Also feather bed, furniture. etc.
414-415. Zadock Dickerson recorded 9 February 1803, from James Suter, deed for 1/3 of all my land and also 1/3 of land in Frederick County, Commonwealth of Virginia. Signed before Ozias Offutt, Elemelech Swearingen.
416-418. Zadock Holland recorded deed16 February 1803 from Archibald Holland of Allegany County, Maryland, for £22..16 one undivided third part of 66 2/3 acre tract called *Gibson's Choice*. Deed ack. Before Robert Armstrong of Allegany County. Eleanor Holland released dower rights.
418-419. Laurence O'Neale recorded deed 17 Feb. 1803 from Honore Martin, for £50, lots #42 and 43 in Town of Rockville, part of *Exchange and New Exchange Enlarged,* beginning at NE corner of lot owned by Lawrence O'Neale, but under lease to Francis Moore. Sarah Martin released dower.
419-421. Richard Bennett Hall of Prince George's County, recorded deed 22 Feb. 1803, from Osborn Williams, of Anne Arundel Co., for 6500 pounds crop tobacco, *Fatique,* beginning at tract called *Blue Hill,* containing 100 acres. Signed before Isaac Dorsey. Elizabeth wife of Osborn Williams released dower right.
421. Commission for Associate Justices of Montgomery County Court recorded 22 February 1803 to Richard Turner and William Holmes.
421-423. John Burgess recorded 26 February 1803, from Thomas Pleasants, of Goochland Co., Virginia, for £650, deed made 3 December 1802 for part of tract taken up by James Brooke, bounded by *Hobson's Choice, Addition to Brooke Grove,* containing 65 acres.
423-425. Gassaway Rawlings recorded deed 1 March 1803 from Joseph Cowman and Thomas Tongue, surviving executors of Richard Cowman, deceased of Anne Arundel County, and Gassaway Rawlings, trustee of Richard Alexander Contee, a lunatic, deceased, of Anne Arundel County. Whereas the aforesaid Joseph Cowman and Thomas Tonque and a certain Ann Cowman were appointed executors of the will of Richard Cowman, deceased, and they did on or about 11 Nov. 1784 sell land hereafter mentioned to the said Richard Alexander Contee, but Ann Cowman, executrix died before any conveyance of the land, and whereas the aforesaid Richard Alexander Contee afterwards became a lunatic and Richard Gassaway was appointed trustee by a court of chancery, and by another decree the surviving executors were directed to make a good deed to Richard Gassaway for the benefit of the creditors or representatives of the said Richard Alexander Contee deceased. For 5 shillings deed made for part of *Snowden's Manor Enlarged,* at the north easternmost corner of *Batchelor's Forrest,* excepting part sold by Richard Cowman in his lifetime to Richard Thomas, containing 313 3/4 acres. Signed before Sam Harrison, Benj. Allison.
425. John Cushman recorded bill of sale 2 March 1803, from Charles Cushman, for £24, one mare and colt, bed and furniture, bedstead, 400 weight of meat, 7 barrels of corn. If sum paid, sale void.
426. John Fleming, William Riley Jr., and John Campbell recorded 3 March 1803, qualification as deputy sheriffs
426. Benjamin Ray Jr., recorded on 3 March 1803 bond as Sheriff, signed by Benjamin Ray Jr., Joseph Slater, Henry O'Neale, William Magrath.
426-427. Ann Clagett relict of Samuel Clagett recorded deed 4 March 1803 from Benjamin Ray Senior, for £11..5, one undivided twelfth part of tract *Fountain,* and resurvey thereon, on main road leading from Montgomery Courthouse to Mouth of Monocacy.
427-428. Negro Harry recorded 7 March 1803, from David English of Georgetown, manumission to Harry, whom I lately purchased of Basil Darby, after 7 March 1806. Signed before John Candler, Wm Smith.
428. Charles Gassaway with Solomon Simpson and Hezekiah Thompson, recorded bond to the state of Maryland 7 March 1803, that he shall execute the office of coroner.

428. James Dick Tucker recorded 8 March 1803, from Jacob Tucker and Margaret Tucker, deed of gift to our son, a Negro girl named Flory about 13 years old. Signed before Richard West, Jane Offutt.
429-430. John Clarke from Dorcas Coffee, relinquishment of her dower rights, recorded 9 March 1803, from the State of Kentucky, Mason Co.
430-431. Arnold Warfield recorded deed 9 March 1803 from John W. Warfield, for £50 lot on tract called *Moneysworth,* Mary, wife of John W. Warfield released dower.
431-432. John Read recorded deed 9 March 1803 from Meshech Tucker, for £93..15, lot #7 in Clarkskburgh, on SE side of road. Lot sold by Matthew Read to the said Mesheck Tucker.
432-434. John Richards & Ann, his wife recorded Mortgage from Joseph Newton Chiswell, for rents and covenants herein, grants a part of *Resurvey on Wolf's Cow,* beginning at 3d line of a part conveyed by Joseph N. Chiswell to Doct. William Brewer, at *Resurvey on Hanover,* containing 12 acres, to hold during their natural lives. John Richards is to plant and maintain 5 apple trees, 5 peach trees and 2 cherry trees provided by Joseph N. Chiswell.
434-435. Samuel Clapham records on 10 March 1803, list of Negroes brought into the state from Virginia on the 1st January. George age 25, Sall age 21, and their children ___ 2 years old and Moses 6 months of age, residents of Virginia on 21 April 1783 or their descendants.
435-436. James Magruder recorded deed 12 March 1803 from Harry Woodward Dorsey, for $609, tract beginning at 12th line of Thomas Pleasant's *Addition to Brooke Grove,* and *Fair Hill,* it being also the 3d line of *Resurvey on Benjamin's Square,* to the 6th line of Magruder's *Cow Pasture,* 61 acres. Mary Dorsey, wife of Harry W. Dorsey released dower.
436. Samuel Clapham of Loudoun County, Virginia recorded bond of conveyance 12 March 1803, from John McDonald, of Frederick County, Virginia, heir at law of Angus McDonald, for $10,000, bonds himself to make good deed for *Fair Island.*
436. Clement Thompson recorded deed 12 March 1803 from Eleanor Palmore of Montgomery County, and Amos Davis, her son, of Baltimore County. Whereas Eleanor is entitled to 13 acres of *Resurvey on Benjamin's Square* by deed from Jeremiah Davis, and 12 ½ acres during her natural lifetime by dower right, to which Amos Davis is heir in fee simple, the 25 ½ acres being bounded by George Culp and by Harry W. Dorsey, on the north by a tract called *Addition to Brooke Grove,* and on the east by part of *Resurvey on Benjamin's Square,* conveyed by Elijah Williams and his wife Eleanor, and Rezin Davis to the said Clement Thompson in November 1802. This deed conveys their right to 25 ½ acres for £47..16..3.
438. Francis Perry of Montgomery County, recorded power of attorney 12 March 1803, to recover my Negro woman Bett, supposed to be in the county and state. Signed by mark of Elias Arvin.
439-441. Joseph Ward's heirs by Thomas Peter guardian and Henry O. Neale, plot re part of commission. Will of Joseph Ward recorded named loving wife Anne Mary Ward, and three sons, Benjamin to receive Negro Daniel, Joseph to receive Negro lad David, John to receive Negro lad Denboe; daughter Elizabeth wife of William Spencer to receive slave Hannah, and she is not to be sold, hired out or disposed of; Daughter Ann Ward to receive Negro girl Doll; daughter Mary Ann Ward to receive girl Nell and boy Jermond, to wife, and after her death to sons and daughters as named above. Signed 18 August 1780, before Ans Campbell, Patrick Aughtectory and Bennett Greenwood. Will followed by division of land. Benjamin and John Ward sold undivided parts to Henry O'Neale, 78 1/3 acres, the said Thomas Peter accepts as the guardian for the children of Joseph Ward Junr. deceased, 2 September 1820. Witness Michael Harper. Division by Wm Smith, Wm Vinson, Thos B. Evans.
441. Thomas Davis recorded 16 March 1803 from Isaac Miller, bill of sale for one grey horse, 8 years old and one bay horse. Signed before Richard Green.
442-444. Upton Beall recorded 17 March 1803 from Thomas O. Williams of Prince George's County, for £15 deed for lot #58 in town of Williamsburgh, also known as Montgomery Court House. Mary Clagett Williams released dower rights.

444-447. *Fair Island* Commission to mark and bound tract, for Anna McDonald and others [John McDonald, Angus McDonald, Thompson McDonald, Elias Langhorn and Mary Lanhorn, Richard Holliday and Anna Holliday, James Tidball and Eleanor Tidball], heirs of Angus McDonald, issued to Lawrence O'Neale, Joseph N. Chiswell, Thomas Fletchall, Samuel H. Wheeler and Alexander Whitaker, who appointed for their surveyor William Smith; and Vincent Whaley and Thomas Davis for chain carriers and John Ellis consented to be pole bearer, meeting on island. Deposition of John Ellis, about 50 years old mentions Wadsworth Willson and Zachariah Ellis some time before. William Bailey, aged about 60 years old, deposes about survey 30-40 years before and Hezekiah Veatch about 15-20 years before. Survey plat completed and recorded.

447-448. Absolom Beddo recorded deed 19 March 1803, from Peter Kemp for 5 shillings, part of *James and Mary,* a part of *Kemp's Discovery,* beginning at 2nd line of *Deer Park,* to *Addition to Austruther,* 9/10 of an acre. Signed in German script.

449-450. Absalom Beddo recorded deed 19 March 1803 from James Willson Perry of Prince George's County, for 5 shillings, part of *Deer Park,* conveyed by John Sheffel to Joseph Perry, father of the aforesaid James Perry, containing 1 3/4 acre.

450. Peter Kemp recorded deed 19 March 1803 from Absalom Beddo, for 5 shillings, part of *Addition to Anstruther,* adjacent to 55th line of *James and Mary,* 9/10 of an acre.

451-453. James Willson Perry of Prince George's County, recorded deed 19 March 1803 from Absalom Beddo, for 5 shillings, parcel called *Second Mistake,* 6/10 of an acre; also part of *Deer Park,* and *Bear Garden,* conveyed by Shekel's to Joseph Perry for 1 3/10 acre.

453. William Higgins recorded release from bill of sale 19 March 1803 from William Willson for Negro woman, Mill, in bill of sale made 20 August 1802. Signed William Willson.

453-454. Richard Thomas recorded 21 March 1803 from Samuel Clements, bill of sale for £88 one roan mare, colt, two cows, other items.

454. James Case recorded receipt 21 March 1803 from Anthony Ricketts for £40, Negro girl, Henny, 3 years old the daughter of Suk. Signed Anthony Ricketts.

454-456. Francis Murphy recorded deed 26 March 1803 from Hezekiah Veatch, for £87, tract called *Timber Neck,* beginning at 4th line of *Locust Spring,* granted Robert Constable 2 May 1761, for 29 acres. Verlinda Veatch, wife of Hezekiah released dower.

456-457. Benjamin Williams recorded 29 March 1803 from Samuel Sprigg, bill of sale for £55..12, Negro boy Isaac, 4 years old, one cow, calf, bed and furniture. Signed before Philip Harding, Martha Sprigg, James Simmons.

457. Phillip Harding recorded 29 March 1803 from Samuel Sprigg, bill of sale for £84..18, for Negro woman Nell, 35 years old, one bed, furniture, one desk, 4 iron pots, 6 chairs, 7 shoats, one sow 6 pigs. Signed before Benjamin William, Martha Sprigg.

457-459. Benjamin Berry recorded deed 29 March 1803 from Thomas Waring, for £500, part of *Younger Brother,* 203 acres, where Thomas Waring now resides.

459-460. Benjamin Berry of Prince George's County recorded bill of sale 29 March 1803 from Thomas Waring, assigns Negro slaves: Negro woman, Mary, Negro woman Nell; girls Suk and Kitty, girl Sophy; two boys Davy and William together with their increase.

460. Thomas Peter of the City of Washington, recorded 2 April 1803, to the Clerk of Montgomery County, list of slaves acquired from his marriage with Martha Custis of Virginia, to work on his farm in Maryland: Hugo, yellow man, 20; Ralph, yellow boy 12, Andrew, yellow boy, 14 on 1st April 1803; John, Negro man 30, Nat 23, Sal (woman) 40, Hannah 7, George 6, Fender (boy) 5, Burel (boy) 3, Rachel 34, Beck 10, Gustavas 5, Ennis 3, Nancy 1, Jim 28 and Celia 19 years old.

460-461. Richard Jones and Burgess Culver, to State of Maryland, bond for building a bridge over Northwest Branch.

461-462. William Culver recorded bond of conveyance, and plat, from Evan Thomas, bound in sum of £1753..4..10 to make deed for tract *Two Farms,* by certificate of survey made by William Stabler, beginning at 2nd line of *Drumeldry,* containing 155 3/4 acres of land, to be sold for sum of £1475. Plat recorded shows mill race on west side.

462-464. William Willcoxon of Jesse recorded deed 13 April 1803 from Joseph Harris, for £3..10, *Mount Zion,* on 26th line of *Resurvey on Jeremiah's Park,* ½ acre. Mary Harris released dower.

464. Peter Bowie recorded deed 13 April 1803 from Thomas Fletchall, parcel called *Mount Ararat,* running to Sycamore on bank of Potomac River, containing 12 15/100 acres. Sarah Fletchall released dower.

465-467. Elizabeth Beall wife to Lewis recorded deed 27 April 1803 from Richard Wootton, in consideration of the natural love and for £5, conveys to Elizabeth Beall and her heirs and assigns, part of *Exchange and New Exchange,* adjacent to William O'Neale's part, containing 400 acres.

467. James Barnes recorded deed 27 April 1803 from Vachel Hall, for £11..5, tract at end of *Resurvey on Jeremiah's Park,* at end of 3d line of lot #8, the lot of John Summers, in new town of Barnesville, on road leading from Monocacy to Green's Bridge, 1 ½ acres. Margaret Hall released dower.

468-470. Peter Bayor and James Day recorded deed 27 April 1803 from William Harrison, of Baltimore Town, for $2323.46, tract *Flag Patch,* granted 22 Nov. 1754 to Thomas Beans for 140 acres; also *Solomon's Roguery,* granted 2 March 1774 to George Cook for 495 acres.

470-471. Enoch Busson recorded deed 29 April 1803 from Honore Martin, for £50, lots #42 and #43 in town of Rockville. Sarah Martin released dower rights.

471-472. Basil Trundle of Bourbon County, Kentucky, recorded deed 29 April 1803, from Evan Trundle, for $150, his undivided share of *Trundel's Inheritance,* granted him by his late father, Thomas Trundle. Ann, wife of Evan Trundle released dower.

472-474. David Trundle recorded deed 2 May 1803 from Jesse Burch, of Washington, D.C., for £402..13, tract *Friendship,* to 10th line of *Resurvey on Jeremiah's Park,* to tract called *Hobson's Choice,* 214 3/4 acres. Jane Burch released dower.

474-475. William Norris son of George recorded deed 2 May, 1803, from Charles Beatty of Washington County and District of Columbia. Whereas Charles Beatty did sell on 10 April 1799, two pieces of a tract of land called the *Resurvey on That's It,* for 14 1/4 acres more or less for £21..7..6, and passed his bond of agreement to the said William Norris, for conveyance thereof bearing the said 10 day of April 1789, and William Norris has paid the said consideration. Deed is confirmed. Signed before Ozias Offutt, Richard West. Ann Verlinda Beatty released dower.

476-477. Doctor Ozias Offutt recorded deed 2 May 1803, from Charles Beatty, of Washington, D.C., for $3000, deed, two tracts, *New Harbour, and Resurvey on That's It, Resurveyed,* on west side of tract *Hopewell,* the beginning of tract called *Father's Gift,* containing 300 acres. Signed before Adam Robb and Patrick Magruder.

477. Jesse Burch recorded acknowledgment of dower, 2 May 1803 from Elizabeth Stewart, wife to David Stewart.

478-479. William Hammond Dorsey of Georgetown, Washington, D.C., recorded deed 4 May 1803 from Walter Dorsey of Baltimore County. Whereas William H. Dorsey and Ann Dorsey, conveyed to Walter Dorsey, tract *George the Third,* 47 acres and plantation, *Fair Hill,* part of *Charley Forrest* and *Brother's Content,* containing 397 acres, for $1. Walter Dorsey assigns tracts back to William H. Dorsey. Hope Dorsey, wife of Walter, released dower.

479. Negro Sally from Samuel Brooke, manumission recorded 4 May 1803 for Negro girl Sally, 8 years old on the 20th of the 11th month next, to be free from the 20th of the 11th month 1813. Signed before Richard Green.

479-480. Samuel Clapham of Loudoun County, Virginia, recorded bond 6 May 1803 for $2000 from John McDonald, that he will make good deed for *Fair Island,* recently laid off by commission, as Samuel Clapham has received threatening letter from Elizabeth Luckett, dissatisfied with survey.

480-481. Thomas Swearingen recorded 6 May 1803 from Rezin Harding, for £300 bill of sale for Negro Pegg, 23 years old; Negro Jacob 4 years old and Negro Cassa, 1 year old.
481-482. Samuel Clapham recorded deed 7 May 1803 from John McDonald, of Frederick County, Virginia, son and heir of Angus McDonald who married Anne Thompson, and died intestate; for $7120, sells *Fair Island.*
482-484. Philip B. Key recorded trust deed 10 May 1803 from John R. Plater, of Georgetown. Whereas he has credit in bank of Columbia for a large sum, for 1005 3/4 acres of *Bradford's Rest,* and 600 acres in Calvert County, part of *Elton Head Manor;* and other tracts, to sell for $3650 payable to Uriah Forrest.
484-485. Mordecai Boone recorded deed 12 May 1803 from Thomas Blacklock, for $800, sells two tracts, *The Remains,* and *Addition to the Remains,* adjacent to division line with Ignatius Mitchell, except for 100 acres formerly conveyed by Richard Lanham to Thomas Blacklock and Charity his wife, 26 Feb. 1738/9. Sarah Blacklock released dower.
485-487. Richard Lowe Hall recorded deed 12 May 1803 from Richard Bennett Hall, for natural love and affection, he has for his son and 5 shillings, tract purchased of Osborn Williams called *Fatique.* Margaret Hall released dower.
487-488. Elizabeth and Catharine Culp recorded deed 14 May 1803 from George Culp, Senior, in consideration of the natural love and affection he has for his daughters, tract whereon he now lives bought of John George, and vacancy added thereto called *Friends Loss,* containing 176 acres. Signed in German Script, Johan George Kulp. Acknowledged before Elemelech Swearingen and Ozias Offutt.
488-490. John Culp recorded deed 14 May 1803 from George Culp, Junr. For 5 shillings, and natural love and affection, assigns land at head of Seneca, purchased from Thomas Aldridge and Edward Crow, also one other tract lying between the mills of Mr. Crow and Mr. Dorsey, purchased from Gideon Davis and George Ellicott.
490-491. Ephraim Gaither recorded deed 16 May 1803 from Nathan Musgrove, for $33.82 ½, part of *Addition to Brooke's Grove,* adjacent to *John and Sarah.* Ann wife of Nathan released dower before Richard Green, John Burgess.
491-493. Thomas Benson recorded deed 17 May 1803 from John Benson, for £364..10, called *Forrest,* part formerly conveyed to Elias Harding, 121 ½ acres. Ann wife of John Benson released dower.
493-494. John Linthicum recorded 17 May 1803 from Charles Rogers, for $300 bill of sale for Negro girl Charlotte, 17 years old, one black horse, chaise and harness, but sale void if sum paid back with interest.
494. John Linthicum recorded deed 17 May 1803 from Benjamin Ray Junr., sheriff. By writ of fi fa executed after suit of Alexander McDonald and John Holmes, plaintiffs, against Charles Rogers, lots 27 & 28, town of Charlesburgh in Montgomery County, sold for £143..9.
495. Benjamin Darby, qualification as Deputy Sheriff on 19 May 1803.
496-497. William Buxton recorded 20 May 1803, from Archibald Trail, for £22..10, bill of sale for Negro boy, John 6 years old, and girl Nance, 11 years old.
497. Allen Green of Anne Arundel County recorded 20 May 1803 from Thomas Grimes, for £19..1, bill sale for a black mare and colt.
497-498. Washington Owen and James White Ward recorded 22 May 1803, from Anthony and Francis Domminy, bill of sale for livestock and furniture.
498-500. James White Ward recorded deed 22 May 1803 from Sykes Beckwith, Watson Beckwith, Ally Beckwith and Benedict Beckwith for $171..87 sells *Beckwith's Mill Seat,* beginning at *Resurvey on Beckwith's Range,* also the beginning of *Paradise,* to a tract called *Rickett's Folly,* to the 11th line of *Rattlesnake Den.* Hessy, wife of Sykes and Elizabeth wife of Benedict Beckwith released dower.
500-502. Nicholas Gassaway recorded deed 22 May 1803 from Richard Berry Senior, for $6 and natural love and affection, to him part of *Charles and Benjamin,* 31 acres.
502-503. Nathan Ricketts recorded bill of sale 25 May 1803 from Zadock Ricketts, for £46..5, a quantity of tobacco in bulk, and one black mare colt. Signed before Benjamin Gaither.

503-506. John Glasco & Thomas Robertson Junior recorded lease 24 May 1803 from William D. Beall, guardian to Thomas A. Brooke, and Thomas A. Brooke, part of *Resurvey on Jacob,* near ditch into Falls Branch, where it empties into the Potomac, for 15 years for the purpose of erecting a mill seat and saw mill of best construction, near Falls Branch, to work with cast iron and cog wheels; and to have two pair of mill stones for grinding corn, rye and plaster of paris. Signed by all parties.
506-507. John Rogers recorded deed 20 May 1803 from Charles Rogers, for £112..10, two lots in Charlesburgh.
507-509. Jonathan Granger, legal representative of Barton Harris, deceased, recorded deed 27 May 1803 form James McCuloch, of Anne Arundel County, surviving executor of James Dick, dec'd, who sold in his lifetime part of *Exchange and New Exchange,* to Barton Harris, but deed not made, for sum of £151 paid, 100 acres.
509-511. Henry Winemiller recorded deed 27 May 1803 from John Anderson, for £120, 4 acre part of *Exchange and New Exchange.* Mary, wife of John Anderson released dower.
511-512. Abraham Umpstattd recorded deed 27 May 1803 from Laurence Snyder, for £16, lot #5 in Addition to Clarksburgh. Eve, wife of Lawrence Snyder released dower.
512-513. Samuel Pennybaker recorded deed 28 May 1803 from William Ballinger, for £312..10, part of *Henry and Elizabeth Enlarged,* 132 3/4 acres. Lydia wife of William released dower.
514-515. Jacob Bowman recorded deed 3 June 1803 from Thomas Pleasants, for $595, tract taken up by James Brooke the elder, beginning at 2nd line of *Hygham,* to 7th line of *Joseph and Margaret's Rest,* to tract reserved by me for a mill seat, 50 ½ acres.
515-520. Thomas Brown, miller, recorded lease 2 June 1803 from Evan Thomas, for rents and considerations herein, tract by name of *Two Farms* and *Addition to Culver's Chance,* and *Berry's Meadows.* Metes and bounds given beginning at Northwest Branch, below the mill dam, containing 44 ½ acres, for the use and benefit of a mill for term of 99 years. Signed by both parties.
520-521. Jacob Stier Junr. recorded deed 6 June 1803 from Joseph Harris, of John for £15, assigns part of *Mount Zion,* south of the main road leading from Monocacy to Green's Bridge. Martha wife of Joseph released dower.
521. Leonard Hays to State of Maryland, Constables bond 6 June 1803, with Adam Robb.
521-522. John Shook to the State of Maryland, constables bond on 6 June 1803 with William O. Lodge
522. Jesse Phillips to the State of Maryland, constables bond recorded 6 June 1803 with Aeneas Campbell.
522-523. Gerrard Gaither to the State of Maryland, constables bond recorded 6 June 1803 with Benjamin Gaither
523. Basil M. Beall to the state of Maryland, constables bond recorded 6 June 1803 with Hazel Butt.
523. Robert Soper to state of Maryland, constables bond recorded 6 June 1803, with John Roberts and James Wade.
524. Clement Jarboe to State of Maryland, constables bond recorded 10 June 1803 with Henry Belwood.
524-525. Peter Kemp recorded deed 11 June 1803 from Nathan Musgrove and Ann his wife, for $868, tract called *Snowden's Mill,* their one half interest, in tract possessed by William Selby, deceased, who devised one quarter of tract to his daughter Ann, wife of Nathan; and one quarter to his daughter Mary Blackwood, who conveyed same to Nathan Musgrove.
525-527. William Hilton recorded deed 14 June 1803, from William Hempstone, for £150, tract *It May Be Good in Time,* 100 acres. Susanna Hempstone released dower right.
527-530. Rachel Hollyday and Angus McDonald recorded deed 16 June 1803 from Anna McDonald, executrix of Angus McDonald, James Tidball & Eleanor his wife, and Thompson McDonald, all of Frederick County, Virginia, for $1735, sells tract *Long Looked For,* adjacent to *Invention,* containing 128 acres, granted to Angus McDonald in March 1772.

530-534. George and Christopher Lindenberger recorded deed 16 June 1803 from Richard Holliday and Anna his wife, and Angus McDonald and Mary his wife, for £194, grants *Long Looked For*, 45 ½ acres. Signed by all four.
534-535. Commission for justices of the levy court recorded 20 June 1802 [1803], issued to Henry Brookes, Edward Burgess Junr., Richard West, Thomas B. Owens, Ozias Offutt, Henry Dorsey and Thomas Lincet.
535-539. George Ellicott and Elizabeth his wife of Baltimore County recorded deed 24 June 1803, from Samuel Brooke. Whereas a certain Richard Brooke was seized of tracts called *George the Third,* and a plantation called *Fair Hill,* being part of *Charley Forest* and *Brother's Content,* said farm awarded to Ann Brooke, daughter of and devisee, for her part of real estate, part of the real estate of James Brooke, the elder, her grandfather, and whereas William H. Dorsey and Ann his wife, the daughter and representative of said Richard Brooke, did 9 June 1802 convey to Walter Dorsey, and he conveyed to William H. Dorsey; and whereas he sold to Peter Casanave, who departed this life intestate, without paying the consideration, and by a bill in chancery against Peter and Johanna Casanave his infant heirs and Ann Casanave and Nicholas Young, administrators, 19 Feb 1803 ordered tracts except for 1/4 acre enclosing the family burial grounds should be sold with Samuel Brookes appointed trustee. For £1350 sells to George T. Warfield the highest bidder, and to George Ellicott and his heirs. Metes and bounds given. Signed before Jno Thomas 3rd, Richard Green.
539-541. Samuel Willson recorded deed 25 June 1803 from William Willson, for $300, lots #40 & #41 in town of Williamsburgh, alias Montgomery Court House, but now called Rockville, sold to William Willson by Honore Martin 29 March 1798 (recorded H:96-98), adjacent to lot sold James Day and now in the possession of Lawrence O'Neale, to corner of piazza of dwelling house on aforesaid lot, west to end of house, the paling, granary and stable; past paling of Honore Martin's garden, to NE corner of Samuel Willson's lot. Rebecca Willson wife of William released dower.
541-543. Harry Woodward Dorsey recorded deed 29 June 1803 from George Ellicott & Elizabeth his wife of Baltimore County, for $1700, sells tracts originally granted Richard Brooke *Dublin,* for 84 acres; *Carlisle,* 74 acres, *Brooke's Plains,* 72 acres, Signed before Gerard Brooke, John Ellicott.
543-545. Richard Wootton recorded deed 4 July 1803, from Saml & William West, for £30..18 . Two parts of *Two Brothers,* 2 1/4 acres and 1 3/4 acres. Signed before Ozias Offutt, Richard West. Nancy wife of William West released dower rights.
545. Edward Owen as trustee for benefit of creditors of debtor, recorded 4 July 1803, from John Thomas 3d, deed made 18 June, for all his property. Signed before Wm Culver and John Adamson.
545. John Wilson recorded deed 5 July 1803, from Nathan Musgrove, for $600 part of tract known by name of *Snowdens Second or Third Addition to Snowden's Manor,* for 200 acres. Signed before Richard Green, John Burgess. Ann Musgrove, wife of Nathan released dower.
547-548. Absalom Beddo recorded deed 8 July 1803 from Peter Kemp, for £363..10 his interest in tract called *Snowden's Mill,* 134+ acres. Signed before Wm Culver, Wm Smith. Sarah Kemp released dower.
548-549. John Aldridge recorded bill of sale15 July 1803, from Daniel Walter, for valuable consideration, assigns one Negro boy named Sandy, nevertheless, if I well and truly pay sums due (£22..15) by 1st December next, sale is void.
549-550. Benjamin Oden recorded deed 19 July 1803 from Alexander Beall, for seven shillings, one pence, part of tract called *Long Looked For,* 193 acres. Elizabeth, wife of Alexander released dower right.
550-551. Gerard Brooke recorded bill of sale 20 July 1803, from Richard Contee (a black man) for £19..5, all my crop of corn now growing, a crop of flax in the house, one cow and calf, two sows and seven shoats, housewares enumerated, all by delivery of one spoon, 11 July 1803. Signed by mark before Jno Thomas 3d.
551. Negro Rachel recorded 21 June 1803, from Joseph Howard, manumission, she to be free from this day forward. Signed 27 April 1803 before Jno Thomas 3rd. Saml Thomas, Jr.

551-552. Commission recorded 21 July 1803 to Henry Brookes, Edward Burgess Junr., Richard West, Thomas B. Evans, Ozias Offutt, Harry Dorsey and Thomas Linstead, appointed Justices of the Levy Court of Montgomery County.
552-553. Ann Clagett recorded deed 21 July 1803, from John Orme, for £13..15 tract called the *Two Republics,* M&B to second line of *Mount Pleasant,* resurveyed for Benjamin Edwards, 12 July 1784, to tract called *Resurvey on Gravely Ridge,* containing 5 1/4 acres. Sarah, wife of John Orme released dower.
553-554. Ann Clagett recorded deed 21 July 1803 from William Leach, for £749..5 assigns part of *Leatches Lot,* being a resurvey, and part of *Cole's Chance,* part of *Mitchell's Range,* and part of *Resurvey on Rays Chance,* beginning at the beginning tree of a tract of land now the property of Zachariah Offutt called *Coopers Choice (alias) Cooper's Folly,* for 166 ½ acres. Mary, wife of William Leach released dower.
554-555. Basil M. Beall recorded bill of sale from Isaac Russell, for £50, one black mare, one cow and calf, one yearling, 16 hogs, all my crops of small grain and corn now growing, and one feather bed, one straw bed, two shovels, ploughs, one bar plough, other items. Signed by mark.
555-556. John Sprigg recorded deed 22 July 1803, from Vachel Hall, part of *Resurvey on Jeremiah's Park,* beginning at end of the lot #5 of Barnesville, contains 1/4 of an acre of land. Margaret, wife of Vachel Hall released dower.
556-557. Jacob Lowman recorded deed 22 July 1803 from Leonard Hays, for $114 part of tract called *Woodport,* Eleanor Hays wife of Leonard released dower.
557-558. Samuel Leeke recorded 23 July 1803, from Israel French Junr. For $16. Lot #40 in town of Brookeville as surveyed by Richard Thomas Junr. Signed before Richard Green, John Burgess.
558. Lenox Martin recorded 23 July 1803, to Negro Sam, manumission to be free after 1 January 1815. Signed before Peter Davis, Wm Smith.

NB. The plat of Rockville rec'd 16 July 1803 and a deed from William O'Neale to Thomas West, William Oden To Evan Jones, same to Richard West, same to Wm O'Neale Junr., Sam'l Hepburn to Lawrence O'Neale, all of which deeds are recorded in Liber L, Folio 173, etc.

END OF BOOK K

INDEX To Libers H - I/J - K

This page includes a quick guide to occupations, and lists several ships, schooners, etc., involving shipping interests from Georgetown, as well as a list of towns, and some town lots. An index to tracts, roads, waterways, and other types of locations, follows the every name index. Please note, that the index combines names, and often uses only the most common spelling, but variants may be found in the text. Deeds for Georgetown in Washington, D.C. continued to be recorded in Montgomery County, until about 1800. Until after 1800, Rockville was known originally as Williamsburg, and then Montgomery Courthouse.

TRACT INDEX

www.ingramcontent.com/pod-product-compliance
Lightning Source LLC
LaVergne TN
LVHW061247100826
845148LV00008B/1048